The foe claims in vain a philosopher I am.
God knows I am not what he says I am.
But, having endured this sorrow's nest, I ask:
Why should I not know at least what I am?

—Omar Khayyam

HUMAN ARCHITECTURE
Journal of the Sociology of Self-Knowledge

Editor: M.H. (Behrooz) Tamdgidi

Human Architecture: Journal of the Sociology of Self-Knowledge (ISSN # 1540-5699) is published biannually (Spring and Fall) by the Okcir Press, of the Omar Khayyam Center for Integrative Research (OKCIR) in Utopia, Mysticism, and the Academy, 1803 Newell Road, Endicott, NY, 13760, U.S.A., tel/fax: 1-607-786-3274, website: www.okcir.com, e-mail: journal@okcir.com. OKCIR is an independent research and educational project of Ahead Publishing House (APH), Endicott, NY; Okcir Press is an imprint of APH. Copyright © by Mohammad H. Tamdgidi, 2002. All rights reserved.

Submissions: *Human Architecture* publishes both submitted and invited manuscripts as well as the working papers of OKCIR. Contributors extend permission in writing to *Human Architecture* for publication of their work in the journal. They retain copyrights to their work and may publish them elsewhere. If the submitted article has been published elsewhere before, written permission from both the author(s) and publication(s) where it earlier appeared should accompany submission to *Human Architecture*.

Editorial decisions: Selection of papers from submitted manuscripts will be based on their substantive relevance to the editorial perspective of the journal. Views expressed in the journal by contributors are those of their authors and may not necessarily coincide with one another or with the journal's editorial perspective. Authors are responsible for the accuracy and integrity of factual, bibliographic, and referential materials used in their own articles. Empirical, theoretical, as well as methodological discourses are all encouraged. The primary language used is English, but material in other languages may be included if relevant to the purpose of the journal.

What to Submit: All text should be submitted in both electronic and printed formats accompanying a completed and signed submission form obtainable from the Okcir Press. The paper should be double-spaced in Times 12 typeface and printed on 8-1/2 by 11 inch white paper, one-sided. Margins on all four sides must be 1 inch. In general, please follow the University of Chicago Style Guide.

Where to Submit: Editor, *Human Architecture*, Okcir Press, 1803 Newell Road, Endicott, NY, 13760. Tel/Fax: 1-607-786-3274. E-mail: journal@okcir.com

Subscriptions: The individual and institutional subscription rates for *Human Architecture* are $30 and $60 per two-issue volume sets respectively. New subscriptions are applied on current-volume basis only. Single issue individual and institutional rates are $15 and $30 respectively. Rates include domestic shipping and sales tax, where applicable. For international orders, or bulk orders of single issues, please inquire for special rates & shipping charges. Non-institutional orders must be accompanied by prepayment. Make checks payable in U.S. dollars to Ahead Publishing House, and send payments to the Okcir Press, 1803 Newell Road, Endicott, NY, 13760, U.S.A. Back issues or additional copies of the journal are available upon request at the same per single issue rates as indicated above. Contributors each receive one free copy of the issue in which their articles appear and a 20% discount on individual single issue or subscription rates.

Advertisements: Current rates and specifications may be obtained by contacting the Okcir Press, 1803 Newell Rd., Endicott, NY, 13760. Tel/Fax: 1-607-786-3274. E-mail: journal@okcir.com

Inquiries: Address all correspondence and requests to Editor, *Human Architecture*, Okcir Press, 1803 Newell Rd., Endicott, NY, 13760. Tel/Fax: 1-607-786-3274. E-mail: journal@okcir.com

Changes of address: Six weeks' advance notice must be given when notifying change of address. Please include both the old and the new address in your written/e-mailed request. **Postmaster:** Send address changes to the Okcir Press, 1803 Newell Road, Endicott, NY, 13760.

ISBN 1-888024-18-6

Human Architecture:
Journal of the Sociology of Self-Knowledge
Volume II, Number 1, Spring 2003
ISSN: 1540-5699
ISBN: 1-888024-18-6

Contents

HUMAN ARCHITECTURE
Journal of the Sociology of Self-Knowledge

Volume II	Number 1	Spring 2003

v   *Editor's Note: "Social Theories, Student Realities"*

Emily Margulies
1   **Why I Smoke: Sociology of a Deadly Habit**

Neo Morpheus
12   **The Drinking Matrix: A Symbolic Self Interaction**

M. Goltry
19   **Theoretical Reflections on Peer Judgments**

James McHugh
27   **It's Worth Living in the World**

Anna Schlosser
34   **My Image Struggles in Capitalist Society**

Charles
42   **"It's Not My Fault": Overcoming Social Anxiety through Sociological Imagination**

Megan Murray
50   **Treading Water: Self-Reflections on Generalized Anxiety Disorder**

Colin Campbell
58   **Sociology of Shyness: A Self Introduction**

Sherry Wilson
65   **"Let Me Introduce Myself": My Struggles with Shyness and Conformity**

Jillian E. Sloan
73   **Religion in an Individualistic Society**

Jennifer S. Dutcher
81   **A Precarious Balance: Views of a Working Mother Walking the Tightrope**

Ira Omid
90   **Links in the Chain: Untangling Dysfunctional Family Ties**

M. H. (Behrooz) Tamdgidi
102   **Marx, Gurdjieff, and Mannheim: Contested Utopistics of Self and Society in a World-History Context**

121   **Contributors**

Editor's Note:

"Social Theories, Student Realities"

M.H. (Behrooz) Tamdgidi

Teaching that begins with experiences distant from those of students devalues the personal experiences of students, contributes to an uncertain self, and academically constructs a person who cannot reflectively judge. This is particularly easy in international relations, which has had a tradition that says efforts to make the general public understand it is a waste of time. To teach students effectively, however, one must begin with some of their personal experiences so that they can have the sense that it is "safe" to use those experiences as a basis for judgement in things considered important by persons (like professors) who are viewed as significant. By teaching students in this fashion, the professor simultaneously does a number of things. She helps the student to link the personal with other experiences that are not personal; she helps the student to see and hear his or her own voice in distant persons and things; and she helps the student understand that it is out of the aggregate of specific experiences that general conceptions are constructed and to which those conceptions must return to ensure their continuing validity. Further, she will help students understand that their own reflections (which they author and for which they can safely claim authority) can become part of the modes of thinking that characterize university—as earlier defined. Residing in those reflections on their experiences, there may be something new in nature—something to be added to the human conversation. ...

—Winston E. Langley, "Teaching, Learning, and Judging: Some Reflections on the University and Political Legitimacy"

I was quite fortunate recently, while editing the present issue of *Human Architecture*, to be reading and reflecting on a collection of wonderful essays by an array of teacher-scholars across diverse disciplines at UMass Boston. The book, *Achieving Against the Odds: How Academics Become Teachers of Diverse Students* (Temple University Press, 2001), edited jointly by Esther Kingston-Mann, professor of history and director of the Center for Improvement of Teaching (CIT) at UMass Boston, and Tim Sieber, associate professor of anthropology in the same institution, was kindly extended to me by Louise Z. Smith, Interim Dean of Liberal Arts at UMass Boston, as a welcoming gift for the occasion of my forthcoming appointment in Fall 2003 as an Assistant Professor of Sociology at UMass Boston.

I must say that I could have easily epigraphed the present editorial introduction using an excerpt from any of the essays in the volume. I could have, for instance, begun from that of Estelle Disch, professor of sociology at UMass Boston, whose disciplinary location I share and her pedagogical application of C. Wright Mills's "Sociological Imagination" (i.e., the ability to link personal troubles and public issues) nicely echoes not only my own teaching style, but also the spirit of what Winston E.

Notice: Copyright of *Human Architecture: Journal of the Sociology of Self-Knowledge* is the property of Ahead Publishing House (imprint: Okcir Press) and its content may not be copied or emailed to multiple sites or posted to a listserv without the copyright holder's express written permission. However, users may print, download, or email articles for individual use.

Langley eloquently expresses above regarding his experience of teaching political science and international relations at UMass Boston. However, in the spirit of welcoming diversity (in this case in terms of dialogue across disciplines), I chose to begin with an excerpt from Lengley's chapter in the volume.

Although the issue of achievement against the odds in the midst of a diverse student (and faculty) population in an urban public university such as UMass Boston is the central theme of the book as reflected in its title, what drew my attention across all essays of the volume was the common strategy adopted by all in meeting that challenge—a strategy that is quite similar to my own teaching style as reflected partly in the purpose and mission of the present journal. The common strategy is that of taking up the challenge of diversity among students and faculty by establishing a dialectic between the common public issues brought up in course contents and the diverse personal troubles of both the students and faculty as explored during the semester. All the essayists in *Achieving Against the Odds*, commonly but in diverse ways, report the discovery and use of such a dialectic to be the central theme of their pedagogical strategy in meeting the challenge of diverse academic (and broader urban) environment. It will certainly not do justice to the complexity and cogency of each essay to summarize them in a brief introduction such as this. However, to acquaint the readers who may not have yet consulted the book, let me very briefly review each piece only to highlight the common concern with the dialectics of personal concerns and public issues running throughout the essays.

In "Coming Out and Leading Out: Pedagogy Beyond the Closet," Kathleen M. Sands, associate professor of religious studies at Umass Boston, addresses the conflicts arising from teaching of religious texts (or to religious minds) which are closed to diverse forms of sexuality. She finds that the conflict is managed more effectively through establishing a comfortable pedagogical spacetime where the subject matter is brought out of the closets of personal narratives into public discourses of student/faculty readings, learning, and discussions. "The broadest change in my relationships with students is that I now hear many more stories about their struggles to make moral sense of sexual complexity. It is as if the opening created by my coming out allows their unmetabolized suffering and unspoken confusion to find light and air. ... My self-understanding as a teacher also has had to grow in the movement out of the closet. ... I could name many similar instances in which my being available as an out teacher made a constructive impact on the lives of lesbian and gay students ... For my straight students as well, my coming out enriches not only their social sensibilities, but also their study of religion" (28, 29, 30).

In her essay, "Three Steps Forward, One Step Back: Dilemmas of Upward Mobility," Esther Kingston-Mann discusses how her own past personal experiences in the academia confronting class, gender, and ethnic snobbery that sought to silence her voice, led to the discovery and learning (from students and colleagues alike) of a pedagogy that involved teaching world-history through exploration of personal and local narratives. Her assigning students to conduct interviews with Vietnam veterans in the area, for instance, revealed what original and first-rate work students can produce as researchers, leading to rich intellectual exchanges with her about historical research and her own work. "While I could have predicted that student interview data might challenge my own assumptions about U.S. Vietnam veterans, I did not foresee how much this assignment would teach me about student abilities and potential. Skills and talents that are invisible in conventional classroom settings began to emerge into the open. In researching a topic that deeply interested them, students usually categorized as "unprepared" revealed strengths that are seldom utilized in the world of academe" (40-41).

The dialectic of the personal and the public is also strongly present in the voice of the "academic anthropologist" Tim Sieber as narrated in his piece "Learning to Listen to Students and Oneself." Trying to understand why he de-emphasized students' personal lives from their learning experiences earlier in his teaching career, he traces the causes to two major factors, personal and public: 1-dissociation from his own past as a first generation college graduate grown up in rural environment and transitioning to an urban public university setting, 2-impersonalized traditional teaching methods to which he had himself been exposed as part of his training. Sieber effectively narrates how, through listening to his students and himself, he finally discovered an alternative pedagogy, one centered on student journal writing, that allowed a dialogical teaching experience to emerge in contrast to the one-sided lecturing style of the earlier period. "Colleagues and my students increasingly helped me to understand how much my teaching constitutes a dialogue with students, a dialogue in which who the students are and what they think is central to the learning equation and to shaping the faculty's contributions to the educational encounter. It was becoming more and more clear to me that to be an effective teacher, I had to offer more support for my students to tell me about themselves and their own thinking" (64).

In "Language and Cultural Capital: Reflections of a 'Junior' Professor," Reyes Coll-Tellechea, associate professor of Hispanic studies at UMass Boston, narrates (as translated by Mark Zola) her surprising experience of discovering that the most important obstacle to her teaching Spanish literature to a class of Spanish speakers from diverse ethnic/national backgrounds was the (painful) history of Spanish conquest of the Americas. For her, though, the bigger shock came when she discovered that in the dialogue of class readings, discussions, and writing assignments, students were as much understanding of her own personal identity troubles as she tried to be of theirs. The historical discomfort of having to teach Spanish, as a Spaniard, to Latin/American native speakers of the language, implying a renewed linguistic "conquest," turned into an alternative exercise in mutual understanding and caring at the personal level—one which the earlier larger historical events desperately lacked. "After reading pages and pages [of student papers] full of Spanish and Native American words unknown to me (those of plants, cities, animals, smells, and textures that I had never experienced), I had to pause to call a friend. I needed to talk, not about the unknown vocabulary, but about a shocking experience; as my students were writing their own short autobiographies (loves, struggles, secrets, and all), they all left space for mine. They all wanted to tell me that they knew what I meant when I was talking about my bittersweet feelings regarding Spanish, and some wanted to advise me on how to deal with them" (85-6).

In his "Racial Problems in Society and in the Classroom," Castellano B. Turner, professor of psychology at UMass Boston, relates his experience with the dialectics of racism in society at large and in his classrooms. Sensing over the years that the basic disagreements in both have been on "the extent and pace of change in race relations," Turner reports on a significant discovery he made in making it possible to establish a constructive classroom environment for confronting such disagreements: "I had made a fundamental pedagogical error: I expected the students to meet me where I was, presenting abstractions such as stratification and domination, rather than meeting students where they were—struggling with the developmental transition from family into the larger world of intimacy and of getting along with others. ... When students see themselves as agents within an interpersonal encounter, they become more open to accepting the general dynamics of intergroup relations, especially in terms of power" (98, 99).

In her "Teaching (as) Composing," Vivian Zamel, professor of English and director of the ESL program at UMass Boston, effectively relates how the transformation of her pedagogy from teaching of public rules and techniques of writing to that of substantive engagements of students (and teacher) with communication of their personal lives and troubles opened a completely new way of learning for her students—one that was less concerned with finding the "right answer" and more concerned with active and ongoing investigative and substantive learning of language. Zamel invited students to "bring themselves to the texts they write" (111), to empower themselves as "authors," and learn that writing is not separate from and does not "proceed" a thinking and idea-generation stage but is and can be identical with it. "Students became authors alongside the authors they read, thus reclaiming authority for themselves. In short, their work represented the dialectical interplay between themselves and the course content, indicating not only the way the material affected them, but also the ways in which they were contributing to the material" (118).

Peter Nien-Chu Kiang, professor of education and director of the program in Asian American studies at UMass Boston, relates in his piece "Teaching, Tenure, and Institutional Transformation: Reflections on Race, Culture, and Resilience at an Urban Public University," his experience of how he learned from and taught his students about the importance of wanting "to go on" despite and beyond the challenges of inherited social structures within and outside school. By redefining the expected tenure requirements of scholarship, teaching, and service in terms of "sharing voices," "crossing boundaries," and "building communities," Nien-Chu Kiang usefully problematizes university's structures in an effort to enrich it with new and better structures for evaluating faculty and student work. Moving on the path of catering to the personal education needs of real students and faculty members in everyday life allows Nien-Chu Kiang certain detachment from institutionalized norms and procedures which in turn renders them less powerful when confronted with the voices of his colleagues, students, and his own. Even when metaphorically applying the strategy and tactics of Chairman Mao to classroom debates, he does not refrain from humbly admitting that the key to his success (or failures) lay in how he failed to take into account *all* the constituencies of the people (in this case students) to which he needed to reach out. "I had mistakenly assumed that they [the advanced students] saw themselves included in both the content and process of my organizing and teaching, but I had not talked directly to either of them about what I was doing or why. I was so concerned with reaching the middle and neutralizing the resistant core that I failed to affirm and invest in those students who could most benefit from working together with me. The course had not empowered them, and their feelings of frustration and disappointment still move me today, nearly a decade later, to think clearly about my priorities as a teacher and mentor" (137). I think it is this critical self-reflexiveness that best exemplifies and appreciates in practice the finding of Tim Sieber in his piece on "Listening to Students and Oneself." More on this later.

Lois Rudnick, professor of English and director of American studies at UMass Boston, narrates in her "Teaching American Dreams/American Realities: Students' Lives and Faculty Agendas" how in the course of ongoing contestations of diverse

American dreams among student and textual voices in her classes, she identified three important dimensions to the representational barriers that often freeze personal dialogues in debates: the barriers of mainstream vs. marginal dreams, the cross-cultural barriers of dreams (the "multicultural" in contrast to "intercultural" attitude), and the conflict between victimization and agency. Rudnick relates how in dealing with such barriers, her pedagogy was significantly enriched when she incorporated the dialectic of students' personal notions of the American Dream with the broader historical literature and practices that are associated with the idea. "What has taken me the longest time to accept is that my students' agendas are not and do not have to be the same as mine. It is this course, which begins and ends with student definitions of the American Dream, that has taught me this hard-earned lesson" (143).

The voice of Winston E. Langley in "Teaching, Learning, and Judging: Some Reflections on the University and Political Legitimacy," an excerpt of which is epigraphed above, is powerful. However, the nuance of his message and how he arrived at it by experience, is itself worth telling. Langley relates how he was confronted with a puzzling low-performance result when administering abstract/applied conceptual examinations to his students, when in the course of in- and outside-class discussions, it seemed that students had much higher grasp of the meaning of concepts and issues than what their test results indicated. Tracing the matter to the heart of the meaning of democracy in practical terms, Langley soon realized—thanks to the brilliant linking by a student on welfare of the theory of money to her personal everyday experiences with "food stamps" and "Women as Third World"—that the problem lies in the separation of academic learning from personal "safe grounds" of everyday knowledge. Their fractured selves being alienated from their personal lives in favor of an abstract notion and practice of democracy, citizens (and students) lose the ability to judge matters and make decisions, even when they "know the subject." Langley proceeds to elaborate on how the production of fragmented and fractured selves serves the promotion of not real, but rhetorical democracy, and it is through the relinking of the substantive knowledges of citizens/students with their personal experiences that an effective and real democratic process may emerge.

As a sociologist of gender, Estelle Disch's account, "Gender Trouble in the Gender Course: Managing and Mismanaging Conflict in the Classroom," provides a vivid example of how self-critical reflexivity is a crucial and indispensable part of the personal-public dialectic in the conduct of meaningful academic pedagogy. Good sociological imaginations cannot dispense with it. Through persistent (and humble) critical self-inquiry, Disch not only illustrates how, despite painful classroom clashes and conflicts, open dialogue with the resistant voices can be accommodated inside and outside classroom, but also, through various exercises of weekly "response papers" and regular in-class feedbacks, preventive dialogues on gender can be generated across faculty-student axis before breaking out of control in the classroom. "These three incidents illustrate the complexity of silence and voice—how voice is expressed, how it has power to silence some people and not others, how it can sexualize the atmosphere in uncomfortable ways, and how central the teacher's role is in attempting to establish a setting in which a maximum of voices can be heard in a respectful context. The learning that I am most struck by as I write about these three incidents is the need for frequent reassessment of what is going on in class—not just in terms of learning, but in terms of individual experience and classroom process" (197).

Finally, Pancho Savery, professor of English, humanities, and American studies at Reed College in Portland, Oregon, relates to us in his "Odd Man Out" how the process of his employment transition from UMass Boston to Reed College showed him the variabilities of regional, urban, campus, and class contexts affecting the teaching and learning about racism in the U.S. Having mixed feelings about both academic environments, Savery compares the immediate vs. the mediated experiences of the "real world" across the UMass and Reed campuses respectively, illustrating how the same academic texts and syllabi are confronted and enjoined differently by the different audiences of the two environments. In his words, "You can't teach at UMass without bringing the real world into the classroom. What I mean by this is that the classroom is always an extension of one's experiences in the real world. The middle and upper classes have layers between themselves and the world that insulate and protect. The working class has no such layers" (210). Savery's account thereby problematizes the dialectics of private troubles and broader public issues as being themselves dependent on diverse spatiotemporal, social, and stratified contexts in which they are studied and pursued.

My effort above in identifying the common underlying theme of the essays collected in *Achieving Against the Odds* is not simply an exercise in book review. As I proceeded to carve out, in my own mind, the essential arguments of pieces as they relate to the central theme of the book, I begun asking the question, Why is it, really, that the dialectic of the personal and the broader social issues is deemed by the experienced voices of the authors to be the key for meeting the challenge of teaching in a diverse student/faculty academic environment? Soon it became increasingly clear to me, as I linked the question to the "safe grounds" of my own teaching experience, that only a dialogical tension of the personal and the broader social provides an antidote to the abstract and impersonal environments in which prejudices, discriminations and injustices thrive. It is only in the emotionless, insensible, and abstract dialogue of faceless and impersonal voices that the possibility of misrepresentation and misappreciation of class, gender, racial, ethnic, religious, ability, age, and national diversities can take place and flourish. So long as voices of difference remain closeted, hidden, unspoken, (self)censored, and silent behind the abstract discourses on history, humanity, society, language, nationalism, politics, economics, and religion, there will always be potentials for misrepresentation and misinterpretation of human diversities in favor of discrimination, prejudice, and injustice.

Of course, this does not mean that abstract discourse and conceptual experimentation and creativity should be abandoned. On the contrary, to use Coll-Tellechea's vocabulary, it is the production, distribution, and consumption of fragmented and "disciplined" theoretical knowledges that often in and of themselves reproduce the concrete historical misrepresentation and misappropriations of difference and diversity. The key here is not to abandon theoretical and abstract discourse, but find ways of integrating them with the concrete fabrics of everyday personal troubles of real people, student and faculty alike, in broader social and world-historical contexts. As a soon-to-be "junior faculty" recruited to teach sociological theory (among other subjects) at UMass Boston, I think the lesson commonly conveyed through the essays of the volume centrally hinges upon the need for integrating broad social theorizations with the diverse personal realities of students, faculty, and administrative members of the university to which I will be devoting a substantial part of my time and energy in the years to come.

Another important question that also crossed my mind and is worth bringing up here (only briefly) as I listen to and reflect on the essays' voices—voices of their authors and of the students they often quote—are the notions of "teacher-scholar" or "teacher-learner" that often appeared in the narratives. Given that all essays without exception revealed the value of listening to and learning from the personal lives, experiences, and voices of students—"politically correct" or not—it would appear logical and fruitful to also speak of "student-scholars" as well as "student-teachers"—terms that were absent in the authors' vocabulary, though in substance and content were present in almost all the essays. Related to this, and also useful, would be experimentations with books and publications that combine voices of faculty *and students* (undergraduate and graduate) in their pages, in such a way that students' contributions could be as much stand-alone authorships of their own voices as they may be cited within the narratives of insightful faculty voices. It will certainly enrich the authors' dialogue, moreover, if students could be somehow integrated into CIT seminars, making them more diverse in a "reverse" way, of treating students as teachers of these seminars, as guest speakers, contributors, and advisors, and their articles (as well) be incorporated in the publications and proceedings of seminar participants.

As I reflected on the above, I was reminded of the wisdom of my late dissertation advisor, professor Terence K. Hopkins, who founded the Graduate Program of the Department of Sociology at SUNY Binghamton. A specialist in social theories and methods, and also in the sociology of small groups on one hand and of world-systems on the other, Hopkins used to emphasize that a more fruitful way of conceptualizing the relationship between students and faculty is in terms of the relationship of young and not-so-young *scholars*. Of course, as graduate students, we associated "students" with ourselves, but from my own experience of undergraduate teaching, I think it would be fruitful to do the same in terms of faculty and undergraduate student relations as well.

But then, here, several important and interesting theoretical issues arise that may be at least touched upon here, if only briefly.

What the authors' essays vividly illustrate in *Achieving Against the Odds* is that, given the chance, students' voices and their intentional articulation in the process of academic instruction are indispensable for the creation and conduct of new and alternative pedagogical strategies of teaching amidst diversity. If we see the faculty as "teacher-scholars" and "teacher-learners," of persons who both teach and learn, from other colleagues *and students* alike, and if, moreover, we also believe in "student-scholars" and "student-teachers," who can be equal partners in authorship and practice of alternative pedagogies, then we may begin to see the value of transcending our inherited traditional sociological imaginations of "diversity" in terms of diversity among "persons" and begin to embrace diversity in terms of diversities of selves, within as well as across persons. If we recognize and see our intrapersonal as well as interpersonal diversities, it may in fact be more possible to transcend the dualisms and barriers Lois Rudnick encourages us to accomplish about our utopistic dreams of better worlds. This is because, we begin to see that the contestations of status quo and change, of mainstreamness vs. marginality, of victimization and agency, and of cultural identities do not exist simply across seemingly separate persons, but also have reality in terms of the contestation of multiple selfhoods.

If we readjust our theoretical lenses to this deeper quantal notion of society as a system of *self*-interactions rather than simply of assumed "individual" interactions, we may find that all "persons" involved in the academic discourse are more or less developed or integrated ensembles of teaching and learning *selves*. Once we embrace new sociological imaginations of the academe as a landscape of interacting selves within and across "teacher" and "student" bodies, once we see "diversity" of traditional dichotomies as breaking down in the complex intrapersonal architecture of multi-classed, multi-raced, multi-gendered, multi-faithed, multi-nationed, and multi-abled persons, then teaching diversity becomes as much a teaching (and learning from) one's own selves as it is traditionally identified with the teaching of (and learning from) "others." Then the "odds" facing "faculty" and "students" become as much an engagement with diversities *of others* as it will be an engagement with the inner diversities of our own voices within. Contestations across separate body organisms become re-imagined as contestations of inner voices, within and without. I think it is in this light that the most intriguing aspect of the essays in *Achieving Against the Odds* comes to light: the strength and courage with which each and every one of the authors has publicly subjected their own diverse inner voices to conscious and intentional self-critical scrutiny.

Since its inception *Human Architecture: Journal of the Sociology of Self-Knowledge* has devoted its pages to the empowerment of searching souls, students and faculty (and non-academic) alike, in search of critical global self-knowledge and change. The articles chronicled in this issue of the journal, produced by undergraduate students of diverse standing enrolled in my courses during the Spring 2003 semester at SUNY Oneonta, also narrate struggles of self-critical voices seeking to problematize their personal troubles in the context of introductory and more advanced sociological theories to which they were exposed in various classes. What they reveal above all is that sociological perspectives and theories are best learned in the context of concrete explorations of personal issues in the context of broader public and social forces. Social theories are best learned by students through empowerment of their voices as authors exploring issues that has fractures their "safe grounds" in the distant or near past, but are subject to remedy, repair, and renewal. As the articles contained herein demonstrate, for the first time previous issues of *Human Architecture* were used as semi-required readings in these classes, exposing students to their own writings and voices across classes, semesters, and campuses. Representative student-scholars in the present issue grapple with important personal issues ranging from habituations to smoking and drinking, to challenges shyness, family obligations and dysfunctions, peer judgments and discriminations, gender conflicts, and family planning considerations pose to their academic and non-academic pursuits at a crucial stage in their life course. The dialectics of social theories and student realities thereby are learned in an applied sociological environment conducive of both student and teacher learning.

Given what I have read in *Achieving Against the Odds*, I am certain that the tradition of *Human Architecture* will continue to take root on the soil of UMass Boston as well. Now I understand why I was presented the book to read in preparation for my arrival at the university in Fall 2003. For this, I pass on the gift of *Achieving Against the Odds* and dedicate the present issue of the journal to the sociology faculty at UMass Boston whose warm reception and subsequent support will make the continuity of *Human Architecture* possible.

Tamdgidi
July 2003

Why I Smoke:
Sociology of a Deadly Habit

Emily Margulies

Smoking is the number one cause of preventable death in the United States. In the twenty first century everyone knows the harm that smoking can cause and yet people still willingly risk their lives for the habit. I am one of these people. I would not throw myself in front of a bus; I would not take Drano from my kitchen and choose to ingest it. One of human being's greatest instincts is survival. So why do I engage in this life threatening activity?

The question cannot simply be answered in one way. There are physical, biological, social, and psychological reasons for the attraction of cigarettes. For our purposes I will use various sociological theories to understand why smoking has become such a huge force in my life and how society has played a role in this manifestation. Perhaps through researching why I smoke I will be able to see how I can stop.

To people of my generation smoking carried along a million perceptions of what it symbolized. Smoking was cool and sexy. When we used to play house in third and fourth grade part of the game was to make fake cigarettes and pretend we were smokers. One of the most popular candies among my friends was candy or gum cigarettes that our parents would buy us. When my dad was a smoker I used to steal his packs and throw them away because I was taught in school how bad cigarettes were for you. As I got older and my parents became less and my peers more significant, it mattered more to me what kind of persona smoking illustrated than what I had been taught.

I remember the first cigarette I ever smoked. I was in the seventh grade, twelve years old, behind a tree in my back yard with my best friend. She had smoked before, I hadn't. The girl I was with was a new friend. Until I met her I wasn't much of a rebel; I was more of a drama kid violin player who did what her mother said. This new friend was different from any I'd ever had. When she lit the cigarette and taught me how to inhale, I did not hesitate—as far as I can remember. It was too exciting; doing something I knew I shouldn't. It wasn't about smoking the cigarette, it was about what that symbolized in the life of junior high kids trying to find their place.

I didn't start buying my own packs of cigarettes until the end of eighth grade. It became a pastime, a social event. We'd all go buy cigarettes after school and sit in the woods or at the park, or outside the mall and smoke them together. We'd practice how we smoked and look at ourselves in the mirror. When I was young the anti-smoking campaigns you see today weren't around. We knew it was bad for you but it was still cool. It said something about who you were and almost defined the kind of person or group you fit with. In ninth grade I began to be loyal to a certain brand of cigarettes, Parliament Lights. Despite what common research says I had never even seen these brands advertised before. I started smoking them because it was what all of my friends smoked not because Joe Camel told me to. Throughout my first two years of high school I was still a social smoker and could smoke and quit as many times as I wanted to. The fact of the matter is addiction sneaks up on you.

Nicotine is an addictive substance. Obviously some of the reasoning for my becoming a full fledged smoker had to do with my body's dependence on the drug. At the same time cigarettes are addicting in other ways. I became socialized into and addicted to the smoking lifestyle. After all of my friends would sit down to eat, or when we were bored, upset, needed a break from work, or were drinking at a party, we would smoke a cigarette. It's a social thing. Sitting down with friends, smoking and talking is something that has occupied a great amount of time in my life. Smoking is even a way to make new friends. Asking for a lighter is a great pick up line at a bar. At Orientation before my first year of school I didn't know one single person. The boy sitting across from me at the lunch table said he was getting up to go smoke a cigarette. I went with him, and went with him every time after that, and we are still friends to this day.

Today smoking has become a part of my lifestyle, although I don't see it in the desirably sexy way I used to. Cigarettes have been presented to us very differently ever since the new anti-smoking crusade. Yet I still smoke. I always talk about quitting, but push the idea away—deciding it would be too hard to do now. "I'll wait until I graduate." I see smoking as helping me function almost. It is a part of me. I don't say I *want* to smoke a cigarette; I say I *need* to smoke a cigarette. What is strange about it is that when I am at home, or with family, or in an important place, I will not smoke. In those places I never say I need a cigarette. But for some reason, sitting on my living room couch or in my school's computer lab, I do.

I have many unanswered questions about this habit and hope that soon I will be able to rid myself of it. Perhaps through sociological inquiry I will be able to see how exactly society has influenced me to become a smoker. By becoming conscious of the reasons for which we do things it is also possible to become aware of reasons why we should stop.

Phenomenological sociology views the world from the point of view of the acting subject. It seeks to explain how the world is given meaning. It follows a social process of how things become **externalized, objectified, and internalized**. So in the case of smoking cigarettes I would start by smoking with my friends, then start to see smoking with my friends as a prearranged process that I simply take part in, and finally internalize that socialization so much that it becomes a part of my life. Smoking cigarettes then has meaning to me in a social sense. Through **reification** I would forget that I initiated the creation of my smoking and see it as something separate from me, imposed on me by outside forces. This process comes about because our world is **intersubjective**, or shared. When we share experiences with others they become real. Through face to face interactions we get an idea of who we are by the way others react to us. So if people in our close group react positively to smoking, we will come to see ourselves as smokers and think of this as a desirable trait. The fact that smoking begins and is fostered by social relationships is what makes it such a concrete part of our lives—because social relationships are what society is made of and how it becomes real. Phenomenology also explains why we are not affected so much by the risks of smoking. The main and most imposing part of our consciousness is the **here and now**—what is going on directly around us at a specific time. Things that are in further concentric zones related to time and space do not affect us as much directly. Because the risks associated with smoking are long-term and the benefits are short-term we are more prone to associate with the benefits.

Now that it is understood that social interaction associated with smoking aids in its creation we must see why smoking becomes part of our social interactions. In society we use **symbols** to ascertain the meanings of each other's actions. This is what is studied by **symbolic interactionism**. The human being can act towards himself; he can see what demands are placed upon him socially, interpret them, and decide how to react to them. This is done by taking on the attitudes of the generalized other. The individual acts according to how he wants the **generalized other** to react to him. In order to call upon the desired attitudes of others we must present ourselves in a way that the symbols and attitudes we project will arouse the desired reaction in them. This is known as the **presentation of self** in everyday life. Every human being is acting as if on a **stage**. In the **front region** we act to project an image to the audience. In the **back region** we hide other parts of our character that would give away the performance. This **impression management** usually takes place within a group of constituents. We work to give others a certain impression of us because an impression is a clue about hidden facts of our selves.

So to relate this to my life we must first look at the attitudes of the generalized other, in this case the American society, and how in this society people view smoking. When I started smoking, it was portrayed throughout the media as sexy, attractive, and associated with older, high class, and successful people. Because we were so young smoking was also rebellious and cool. These are all traits that the generalized other of American society deemed valuable and social demands were put on people to acquire these traits. So if smoking would symbolize these characteristics it would be a way for me to give others the impression that I possessed these qualities. I mentioned before that my friends and I used to analyze ourselves smoking in the mirror to see how we looked; to see what we were projecting to others. That is such a telling fact. We weren't smoking for ourselves, we were smoking for the reaction we would get from society and used cigarettes as a symbol to project the image we wanted to others.

In a previous sociological self-exploration titled "From Anti-Man to Anti-Patriarchy" (see *Human Architecture*, Fall 2002 issue), I touched on the concept of a woman's dual consciousness of being at the same time the **surveyor and the surveyed**. In his book *Ways of Seeing* (1995), John Berger explains that a woman is constantly looking at herself to monitor how she is being seen by others. Women are taught from an early age how to control themselves so as to always project the proper image. It is a way of thinking that is embedded in the minds of most women but also unrecognizable to them. In relation to my experience with smoking, I was only twelve years old at the time when I watched myself inhaling and exhaling in the mirror, but I already knew it was important to see what smoking would make me look like to others and to control that image. I was the surveyor of myself and of the action I was taking part in order to be surveyed by others positively.

To further explore how smoking became a part of my character or my self, George Herbert **Mead's theory of the emergent self** is helpful as it explains how our selves are created. In order to form a self people must take on the ideas and attitudes of the generalized other so that they may function in society and interact with its members. This process of **socialization** begins in childhood. Children begin to take on the **role** of others and themselves as they **play** make-believe roles. They practice arousing certain feelings or actions in other people. Next, kids take part in organized **games** in which they must be able to take on the role of every other member and act in accordance to what is expected of them and other members for the good of the team as whole. Finally individuals are able to control their own desires, to self analyze, and correct themselves in order to gain acceptance from others. People take into account the generalized other which is the sum of all of our interconnected attitudes and actions. The self can only come about after internalizing these attitudes. That is how a society controls its members and how people relate to one another. During my childhood the ideas of the generalized other towards smoking were good. When I played make-believe roles I pretended to be a smoker but don't ever remember pretending that it was bad. As I came to take on the attitudes and ideas of the generalized other I simply saw it as cool. I smoked to go along with group norms and gain acceptance from others.

Symbolic Interactionists seek to explain society on a micro level through face to face interactions. They believe in the importance of symbols to give life a shared meaning. Another concept that many of these theorists touch upon is the importance of an individual being socialized into **group norms** in order to function in society. Much of our actions and parts of our personality come from conformity to the group in order to gain acceptance and group membership. A movie that illustrates and challenges how important group norms and conformities are in shaping our lives is *Billy Elliot*.

Billy Elliot is a young boy living at home with his father, brother, and grandmother after the death of his mother. The two male role models in his life are coal miners; they are very masculine, violent, angry, and unapproachable. Although they offer Billy minimal guidance, they expect him to follow in their footsteps doing traditional family pastimes like boxing and probably working eventually in the mine. When they discover that not only has Billy rejected their ideals but those that the generalized other holds in relation to male gender roles they become furious. Billy has to hide his ballet dancing from them because it is an idea that runs against their group norms and is therefore unacceptable. Luckily Billy is able to gain acceptance for his ballet dancing by proving how great his talent is, letting his father see that it can give him a better life. But until his hobby could be accepted by others it was very difficult for him to follow his own desires. It is very important in society to go along with the group, be accepted, and take on the ideas and practices of the society you belong to. Thus I chose to smoke when that was the practice popularized in my group.

In the foregoing, several sociological theories have helped me explore why I started smoking. It was seen as desirable at the time, I wanted to project a certain image and fit in with the group. Why, though, do I continue to smoke? Smoking is not considered desirable anymore. New anti-smoking campaigns have helped to portray it as dangerous and disgusting. It is becoming more expensive and more difficult to do because you can't smoke inside just about anywhere. I no longer want a cigarette to symbolize me because it does not represent what it used to. The fact remains, I still smoke. Not only because I'm physically addicted (there are patches for that) but for other reasons as well.

I think that in order to fully understand why I still smoke it is important to acknowledge when and where I smoke. The times I feel like I need a cigarette are after I eat, when I'm stressed out, when I'm out drinking, or when everyone else is having one. Some of these desires can be explained sociologically by the ideas of George Simmel and also by Exchange Theory.

In his "The Metropolis and Mental Life" (excerpted in Farganis, 146-157) George **Simmel** systematically explains the dialectic of individual and society. Man is not equipped to handle the complexities of today's lifestyle. Modern man must learn to cope with the metropolis in which many different images are bombarding him or her all the time. This creates high stress and intensification of nervous stimulation. Also because the metropolis is a mixture of so many people with so many different interests people need something to tie them together, to set them apart, make them easily recognizable and identifiable to a certain group. This affects my smoking habits in two ways. First of all the **metropolis** of modern life does have a tendency to put people on **sensory overload**. Sometimes, honestly, my brain feels like it may explode. Those are the times I smoke a cigarette. It is a break from everything else. While writing a paper, at work, during an intense conversation or argument, a cigarette is a time out. By smoking a cigarette, I am identifying myself with the group of smokers. Five people standing outside smoking a cigarette are almost guaranteed to start a conversation. Smokers identify and feel comfortable with one another.

This brings me to **Exchange Theory**. People's interests find expression in social groups. People are attracted to a certain group because of the perceived reward they may receive from the association. Sometimes just the association itself is the reward. Often times it is not what people do together, but the fact that they do it with others that makes an experience enjoyable. Most human pleasures have their roots in social life. People are attracted to a social group and then want to prove themselves attractive to them. This can be done by taking part in doing and reciprocating favors. These actions are a huge part of human social life. It is also a huge part of the smoking subculture. One smoker is always quick to give a cigarette or lighter to another smoker. Actions like these bond smokers into social groups who then foster each other's interest in the habit. All of my friends smoke. It is a social thing for us. I think the main thing that keeps me smoking is the fact that all of my friends do. It is part of the social exchange process to us and therefore gains validity.

What interests me deeply is to understand why it took so long for social regulations of smoking to come about. Smoking kills people and not only smokers but also victims of second hand smoke. Suicide is illegal and so is murder so why has smoking not faced serious threats and criticisms until now? Perhaps if smoking had been so widely criticized when I was younger and regulated better, I would not be a smoker today.

Conflict Theories may help give an explanation for the fact that society has condoned a life-threatening behavior for so many years. Conflict theorists see society as being controlled through power and coercion. They also agree that throughout history and historical periods a common thread is the presence of the dominant and the subordinate and conflict between them. Their perspectives on society can help to analyze the role of cigarette smoking in American society.

Max Weber's notion of the iron cage puts an interesting spin on the idea of smoking in America. Weber believed Ascetic Protestantism's favoring wealth, savings, and hard work is what contributed to the genesis of capitalism in Europe and the West. Fostered by the capitalist system, the underlying ideals of America have to do with money, the value of things, and working hard to attain wealth. Everything is boiled down to the rationality of costs and benefits. The personal attachments of traditional society is gone and a cold rational calculating society has taken its place. This rational society is controlled by companies, bureaucracies that derive power from their economic status. The more a business is worth, the more money it makes, the more valuable it is, and the more power it has. Therefore big tobacco business made sense for American society. It put a lot of money into our domestic market, and tax dollars in government budgets. The big cigarette producers like Phillip Morris would then gain more control over public policy and life in general because of their money. This is what Max Weber would see as the manifestation of the workings of capitalism. When money and capitalist rationalism—reinforced by a growing capitalist bureaucracy—mean more than people's lives, humans are bound to suffer. Even now that legislation is being passed to control tobacco, it has not been made illegal. The government simply uses this killer to gain more money by putting high taxes on it. Then the medical industry makes money from smokers' hospital bills, and the funeral homes make money off people's deaths.

It may be taking comparisons out of historical context, but **Karl Marx** may have agreed with Weber that allowing people in society to smoke is directly influenced by the interests of the ruling class whom Marx called the bourgeoisie. According to his theory the dominant ideas present at any given time are the **ideas of the ruling class**. If big tobacco companies and the people that have vested interests in them are a part of that class, it is possible to assume that smoking would be one of those dominant ideas. Some smokers see their cigarettes as more than just rolled tobacco. Smoking satisfies many different needs depending on whom you ask. Marx may have attributed smoking to feelings of **alienation** in the individual that stem from being disassociated from one's work. This alienation causes people to seek new forms of gratification and fulfillment, often self-destructive, and one of these may be smoking.

C. Wright Mills's ideas perhaps most directly shed light on my attitudes towards smoking. Mills said that Americans have lost faith in old loyalties and have not yet been able to find new ones. This loss of faith and loyalties makes people indifferent to the state of their lives. He said people just don't care. We go through life content with our physical pleasures and recreational distractions without really taking an active interest in any certain cause or in ourselves for that matter. For instance, people know that a quarter pounder with cheese is unhealthy but they eat it any way because it is convenient and tasty. These are the same people who disagree with the war in the Middle East but never bother to voice that opinion. Along with this group are those smokers who say "I'm going to die someday anyway, I might as well keep on smoking because I like it."

Other conflict theories can help us take our inquiry even farther. In his study of "Social Structure, Group Interests, and Conflict Groups" (Farganis, 266-284), Ralph **Dahrendorf** states that the masses may be excluded from political power but still enjoy a high standard of living, social rewards, and some political activism. So, as American citizens we may not have real power over the conditions of our society and the decisions that shape them but that is O.K. with us because we live comfortably with relative access to the political arena. If Americans feel that they need their voices to be heard about a certain issue they are able to do just that. As industrial society advances this access to politics grows stronger with the growth of communication which not only helps groups to organize but helps information spread to a large group of people. When the masses felt that it was time to take a stand about smoking they were able to. Through the organization of groups and most importantly through advances in communication anti-smoking legislation has been passed, the "truth" ad campaign has been launched, many other regulations put in place, and people educated about the dangers of cigarettes.

But another interesting point one may derive from Mills's perspective at this point. He may say that all of this attention toward the issue of smoking or not smoking, changing legislation, suing tobacco companies, and other ideas surrounding this controversy are all just a bunch of smoke and lights. In the realm of the real world issues like this are focused on to distract the masses from looking at the big picture of the kind of social system we live in—away from seeing who really has power. People may be able to make changes in the middle levels of power-structure like Congress and political action groups but there is a small group of elites in the world who hold a power far greater than that. This group does not care about smoking or not smoking, which is used as an issue to let people feel like they have power, as if they have a voice. The real source of dominance and change in the world lies in the fact that "a few men have access to the means by which in a few days continents can be turned into thermonuclear wastelands" (Mills, in Farganis 286). This inhuman power is so much more than a few laws about cigarettes.

The movie *Erin Brockovich* provides a great illustration for our purpose of exploring how Conflict Theory sheds light on the role of big tobacco companies in American society today. The movie depicts a large corporation and the power it can exert over the common citizen. PG&E is a 28 billion dollar a year company. They knowingly exposed citizens of their surrounding town to toxic substances. They were able to make people believe that chromium six, a chemical they used in their plants, had many physical benefits when really it was infecting people with deadly diseases. They even destroyed and hid evidence linking the chromium to the illnesses. They were able to get away with all of this for twenty five years because they had power, money, and people's trust in a system that actually dominates them. Eventually Erin Brockovich, along with the help of a few insiders from the company and those harmed by the company, was able to implicate PG&E in the illnesses and deaths of many citizens. Lawsuits and new regulations followed.

The path followed by PG&E resembles that of many cigarette companies. Tobacco is a forty five billion dollar a year industry. This indicates that many people smoke cigarettes. For years no one even knew they were harmful. Watching the movie *Twelve Angry Men* is a tell tale sign of this. The majority of the men in the movie are not only smoking but *chain-smoking* cigarettes. There are several times when the camera zooms in on the full ashtrays before fading to the next seen as if it is a necessary prop. Throughout the entire movie one of the men has a hacking cough, as cigarette smoke is blown in his face; people keep asking him what could be wrong with his health. During the time when this movie was made people weren't fully aware that nicotine is a poison, or that benzopyrene causes cancer, or that tobacco would end up causing 430,000 premature deaths each year. Finally in the early nineties all of that changed. For a few years people had known that smoking was dangerous and that it caused lung damage and cancer but no one was able to prove that the tobacco companies were aware of these dangers the entire time they were marketing the product. In 1994 a paralegal at one of the tobacco companies stole documents that proved the heads of the corporation knew cigarettes were addicting and had lied under oath. In 1996 a biochemist came forward with information that he had pushed one of the companies to make safer cigarettes (informing them of the dangers smoking had for people) but he had been denied. Later that year the first lawsuit against tobacco companies was filed and won, and the first legislation controlling tobacco was passed. Since then the controversy has continued to unravel and tobacco companies have lost much of their power, money, and especially the trust of the people.

On the opposite side of the spectrum from conflict theorists we find **functionalists**. Functionalists view society as emerging from consensual agreements based on shared values and norms. Through these agreements people view the society they live in as legitimate and it becomes their bond. Where conflict theorists would say that smoking is a projection of the interests of the elite, functionalists would say it serves a purpose and function for members of society.

Emile **Durkheim** was a functionalist, though the label emerged much later. He was one of the first people to view society as an entity in and of itself. It is external to individuals and forces them to conform. He also introduced the idea of "**social fact**," of what exists independently from individual human acts and induces their conformity to "objective" social norms. Smoking cigarettes in order to gain acceptance would be, Durkheim may argue, one of these "social facts." I was not born with that idea; it was taught to me by society and existed independently of me. Somewhere I learned that smoking would lead to acceptance. This idea exerted a force on me and in turn I began to smoke. When studying **suicide** Durkheim realized that a person's decision to take his life had a great deal to do with the degree of his integration in and bond with social groups. His study may reinforce the idea that human beings smoke because they have too much or too little social solidarity.

Talcott **Parsons** is another functionalist. One of his studies had to do with age and sex in the social structure (see Farganis, 236-246). Although his work is a little outdated in its application to modern society it does contain some valuable points of interest. For instance, Parsons writes about the "youth culture," the time in life when adolescents rebel against adult norms. At the time when Parsons wrote this study he found that there was no female counterpart to the "bad boy" that is ever present in adolescence. His reasoning for this finding was that girls were in direct contact with their mothers at all times because women stayed at home with the children. This allowed females to more readily observe and replicate their roles as adult women. Males lacked this contact with their future gender role because fathers spent most of their time at work. As a result males were not as directly socialized into the adult role giving them more freedom to break away from it.

In today's society both men and women spend a great deal of time away from the home and from their children especially during their adolescence. This gives both boys and girls more of an opportunity to stray from the path their parents would like to see them on. Smoking is a very common form of rebellion. Parsons also gives an explanation for smoking among adults and how it is differentiated by gender lines. Women are taught all of their lives that the best trait they can have is to be desirable to men so that they may end up with a rich husband whose success will help to define them as a person. Men are taught that they must become rich and powerful so that they may attract a beautiful wife and be judged as successful by others. Smoking has come to symbolize both attractiveness and power in our society which makes adults want to smoke to help to enhance their image.

Robert K. **Merton** provided sociologists and social scientists an interesting way to study society. Merton introduced the idea of **manifest and latent functions**. Manifest functions are those that are intended and latent functions are those that are not. For example a manifest function of smoking may be to satisfy a nicotine craving or to take a social break from work. Latent functions of smoking may be to project a certain image or to fit in with a peer group. When looking at manifest and latent functions together we are able to see the entire picture surrounding an issue. Recognizing latent functions also helps people not to pass naïve moral judgments. Instead of looking at a teenage smoker as a rebel or a "bad boy" one may be able to see them as a person with insecurities seeking to fit into a group.

Conversely, through the influences of the media and people around us smoking takes on the latent symbolism of prestige and power. As L.M. Damian asserts in his essay "Conspicuous Conflict" (2002) that the quest for power and prestige has become a dominant ideology in modern life and is viewed as a means to happiness by many Americans. The movie *Affluenza* also deals with this idea as it shows the American population seeking material possessions in order to fulfill some need and to give off an aura of dominance over those who have less. Smoking has come to represent these ideals; even the brand of cigarette one smokes can contribute to a person's ranking of power and prestige. Damian suggests that in order to dispel such ideologies in our lives and not take part in actions that foster them we must have "extensive" perception. This will allow us to see things as they are not as they are labeled. I must be able to recognize a cigarette not as a rolled stick of tobacco, but as a status symbol.

Jürgen **Habermas**, a Critical Theorist, believed that despite the limits of capitalism, modern rational knowledge can be accessible to all people and thus help shape society into a just and democratic order. The current anti-smoking campaign, providing people with knowledge regardless of the power of the tobacco companies supports Habermas' idea. As a postmodernist, however, **Foucault** may argue the opposite. Postmodernist theories arose almost in opposition to all those that came before them. Most **postmodernists** also seek to problematize and question the relationships among knowledge, science, and power in industrial society. Foucault brings up the notion of "carceral society" in which every social institution reinforces the coercion and power of society as a whole. Scientific knowledge has had a huge impact on these arenas because of the control it exerts over people. Psychiatrists, schools, teachers, medical doctors, scientists and others are all putting their knowledge to work in order to define and determine what is "normal." Foucault believes that we let scientific knowledge and those who spread it dictate the path of society. My medical doctor has told me repeatedly to quit smoking and so I believe that it is bad for me and I'm harming myself. During therapy for panic attacks my psychiatrist told me not to quit until I had dealt with my anxiety, so I didn't. We see these people, professionals, as being accredited with a form of elite knowledge. We trust them and allow their knowledge to control our actions.

Postmodernism challenges the idea that the modern human thinks for himself. Our immense reliance on rationalism allows us to accept certain scientific facts to be true and to simply live by them, to let our thoughts and actions be controlled by society. **Nietzsche** is one of the main influences among postmodernists. He believed that rationalism and all of the institutions of society are in place to uphold certain Western Christian ideals which are not necessarily legitimate human truths. Nietzsche's hope was for the *Ubermensch* or superman to overcome the current state of man so humans can become "authors of their own lives" instead of letting society dictate who they were and impose itself on them.

Why is it that people let what is around them control their lives? Why are we so affected by our society? What is it about human nature that allows us to passively give up our own will and accept what we are told?

In his piece titled "From the Author" (excerpted from *All and Everything: Beelzebub's Tales to his Grandson*), **Gurdjieff** criticizes modern man for exactly the questions I just raised. He describes the human organism symbolically as being composed of a carriage, a horse, a coachman, and the passenger representing the physical body, feelings, consciousness, and the "I." Modern man has a broken and run down carriage because he does not take care of his body or do with it what was intended. His horse is wild and out of control because it has been neglected and uneducated. The coachman is drunk with no control over the horse meaning that the organism as a whole is powered by his impulsive feelings and desires and not by his consciousness. Finally there is no definite passenger; one or another comes along for a ride but the modern man has no true self.

Gurdjieff believes that we humans live in sleep throughout our lives reacting to stimuli and ignoring important parts of our composition. Modern man neglects those parts of his character that could lead him to reach his full potential and instead is controlled by desires for food, drink, sex, and pleasure. Perhaps the reason for my bad habit is that my mental self has no intelligent control over my physical and/or emotional selves and desires. One would think that if my consciousness recognized the dangers of smoking it would control my desires. Perhaps if I refine and train the separate parts of myself I will be able to dispel my desires for cigarettes.

All of my questions about smoking have not yet been answered. I have seen that I smoke to fit a certain image and gain a desirable reaction from others. Also I enjoy the social solidarity I feel with other smokers and the relationships I develop through the habit. I continue to smoke because I am led by blind physical desire and because cigarette use is not widely enough condemned by our "rational" society. I have seen how smoking is a social product and how I also am a product of that society. I have recognized the implications of smoking in my life and yet am not ready to reject it. There must be something else besides the issues I am aware of that continues my drive to smoke, that makes it a habit, that allows me to actively engage in the activity without even thinking about it. This something else is discussed in the book *You can do it with Self-Hypnosis* by Charles E. Henderson (1983).

Henderson explores the idea of the subconscious mind controlling our automatic impulses. Because our thoughts are stuck in the conscious state of mind we have no access to the subconscious even though it has control over us. The subconscious is the part of the mind that protects us. It is what pulls our hand away from a hot stove. The subconscious mind is preoccupied with goal seeking and group membership because both of these functions are necessary in the life of a human being. A good example of the subconscious mind helping us to attain both of these things and protecting us when we don't is illustrated in the essay "Repairing the Soul: Matching Inner with Outer Beauty" by Kristy Canfield (2002). The author describes how she was shunned by her peers because of physical differences in her speech. This exile caused anxiety, depression, and hopelessness. As a result Kristy was subconsciously conditioned to isolate herself from the outside world in order to protect herself from rejection.

The subconscious learns and experiences then timelessly holds onto the emotional qualities of each experience. This part of the mind is based on imprints that are learned early in life and remain inside of us, unchanging. The film *Multiple Personalities* features several different patients who suffer from these mental illnesses. In every case the problems are said to stem from childhood. Often times the individual is not even aware of the events which caused their subconscious mind to create the other personalities. In every case early events in life became internalized as subconscious imprints inside of the mind. The beliefs, ideas, and values of the group are internalized as identification imprints and learned without the learner knowing he or she learned them. The habit of smoking usually comes from these identifications. Either the subconscious mind identifies with the role of an adult, with a significant other who smoked, or a group of peers. In any case the subconscious links smoking with these identifications and doesn't let go. Without realizing it, smoking to me may mean being an adult, fitting in, or something I am totally unaware of. It symbolizes something important that the subconscious wants to protect. This is a reason that so many people find it hard to quit smoking. They may consciously reject the habit but subconsciously they are attracted to it because of the emotional response of the original imprint in the subconscious.

Henderson introduces a method with which to explore and control one's own subconscious mind in order to quit smoking and other habits. I have decided to try these methods but because it takes about six weeks to accomplish I will be unable to share the results with you the reader. What I can say is that I find the idea of identification imprints legitimate when looking at my own life and smoking habit in the contexts of role identification (when I used to play house) and group identification (choosing to smoke because of my peers).

Exercising my **sociological imagination**, I can see how society has played a huge role in my decision to smoke. Coupled with my subconscious mind within, broader society has fostered the habit throughout my life. It bothers me that I have acquired a pastime that inflicts such harm onto my person. It bothers me that the habit is so strongly internalized that even after analyzing smoking and cigarettes using many sociological theories and some other helpful references I am unable to throw my pack in the garbage. This paper has once again opened my eyes to the social forces that are at work in our lives everyday and has made me more aware of the role society plays in my everyday life.

Perhaps this knowledge will help me to better control myself and my actions.

References

Berger, John. (1995). *Ways of Seeing*. London: Viking Press.

Canfield, K. (2002). "Repairing the Soul: Matching Inner with Outer Beauty." *Human Architecture: Journal of the Sociology of Self-Knowledge*, I, 2, 20-26.

Damian, L.M. "Conspicuous Conflict," *Human Architecture: Journal of the Sociology of Self-Knowledge*, Vol. I, No. 2, Fall 2002.

Farganis, J. (2000). *Readings in Social Theory: The Classic Tradition to Post-Modernism*. Third Edition. Boston: McGraw Hill.

Gurdjieff, G.I. (1950). "From the Author," in *All and Everything: Beelzebub's Tales to His Grandson.*, First Edition. New York: Harcourt, Brace and Company. pp. 1089-1135.

Henderson, Charles, E. (1983). *You Can Do It With Self-Hypnosis: Achieving Self-improvement, Personal Growth, and Success*. New Jersey: Prentice-Hall, Inc.

Margulies, Emily. (2002). "From Anti-man to Anti-patriarchy," *Human Architecture, Journal of the Sociology of Self-Knowledge*, Volume I, Number 2, Fall 2002, pp. 1-8, Okcir Press, Endicott, NY.

Wallace, R and Wolf, A. (1999). *Contemporary Sociological Theory: Expanding the Classical Tradition*. Fifth Edition. New Jersey: Prentice Hall.

Films:

"Billy Elliot." (2000). Universal Pictures.

"Erin Brockovich." (2000). Universal Pictures.

"Multiple Personalities: The Search for Deadly Memories." (1994). Home Box Office.

"Twelve Angry Men." (1957). MGM.

The Drinking Matrix:
A Symbolic Self Interaction

Neo Morpheus

When our class began to get more in depth and interesting, I learned something about myself. Watching the movie *The Matrix* was extremely fascinating, but the discussion after the movie proved to me to be of more value. The concept "Know Thyself" almost exploded before my very ears. The movie brought up theories and ideas which never occurred to me. I left that particular class that night with a feeling of confusion and doubt. Do I know myself? Do I know who I really am? Before this class I thought I had a firm grasp on knowing myself. The fact is John P. Hewitt, the author of our textbook *Self and Society: A Symbolic Interactionist Social Psychology*, and the movies we have watched have opened for me a window to escape, leaving me with a choice. I can remain in this cave and accept my false "I" who misses the whole picture. Or, I can slowly work myself out of this created cave of uncertainty.

I believed I had a firm grasp on who I am. Life experiences no doubt have made me a mentally tough individual. A way of noticing one's own positive and negative traits is through time. I have traveled numerous times around the United States during which I had a great deal of time for self reflection. I have met all sorts of individuals and have acquired many positive characteristics and left behind numerous flaws. Yet it wasn't until *The Matrix* that I realized how much more there is to know. During the film the concept "residual self-projection" was introduced. A residual self projection is an individual's image constructed by outside forces. It makes an individual believe that he is fine with the surrounding conditions, hence becoming incapable of empowering himself. I now feel as if I am also in some sort of capsule and think of myself as blinded, controlled, and manipulated by outside factors. I feel that unhealthy urges are weights holding me down from getting to know the real "I" within. I am enslaved to an evil alcohol addiction. All Morpheus wanted is to free the minds of individuals enslaved to Matrix. Through the words of Morpheus I realize that I am a drone enslaved to evil corporations profiting on my weakness, and my weakness is preventing me from knowing my real "I."

The way I acquired these characteristics may be explained by the **Learning Theory** in social psychology. At a young age through **model learning** I witnessed alcohol as a progression to fun. **Operant conditioning** made it obvious, and now **classical conditioning** has me craving for a drink when I hear the word "bar." At the bar a process begins to take form that can best be explained by **Exchange Theory**. Social relations have been developed with other heavy drinkers as a way to maintain beneficial encounters. "Exchange relationships develop in an established social world that shapes the way people depend on one another and exchange benefits" (Hewitt 15). Even if I'm broke I know that either friends or the bartender will make me drunk. It's a wonderful yet vicious cycle. In this world that I have created, while the money lasts, my friends and I all look out for one another. The money issue goes through phases, but always comes down to sharing.

There are other **phases of the act** that play parts in my life. After not smoking all day, I rent a movie to keep my mind occupied. When I see a smoker in the movie inhaling, I receive an **impulse** to light up. My internal urges **motivate** me and then **manipulation** takes flight. I'll walk to a neighbor's home and ask for one. I might return to the movie, but unfortunately at this time I might not enjoy the movie until **consummation** is complete. Usually once an impulse is aroused, consummation becomes the next step. I am working towards laughing at that smoker in the movie, while I proudly enjoy my health.

Working towards good health isn't that easy. I have **social objects** that prevent me from achieving my goal. Sometimes I question who my friends are. I have chosen my friends because we all have a great deal in common. Yet, with that said, it doesn't seem to be enough. Without alcohol something is off and the situation isn't as fun and exciting as it could be. Time to ponder over these issues with a broken leg has given me a chance to step **off stage**. Not being around a crowd concentrating on drinking has helped me notice a few things. A social object is not simply peer pressure imposed from outside, but an object created by myself. I do have a **social bond** with my friends. I am beginning to see this bond as artificial. Everyone craves attachment to others. Bonds need to be constantly reinforced through tests. This new test I am proposing demonstrates differentiation within my group. Hewitt claims that a need for personal identity within the group is appropriate.

Alcohol and cigarettes hold the **attention** of everyone I know. That's not to say I can't have fun without them; I'm saying that I won't have as much fun—which is a horrible thing. The notion of **self as object** helps clarify my position. "It is not only the corporeal existence of the person that we have in mind when we talk about the self, but also, and more importantly, a great many intangible attributes and characteristics. ... in short, whatever kind of objects their own acts indicate them to be" (Hewitt 58). Seeing self as object involves concentrating attention on ourselves, because we can be our own object and desire to achieve some goal. Some people are alcoholics because they are insecure or anxious. I have excuses and explanations of why I live the life I do. Yet, as of lately those excuses do not seem to work as well as they did one year ago. In the hour-long documentary *Multiple Personalities: the Search for Deadly Memories*, one of the patients, Gretchen, makes an excellent statement. Gretchen and I both suffer from the same disease, though caused by different factors. We both cope with it, but in different ways. Yet, I feel we both try to block out and alter our selves to deal with some sort of pain. In one of Gretchen's calmest moments she stated that "we are so good at hiding ourselves." She used a journal as a mechanism to communicate among her selves in order to understand and move beyond her problems the way I am using this paper to elevate my life. The notion of self as object helps me step back from my selves and my groups to predict the potential worsening of a disease.

This disease has ruined many relationships. A few years ago my **role** as a boyfriend did not fit an ex-girlfriend's definition. She would get mad that I would leave the apartment to get drunk. In many **situations** I knew she would disapprove of my actions. I would wait for her to fall asleep before I went into the apartment after a long night of drinking. Sometimes she would find me the next morning still sleeping outside the front door. She left me for good one morning because she predicted that I won't change. She helped me view myself as what I was and somewhat still am. By pretending I am not a drunk, I was **role making**; the problem was that I could not really adjust all my behavior—because I have a problem. My **line of conduct** (Hewitt 69) stopped for almost nobody. Unfortunately that sweet girl had to deal with my antics. I usually didn't remember how bad and belligerent I got, so I never really began **role taking,** the role of someone who has a problem. Once I did, I began going to meetings and **talking out** my problems. Talking is the best way to analyze a dilemma. Talking with someone allows the problematic person an outlet to express his or her deepest fears and concerns. Somehow, though, one day I missed the bus to the next meeting and hopped back on the wagon.

The excerpt "From the Author" from the book *All and Everything* by **Gurdjieff** introduces an interesting notion of **Real Man** using the symbol of a coach driven by a horse and coachman, with a passenger in the box. "I," the passenger is supposed to have control over the whole organism, over my life. The "I" tells the coachman (my consciousness) to direct feelings (the horse) so as to lead the coach to its destination. When my horse has feels like drinking and smoking, the "I" in me has difficulty dealing with the coachman. I do not always have complete control over the system, including the reins, the shaft, and the break lever linking my physical, emotional, and intellectual selves to one another. Therefore, my "I" is not always in control—three sheets to the wind so to speak.

I have been involved in many **actions** that have become embedded in the memories of friends and strangers. My actions have caused certain **emotional reactions** in anyone I encounter. I am always a friendly and considerate person, but feel I am expected to produce comic situations for others. "We experience emotion because of our participation in social interaction" (Hewitt 74). I find this to be completely true and also find myself observing the emotions I feel and generate during social interaction. I thought I had my friends fooled to a degree. None of us are really fooling anybody because we all notice how much the others drink. We've never talked about these issues but I imagine we all have deep issues to resolve. No one would guess this, but I'm not all that happy a person these days.

My inside tells a much different story than what I project externally. What I find odd is how I'm coping with a broken leg. I have never experienced continuous physical pain until recently. To add, besides my folks I haven't seen anyone and have only talked to a few people for weeks. I'm extremely lonely, but haven't been drinking. The opportunity is there, but I find myself day after day hatching more and more out of a shell that I have constructed. I'm learning that if I'm strong enough to surpass this unfortunate mental/physical situation without the booze, then I should be ecstatic about simply talking to someone and walking around.

According to Hewitt, I might have low **self-esteem** and **motivation** problems. I don't think my low self-esteem is necessarily the main problem. As far as motivation is concerned, I admit that alcohol does motivate me. It doesn't matter what's going on when I get motivated, because I won't remember it any ways. Admitting that I have low self-esteem probably wouldn't help me. Hewitt's reference to low self-esteem does describe a part of my problem. My problem is perhaps an arubix cube with many different sides that nearly nobody has figured out.

I am only one person and this is the life I live in the State of New York. I am also part of something bigger in the country, or even globe as a whole. I'm part of many problems that are not just personal or local, but national and global. My **self image**, how I view myself in everyday life, points out flaws in my identity. When I begin to drink, drinking overwhelms my situated identity. A lot of other factors hold my attention while I have a drink in hand, but when I've started and become cut off (a sign that my alienated horse has taken over), I become uneasy and focus my attention on obtaining a drink. Sometimes I can't stop myself, and as a result begin to realize that in contrast to other people I have an addictive personality. I no doubt have a lifelong **personal identity** beyond my situated selves; I am a unique and unusual character. But I associate with a group of kids that behave as unpredictably as I do. **Social identity** "places the individual as a member of a social category that differs from other categories" (Hewitt 107). My friends and I are certainly noticed for our social identity of having a lot of fun wherever we go, but at the expense of our health.

When a new day starts, I can't always be honest when discussing the night before. To some I could brag about what I did or what happened, but to the majority of acquaintances I have to lie about my life. I am too ashamed, especially when meeting someone new, to admit some of the things that has happened to me. **First impressions** do not come around again, and so I practice regularly putting **limits on the choice of stories** I report. Everyone does in some form; I just abuse this option so much that I get dizzy.

With the act of breaking my leg I have broken the habit of inebriating myself on a daily basis. I am working on not letting habituation become concrete and cement my "role" in defining myself in situations. My use of **cognitive frames for role making and taking** have allowed me to assume and predict how future actions will affect others and myself. **Probability** is the category that for me stands out beyond the rest. It helps me to assume and predict how others will react to my potential hiatus from drinking. I know that I won't necessarily be in the loop any more. I will still hear about the things that happen on a Tuesday night, but when I no longer create the stories that are being told it proves I have made myself scarce. Although I shouldn't be, I am concerned with **means and ends**. I want to feel healthy, but see my associates as a hurdle. At the same time I desire fun and stimulation and need others to accomplish that. It shows me that means and ends question hiatus.

I see myself performing **aligning actions**. Drinking or not drinking I always seem to try to make my behavior desirable. With my group of friends, on Friday and Saturday nights especially, I will need a strong **motive talk** to explain why I am not partaking in their ritualistic drinking. I have previously projected to them an identity and expectation of doing so, therefore the act of someone asking me if I am thirsty is nobody's fault but my own. I'll have to deal with that, but my group will have to deal with my **disclaimer**. Sometimes people outgrow each other and begin to take on other interests. If my main hobby is no longer drinking, I'll seem to slowly slip away without much notice from the crowd. I would never give the crowd my **account of clarity** when they have been drinking, for I know that it wouldn't go over so well. Not involving myself to the degree in which I am doing so now will invite a variety of reactions. In the long run, nobody will lose sleep over it.

Symbolic Interactionists believe there are wider **constraints on social interaction** beyond personal ones. However, in my life, I have the power to make up my own mind and decide what is best for me. The only power I know I have over others is the ability to empower myself to make my own decisions. My acts also have the power to manipulate someone subconsciously. The **interpersonal roles** I have created with the people with whom I interact repeatedly will undoubtedly continue to produce subconscious expectations in others about me. I might also continue to make roles subconsciously. Conversely, if I redefine my situation and modify the reality around me, I might no longer feel a need to be constrained by a particular lifestyle, which in turn may trigger others to notice their potential power to do the same. My role **altercasting** may induce others to modify their conduct. The way I act toward them will begin to constrain their conduct. In a sense, I'm giving them an opportunity to awaken from the hellish nightmare of a life that has become habituated to a liquid.

I frown and look down upon my own past actions in this period of sobriety. I usually put myself through horrible **routine and problematic situations**. Not eating to save and spend money "elsewhere" became ritualistic. My routine "requires little self-conscious control" (Hewitt) and leads to problematic confrontations mostly with myself but sometimes with others with whom I interact. I feel like a hypocrite because I will eventually fall back into my old routine. Currently I have been awakened. The movie *Awakenings*, about the real life based story of Dr. Sayer's catatonic patients coming alive for a short period, showed patients that do not symbolically interact on the outside, but inside are nevertheless amply aware. Their awareness becomes brought to life for a period of time. The patients just sort of snap out of it, similar to the way I have awakened due to a leg injury. The patients also struggle to maintain their freedom, but find themselves falling back into a constant state of prior horror. Certain diseases are very difficult to cure. I find it especially difficult to say good-by to an element of my life that I have had a love-hate relationship with for so long. I know that I have a choice as opposed to Dr. Sayer's patients—a choice to alter future situations from problematic to non-problematic. Along my recovery some people will notice the changes I have brought upon myself; I hope to cast them along, knowing helpful others will make the struggle easier. In a sense I would be forming a **boundary line**—like the woman in the movie, who was constrained by a routine floor pattern. Once the constrains were removed with the "will" of a helping hand, she was able to move beyond prior limitations and restrictions. This paper may be that helping hand "I" am giving myself.

The mental line I have begun creating for myself has laid the ground work for new boundaries. New subdivisions of social life will help emphasize and distinguish those I can more closely identify with. Setting boundaries is a major step to free myself of negative habituations. I get to pick and choose what may become a new beginning. The **problematic boundaries** and ways which have created uneasiness and a lack of happiness in my life need to be changed. I need to redraw my floor plans. I need to focus and concentrate on resolving my current dilemma. Social **Problem solving** starts with me. Defining and acknowledging the problem lets me become aware of my position in society. Most people are unaware of my situation, but I am myself aware of my social classification, and how my conduct is burdened by and burdens society.

My everyday social actions and interactions cause mixed internal emotions. There is a **social order and disorder** that I am very much a part of and which allow me to get caught up in familiar negative ways. People who are classified as drug and alcohol addicts are burdened with a horrible connotation. We are considered symbolic representatives of social disorder. We are **labeled** negatively even though we might be otherwise making valuable and positive contributions to our community. People create images from prior experiences and forever label an act as correct and another act as wrong. It is difficult to maintain one's individuality when people label and stereotype you. Conversely, individuals and groups may question inherited stereotypes and labels. I do feel fortunate that such people speak their minds. Their questioning of particular roles empower actors to change and make a difference.

Society treats people well or badly, as being normal or abnormal. We label others and thereby perpetuate a social order. The social order then implies a distinction between **deviant** and "normal" people. People use the term deviant when they themselves are not pleased with the actions of another. I consider myself to be a deviant. I perceive myself as a threat to myself.

I am also a threat to society. I own an automobile which can be deadly to myself and to others. The act of my friends' taking away my car keys proves there are **variable responses to similar acts**. Driving while intoxicated is not something to consider lightly. It is an object that has a social meaning beyond personal choice. My intention to drive is perceived by most as deviant, thus forcing them to involve themselves in my decision-making. When an actor creates a scene where others perceive the situation as harmful, other members of society make an effort to role take and eliminate a potential threat.

Overconsumption is a threat that is highly overlooked. In a way, I also suffer from **Affluenza**. Drinking is a way to overconsume to achieve temporary happiness. The act of consummation fills an emptiness that lurks within. Each time happiness is achieved, time wears the notion thin. Corporations want to "brand and own" people in order to lure them to their product. The millions of dollars spent on advertisements have helped persuade me to choose my poisons. People are slaves to consuming. Every time I own a bottle that bottle is actually owning me. I need to come back to it, to feel a sense of happiness. Drinking is consuming an idea of happiness. Several people in the documentary *Affluenza* began to awaken. People began to realize that the life they were living was dangerous. These objects of luxury hid the problems waiting to come. Those people did not notice that it is their actions that produce society. We create and re-create social structure through our actions towards our selves and society. This is processed through our minds because we create symbols and give these symbols value and power. I feel that certain people, myself included, created insignificant meanings within a world taken for granted. *The Matrix* tells us symbolically that the world we take for granted is artificial and that we should begin to question our everyday life.

I first took the movie *The Truman Show* for what it is; a movie. However, I found the concept new and extraordinary. The intensity of the notion of life as a show faded after a few days but left a lasting impression. *The Truman Show* is another symbolic portrayal of our artificial world. Others create what one processes as reality, when in reality the individual is fooled. It is "reality" for Truman until his moment of clarity. In a sense, Truman begins to uncover the truth and "learns how deep the rabbit hole goes." The audience in the film watch the "Truman Show" and become so much incorporated into the show that their own lives become an appendage of its episodic doses. Likewise, the War in Iraq became the biggest reality TV show that I have ever seen. On every channel during all hours of the day anyone was able to turn on the television and witnessing hell on earth. The television coverage of the war controlled viewers. People planned eating and sleeping arrangements around the TV, the way people in the Truman Show lived their entire lives. Viewers consumed an idea or notion of happiness, struck with Affluenza. It appears that all people suffer from forms of habituation. I almost feel now that even exercising every other day at three in the afternoon can become an element in a person's life which in fact will wind up owning them and manipulating all aspects of their everyday lives. The producers of the show have complete **social control** over Truman. Manipulating him into becoming habitually frightened of water and in a sense "grounding" him to a specific area demonstrates the producer's power. Rebellion comes into play as a direct result, though, and Truman responds in a deviant way by going against the norms others have constructed.

I feel that this course has helped me question my every day life and how social meanings have become embedded in **significant symbols**. This course is another step towards uncovering constructed associations. I now realize that until I uncover these constructed associations, I can not discover myself. I am unable to discover myself because I continually perpetuate associations which do not question and problematize my habituated conducts. I need to fully awaken—but not just dream that I am awake. My unconscious impulse is a weed infecting my motivation. Lately my "I" seems to be gaining control over and directing my coachman. I have had a firm grasp of the reins and have had my sights set on a better looking and feeling tomorrow. I have decided not to let habituations permanently define who I am in a given moment or situation. I know that every act is due to an impulse. I feel that my urges will no longer easily overwhelm my perceptions and manipulations. These are the factors preventing me from partaking in intentional consummation. My inner dialogue, understanding, and questioning of who I am take place through symbolic interaction. Role taking and making, constraining and liberating, would not exist without symbolic interaction.

I was not grown to be a cash crop. As I am writing I am gathering new conceptual building blocks to find myself. As a result of this course I have climbed higher to taste a plateau of happiness beyond habituation. Breaking a leg, ironically, helped me climb on the path of breaking a habit—symbolically speaking.

REFERENCES

Gurdjieff, G.I. (1950). "From the Author," in *All and Everything: Beelzebub's Tales to His Grandson.*, First Edition. New York: Harcourt, Brace and Company. pp. 1089-1135.

Hewitt, John P. *Self and Society: A Symbolic Interactionist Social Psychology,* 9th edition. Allyn & Bacon, 2002.

Films:

"Affluenza." (1997). KCTS-Seattle and Oregon Public Broadcasting.

"Awakenings," (1990). Columbia/Tristar Studios.

"Multiple Personalities: The Search for Deadly Memories." (1994). Home Box Office.

"The Matrix." (1999). Warner brothers.

"The Truman Show." (1998). Paramount Pictures.

Theoretical Reflections on Peer Judgments

M. Goltry

We are all absorbed in a constant struggle to find ourselves. From the time we are born, every experience becomes a piece in the puzzle that may or may not eventually integrate into the whole person. Both society and ourselves play a major role in deciding what kind of people we will be. It is through our interactions with others that we form opinions of ourselves. Throughout my own personal struggle to find myself, society has had an effect on both micro and macro levels.

A significant problem in my life arose at about the time I entered middle school. At this point in my life, I began to more than before take into account the opinions and attitudes of others. The situation was escalated by the fact that I became overweight and had to start wearing glasses, both of which caused me to become tremendously self-conscious. My self-consciousness stemmed from my increasing attention to how others thought of me. Now I see how **symbolic interaction** affected my self-identity formation. It seemed as though all at once I had become the fat, four-eyed girl. For the other children, my weight and the glasses acted as symbols for how they should treat me. They felt that based on these symbols, it was acceptable to treat me with less respect and dignity. This treatment was well illustrated in the movie, *Erin Brockovich*. When Erin begins working in the lawyer's office, she is not accepted by her co-workers because of her style of dress. Her clothing becomes a symbol for the other workers' cruelty towards her. They ignore her, and are rude and unhelpful to her at every opportunity. However, Erin does not let their negative opinions of her stand in her way, and in the end she earns their respect through her hard work and great accomplishments. As can be seen, there are certain symbols in society, such as weight or provocative clothing, which signal to others the opportunity to judge and to behave in certain ways. According to George Herbert **Mead**, "Our actions are always engaged with the actions of others, whose responses to what we do send us signals as to their approval or disapproval" (Farganis 159). I also looked toward others for their opinions of me, and then allowed their reactions to gauge how I felt about myself. As is common among children of middle school age, my classmates were quite cruel toward me. This led me to believe that their harsh comments were true, and that I was truly worthless. These events, in turn, triggered the gradual decline of my self-esteem and overall self-worth.

As time went on, my conceived notions of others' opinions gradually became a part of me, and came to shape my overall self-concept. As hard as I tried to ignore the cruel comments of others, they eventually became subconsciously embedded inside my mind. This was especially the case when this harsh attitude came from my own **significant others**. In particular, I can recall one of my cousins who used to derive pure pleasure from making fun of me. This specific cousin was several years older than I, and she was someone whom I had always looked up to and strived to be like. Charles Horton **Cooley's "looking-glass self"** concept helps explain this. The idea is basically that we judge ourselves based on our perceptions of other people's opinions of us, which in turn, affect our feelings about ourselves. In her article, "Repairing the Soul: Matching Inner with Outer Beauty," Kristy Canfield adds that the looking-glass self, "shapes our ability to contemplate our existence and to project ourselves into the past and future" (Canfield 24). Another concept put forth by Mead is **reflexivity**, which is defined as "the capacity to use and respond to language, symbols, and thoughts" (Farganis 159). This has to do with how we manipulate our actions in order for them to fit the expectations of others. Mead goes on to state, as quoted earlier, that "Our actions are always engaged with the actions of others, whose responses to what we do send us signals as to their approval or disapproval" (Farganis 159). Because of the fact that my cousin was a role model for me and I highly valued her opinion, her comments had a major impact on my self-image. Therefore, I attempted to change myself in order to meet her standards and earn her respect. This relates to W. E. B. **Du Bois**' notion of **double-consciousness**. Du Bois describes this phenomenon as, "a sense of always looking at one's self through the eyes of others, of measuring one's soul by the tape of a world that looks on in amused contempt and pity" (Farganis, 187). In this way, I was constantly struggling to keep my personal values and attitudes, while at the same time attempting to fit in and adopt the values of others.

Throughout my quest for popularity I was very concerned with **status**. Peter **Blau** defines status as "the common recognition by others of the amount of esteem and friendship that someone receives" (Wallace and Wolf 330). In my case, the other children were of a higher status than I, as they were more highly respected and recognized. Blau goes on to make the point that, "people whose status is not very secure are most threatened by being seen with lower-status people" (Wallace and Wolf 330). This was certainly the case among many of my classmates. The reason for this was that shifts in status could occur very rapidly and unexpectedly among the children. Therefore, they were very uneasy about associating with classmates of lower status, as they could quickly be reduced to the level of the lower-status person. In my situation, it was extremely difficult to achieve high-status, but once you had reached that level, it was very easy to slip back down the ladder.

Now that I look back I have realized that in many ways the people who would pick on me were using me as a stepping stone in their own quest for popularity. The more they made fun of me, the more the other kids looked up to them and respected them. This ties into the ideas of **Rational Choice Theories**, which "assume that people are rational and base their actions on what they perceive to be the most effective means to their goals" (Wallace and Wolf 294). Therefore, the other children, who were in pursuit of popularity, saw cruelty as the most effective route to their goal. This idea also fits well with the ideas of **Exchange Theory**, which explains the rewards and punishments that are involved in social associations. Exchange Theory is a rational choice theory, as it encompasses the idea of the means to ends rationality of human behavior (Wallace and Wolf 294). According to this theory, "the gratifications experienced by individuals are contingent on actions of others" (Farganis 298). Basically, people are rewarded either extrinsically or intrinsically. In my case, **extrinsic rewards**, which Peter Blau defines as "tangible things, such as money" (Farganis 295), were not a major factor. Rather, when children made jokes about me, the action of laughter from other children encouraged them to continue with their cruel behavior. Therefore, the other children's laughter acted as an **intrinsic reward**, which Blau defines as "intangible, such as love or respect" (Farganis 295). My feelings of pain and hurt as a result of this cruelty are congruent with another of the ideas of Exchange Theory, which states that, "the rewards individuals obtain in social associations tend to entail a cost to other individuals" (Farganis 299). This fits with my situation, as the cruel kids were being socially rewarded by the attention from other kids, while I was being punished by the same reactions by the children. Further, Blau states that, "processes of social exchange, which may originate in pure self-interest, generate trust in social relations through their recurrent and gradually expanding character" (Wallace and Wolf 331). Therefore, as the other children worked together and participated in social exchange, they became closer and more trustworthy of one another.

Another possible reason for the children's behavior is the issue of **power**. "In discussing friendship and conformity, Homans identifies social approval as the good people offer when they have nothing else desirable to exchange" (Wallace and Wolf 317). It is possible that the more powerful children, who had more to offer, were able to give the other children rewards. In exchange for these rewards, the children followed the powerful kids, therefore compensating them with social approval. This fits with **Homans**' idea that social approval can explain group conformity (Wallace and Wolf 315). The powerful kids were rewarding the others with social approval, among other rewards, which gave them power. Further, "individuals tend to cope with impending imbalances of attraction by seeking to prove themselves attractive to associates they find attractive in order to establish friendly relations and become integrated among them" (Farganis 307). In this way, the children attempted to make themselves attractive to the powerful kids in order to be accepted. Therefore, they stayed together as a group via power and social approval. Throughout this whole process, it seemed that I was never rewarded, but only punished.

Another sociological point of view which somewhat disagrees with the ideas of Exchange Theory, is **Symbolic Interaction**. A basic premise of this theory is that people analyze and evaluate situations, and then make decisions based upon their own interpretations of the situation. If this is true, the other children were picking on me simply of their own will and their own cruelty. Essentially, they judged the situation, and then acted cruelly toward me for their own gain. The concepts of symbolic interactionism are illustrated by the movie, *Twelve Angry Men*. Throughout the movie, each of the men reacted to the same situation in different ways. Basically, they individually summed up the situation, and then reacted based on their own interpretations and their own wishes. For example, the sports fan is anxious to achieve his end of going to a baseball game, and so he attempts to convince the other jurors to rush their decisions. On the other hand, the architect wants to take his time and make careful decisions, as he views the situation differently. Although these men all have different ideas, the world that they live in "already has a structure, and people who occupy that world share meaning structures that make social interaction possible" (Farganis 311). This is illustrated by the fact that the men are all on the jury for the same purpose, which is a part of the society in which they all live. This is true of my situation, as the other children made the decision to make fun of me but they were also influenced by the culture surrounding them.

My reactions to the cruelty of other children can be summed up by the concept of dramaturgy put forth by Erving **Goffman**. He believed that in different social situations people tended to play a variety of different roles (Goffman 351). **Dramaturgy** is the study of everyday life as drama. In this way, individuals are better able to control the situation and exert influence over others as in a play. P. Heim provides support for this idea in her article "Alien Nation" when she says, "each and every person has many different facades, which can also be thought of as having a society within oneself" (Heim 36). Throughout her article, Heim describes the different roles that she played, especially within her family. In my case, when other children would make fun of me, I would usually become quiet and attempt to ignore them. This was different from my behavior in other situations. I had hoped to control the situation through my action of ignoring them, assuming that they may become disinterested and give up. However, this just made them harass me even more in most cases. Realizing that my quiet act was not working, I attempted a different role. In this role, I attempted to laugh with the other children, hoping that it would make them accept me. This also turned out to be a failure, so I tried yet another new character. In this new role I would get mean and nasty toward the other children, hoping that they may begin to understand what it was like to be the victim. However, this role also proved to be a disappointment. At this point, I felt that the situation was hopeless.

This idea of the many different roles and personalities that people assume is illustrated in an extreme sense in the documentary, *Multiple Personalities: The Search for Deadly Memories*. When I switched roles in order to manipulate the other children's behavior, I was showing different parts of my personality. People who have Multiple Personality Disorder actually have several different personalities within them. This is true of everyone to an extent. However, Multiple Personality Disorder is an extreme case of this. In the documentary, the people would switch personalities depending on the situation and the people involved. This behavior can be observed frequently in everyday life, as with my actions toward the bullies.

Another illustration of this concept comes from the excerpted writing of G.I. **Gurdjieff** entitled "About the Author" the concluding chapter of the first volume of his work *All and Everything* (1950). Throughout this piece, the author discusses the idea that we have many different personalities, which come together to develop our "I." Gurdjieff uses the analogy of a carriage to explain this concept, and describes how the parts of a man work together yet are still independent of each other. The three parts of a man that are described by Gurdjieff include the physical, intellectual, and emotional selves. Basically, these three parts each affect man in different ways, yet they all are supposed to come together to form a complete person. This analogy is true for my situation, as my different personalities, although they are all unique, are supposed to come about at different times in different situations to form my "I."

Although so far I have considered many micro social processes that had an impact on my development, there are also macro social forces which have played a role. A major social factor that has contributed to my image of and feelings toward myself has been the rural setting in which I grew up. Georg **Simmel** devoted his article "The Metropolis and Mental Life" to a comparison of rural and metropolitan life and how they affect the interaction of individual and society. Simmel begins his writing with the following observation: "The deepest problems of modern life derive from the claim of the individual to preserve the autonomy and individuality of his existence in the face of overwhelming social forces, of historical heritage, of external culture, and of the technique of life" (Farganis 149). Simmel goes on to discuss how people in **metropolitan** areas are more likely to lose their individuality due to the impersonal nature of the environment. However, in my personal experience, Simmel's deductions do not hold. The area that I grew up in was very much rural. My school was so tiny that my graduating class consisted of 25 people. Since there were so few people and everybody knew everybody else, it was difficult to keep secrets at all. Furthermore, if one person was different in any way from the majority, they were viewed as an outcast. This was the case for me, as I did not fit into the perfect category. It is my belief that in larger areas differences are more acceptable. This is probably due to the fact that there are so many people that it is impossible to analyze and judge everyone.

As a result of my situation, I developed an extremely negative self-concept. This is partly explained by George Herbert Mead's idea of the **generalized other**, which "means that individuals internalize the norms and values generated by the dominant institutions" (Wallace and Wolf 202). A very common attitude of the American people, which is learned very early on in life, is the importance of physical appearance. Basically, "the modern belief that one's body can be constructed is associated with an equally strong belief that the shape one is relates to one's inherent worth" (Wallace and Wolf 373). This was a value that I, along with the other children, had been exposed to for most of my life. Based on this value, I came to see myself as a failure even without the other children's input.

My situation can be further examined using a **functionalist** perspective. "The major distinctive contribution of functionalism has been its view of social order as a consensual agreement reflecting shared values and norms that bind a community together" (Farganis 225). Emile **Durkheim**, inspiring functionalism, emphasized the notion that society creates values which all members are supposed to attain. He believed that, "there are 'social facts' that exist outside of us and that compel us to behave in conformity with norms that are not of our making" (Farganis 59). The idea that women should have certain body types is a norm in today's society. As with other norms, non-conformity leads to social sanctions, such as laughter, stares, and other sources of embarrassment. Through these actions, conformity with the norm of typical gender roles is produced.

This **phenomenon** had a profound effect on me. In my case, I was breaking the **socially constructed** norm of the way that females are meant to look like, and I was punished by the other children's laughter and jokes. However, there was not really anything that I could do in order to conform to the norm. Alfred **Schutz** uses a related concept, which he refers to as the **common stock of knowledge** (Wallace and Wolf 255). He defines the common stock of knowledge as, "social recipes of conceptions of appropriate behavior that enable people to think of the world as made up of 'types' of things" (Wallace and Wolf 255). In this way, people all share similar ideas, and are better able to communicate in social situations. In my case, the other children all felt that it was appropriate behavior to be cruel to me in particular social situations, such as when in the company of certain other children. According to Anthony **Giddens**, "We have a 'generalized motivational commitment' to sustaining the routine and tactfulness of ordinary social intercourse" (Wallace and Wolf 257). Basically, we all strive to keep our lives as routine and simple as possible. For the other children it became **routine**, and almost habit, to be cruel to me whenever in my presence. In this way, their social interactions were standard and did not require a lot of effort.

Friedrich **Nietzsche** adds to the consideration of norms and specified ways of acting by describing "the struggle that an individual must endure in order to break out of societally sanctioned roles and to reject externally imposed values" (Farganis 93). This effort is illustrated in the movie *Billy Elliot* which describes the struggle of a young boy who wishes to be a ballet dancer, rather than a boxer as society expects of him. Despite objections from his family and others, Billy keeps working at ballet with his teacher. In the end, Billy follows his dreams and, breaking with society's ideals, becomes a professional ballet dancer. *Billy Elliot* is an example of one boy's triumph over society's strict gender role norms. The great effort that is required in order to break with society is almost impossible for most people, as society's ideas are so deeply ingrained within each individual.

Further evidence for this phenomenon comes from Talcott **Parsons**, who describes the **"glamor girl"** model (Farganis 238). He states that females have "a strong tendency to accentuate sexual attractiveness in terms of various versions of what may be called the 'glamor girl' pattern" (Farganis 238). Basically, Parsons is describing the socially constructed image that females are supposed to project in today's world. Through the media, and other sources, young girls pick up cues as to how they are expected to act. Women on television are projected as having perfect bodies and being glamorous all the time. The movie *Affluenza* demonstrates this point through its exploration of materialism in today's society. It describes the various ways in which products are marketed toward young children at a very early age. In particular, items such as the Barbie Doll, which is specifically marketed toward young girls, emphasize the "glamor girl" attitude. By adopting today's materialistic attitude, young girls are reinforced to believe that they should look and act in a certain way, which is in most cases impossible. In fact, "Billions of dollars are spent annually on cosmetics, physical fitness, and weight reduction advertising with messages encouraging thinness" (Felts 374). As a result, it eventually becomes ingrained in many young people's minds that if they do not fit this description, then they are worthless as a person.

As stated by Bryan **Turner**, **"to control women's bodies is to control their personalities"** (Wallace and Wolf 380). These ideas that are presented in the media come to shape the views that young people hold regarding self worth. In fact, Parsons also points out that, "The glamor girl pattern has certain obvious attractions since to the woman who is excluded from the struggle for power and prestige in the occupational sphere it is the most direct path to a sense of superiority and importance" (Farganis 243). Although this is less true today than it was in the past, the idea that being glamorous leads to respect and power still acts as a major influence on the attitudes of young girls. In fact, even in my situation, which took place in a school setting, the pretty and glamorous girls were always the most popular. Further support comes from **Berger and Luckmann**, who believe, in the words of Wallace and Wolf, that, "how we view and how we experience our bodies is entirely a social construction" (371). Basically, the culture that we live in shapes our views of how we should appear. These views become ingrained in us and affect every aspect of our lives, including our personal self-image. However, these images that are portrayed within society, as to how we should appear, are often impossible for people in the real world to achieve. This conflict is represented by **Merton's** definition of **anomie** (in contrast to Durkheim's), in terms of "a discontinuity between cultural goals and the legitimate means available for reaching them" (Wallace and Wolf 56). Merton's definition can be utilized to explain the socially constructed gender roles of today's society. Women strive to achieve socially created goals, but are faced with conflict and anxiety as their means of reaching those goals are blocked. This could be the reason behind Talcott Parson's belief that, "The period of youth in our society is one of considerable strain and insecurity" (Farganis 244). Young girls learn early on what is expected of them; yet, these expectations are, in many cases, impossible to realize.

In considering my problem, it is important to understand the other children's motivations and reasons for being cruel. Merton's ideas of **manifest and latent functions** come into play at this point. "Manifest functions are the consequences people observe or expect" (Wallace and Wolf 52). In my case, the other children's laughter and fun, and my sadness and pain served the manifest function of reproducing gender and power dynamics at school, as they were easily observable and understood. "Latent functions are the consequences that are neither recognized nor intended" (Wallace and Wolf 52). In this case, the group cohesion created by the other children was a latent function. It was not easily observable, but was happening nonetheless. Merton provides support for this point when he states that, "Through the systematic application of the concept of latent function, apparently irrational behavior may at times be found to be positively functional for the group" (Farganis 249). The other children's cruelty created tight-knit friendships and cooperation within their group. Therefore, latent functions were at work in creating group cohesiveness, and reinforcing many socially constructed ideals among the children.

In many ways, in my situation at school, both micro and macro forces were at work. My individual personalities and behaviors and those of the other children brought about the micro level of functioning. At the same time, **macro** forces, such as the basic ideas and values of our culture were strongly influencing our actions. C. Wright **Mills** introduced the important concept of **sociological imagination**, which involves the ability to see the interaction of **personal troubles** and **public issues** (Wallace and Wolf 106). The distinction between these two items helps to link the concepts of the micro and the macro levels of functioning. According to Mills, "personal troubles are troubles that occur 'within the individual as a biographical entity and within the scope of his immediate milieu' and relations with other people" (Wallace and Wolf 106). Therefore, personal troubles relate to the micro level of functioning which occurs among individuals. Mills goes on to define public issues as "matters that have to do with the 'institutions of an historical society as a whole,' with the overlapping of various milieus that interpenetrate to 'form the larger structures of social and historical life'" (Wallace and Wolf 106-107). So, public issues deal with the problems of the masses, and the macro level of functioning within society.

In my case, my pain and anger resulting from the other children's behavior engendered a personal trouble within myself. However, if we consider the macro level, the situation is a public issue due to the fact that this was not a problem only for me, but also for many thousands of other children around the world. According to Rebekah Heinrichs, "75% of school-age children report being bullied at least once during the school year" (Heinrichs 200). In this way, it is possible to see the link between the micro and macro levels of functioning in today's society. Generally, micro issues impact the individual, but these issues are themselves shaped greatly by the macro forces of the surrounding culture and conditions. Similarly, the micro level also has a compelling effect on the functioning of the macro level. As can be seen, the individual and society as a whole impact each other simultaneously, and affect the overall functioning of one other.

For a long time, I was very negative and self-conscious, due to perceptions of my physical appearance. According to Samara Cohen, "Our personalities are shaped by interactions we have with people as individuals, and as groups in society" (Cohen 9). This was very true for me, as my relationships with my classmates had a major impact on my personality, and on my view of myself. Suddenly, right before I entered high school, I lost a lot of weight and started wearing contact lenses. It was as if I was a completely different person in the eyes of my classmates. They suddenly accepted me, and wanted to spend time with me. I started ignoring those people who were always friendly to me and stood up for me, and instead became one of the "popular" kids. At the time, I loved my newfound popularity and my acceptance among my peers. I still do enjoy these things, but I now see them in a different light. I realize now that the people who liked me only when I started to look "acceptable" to them were not really my friends at all. They were my friends for a while, but the relationships soon faded away. In the end, I found that only people who were there for me and who stood up for me when I was being bullied that really mattered. Fortunately, my true friends were willing to forgive me, despite my actions toward them. Today these people continue to be my best and closest friends. I cherish them wholeheartedly, as they taught me a valuable lesson that I put to use everyday in my interactions with others. That lesson is that it is never alright to judge people based upon their physical appearance. Rather, people should be valued for their inner beauty and beliefs.

As I look back, I can understand somewhat why the other children acted so cruelly toward me, as there were many forces acting upon them as well at both the micro and macro levels. However, I have found that despite these same forces acting upon me, I have learned to accept others for who they are, and not judge them based upon what they look like. I still sometimes catch myself thinking poorly of a person at a first glance. However, based upon my experiences, I am able to realize my fault, and change these thoughts. In fact, I often find that after meeting the person and getting to know them, their outward appearance does not mean a thing and they are really a wonderful person.

My friends, through their actions, proved to me that what is inside a person is what matters the most. In the end, my middle school experience taught me that true relationships are not based on physical characteristics, but rather the feelings that come from within a person.

REFERENCES

Canfield, K. (2002). "Repairing the Soul: Matching Inner with Outer Beauty." *Human Architecture: Journal of the Sociology of Self-Knowledge*, I, 2, 20-26.

Cohen, S. (2002). "I Only *Thought* I Knew It All: Society and the Individual." *Human Architecture: Journal of the Sociology of Self-Knowledge*, I, 1, 9-17.

Farganis, J. (2000). *Readings in Social Theory: The Classic Tradition to Post-Modernism*. Third Edition. Boston: McGraw Hill.

Felts, M., Tavasso, D., Chenier, T., Dunn, P. (1992). "Adolescents' Perceptions of Relative Weight and Self-Reported Weight Loss Activities," *Journal of School Health*, 62, 8, 372-377.

Gurdjieff, G. I. (1950). "From the Author," in *All and Everything: Beelzebub's Tales to His Grandson.*, First Edition. New York: Harcourt, Brace and Company. pp. 1089-1135.

Heim, P. (2002). "Alien-Nation." *Human Architecture: Journal of the Sociology of Self-Knowledge*, I, 1, 36-44.

Heinrichs, Rebekah R. (2003). *A Whole-School Approach to Bullying: Special Considerations for Children with Exceptionalities*. Intervention in School & Clinic, 38, 4, 195-205).

Wallace, R and Wolf, A. (1999). *Contemporary Sociological Theory: Expanding the Classical Tradition*. Fifth Edition. New Jersey: Prentice Hall.

Films:

"Affluenza." (1997). Bullfrog Films.
"Billy Elliot." (2000). Universal Pictures.
"Erin Brockovich." (2000). Universal Pictures.
"Multiple Personalities: The Search for Deadly Memories." (1994). Home Box Office.
"Twelve Angry Men." (1957). MGM.

It's Worth Living in the World

James McHugh

"Homeostasis and Transistasis… one is a force to maintain the present status and the other is a force for constant change. Anything that lives is composed of these two conflicting forces." Ritsuko Akagi from the anime series *Neon Genesis Evangelion* once brought this point up to explain how all living things, specifically humans, have a need for consistency in their lives and at the same time are in a constant need for change. Ultimately, these two conflicting forces drive our lives and always lead to change, but at a pace that is anything but wanted. Change is something that always happens, and it's always up to the individual to deal with that change if they want to survive. That is simply a fact of life, and my own is no exception.

"I don't understand. I don't know how to live in this world if these are the choices, if everything just gets stripped away. I don't see the point…[when] the hardest thing in this world is to live in it." The character Buffy Summers from the series *Buffy the Vampire Slayer* said these words in the would-be final titled *The Gift*. In the end, she chose death rather than trying to live in this world; she chose to sacrifice her own life so that others could live. I believe that all people have faced a time in their lives when they feel the same way Buffy does. None of us really know how to live in this world, how to be safe and to live a good life in a world that demands so much from us. What's more, we are almost programmed at birth to do things since we are expected to do it. As David Newman puts it in *Sociology: Exploring the Architecture of Everyday Life*,

> The actions of individuals are not simply functions of personality types…they are also a reflection of shared cultural experiences…We [have had] many unwritten rules about which emotions are appropriate to feel, which are appropriate to display, and how intense the emotional display should be under specific circumstances. For instance, we're supposed to be sad at funerals, happy at weddings, and angry when insulted. (87)

Newman explains how people tend to respond to specific situations in a uniformed manner. And despite how the individual may feel, he or she must alter their own perceptions and convince himself or herself that there is a correct way to answer a situation in order to fit in with the rest of the world. In essence, society as a whole forces emotional control and values on us at birth, and despite how hard the society may try to enforce these views, in the end I feel the individual will always have to justify the world for themselves.

Let's start at my beginning. In 1984 I was given a great life at birth. I was handed an older brother and a loving mother and father who, despite the culturally found odds, have yet to part. I lived in an average suburban neighborhood for years. When I was finally old enough, I was enrolled in Holy Name of Mary elementary school. It might seem odd to go as far back as my elementary school, but it does actually play a role in the scheme of things. As David Newman puts it ,

In contemporary industrial societies the most powerful institutional agent of socialization, after the family, is education…the "personalized" instruction of the family is replaced by the "impersonalized" instruction of the school, where the…institution has such extended and consistent access to a person's social growth. (123-124).

In school, I was a below-average student to say the least. I failed, largely due to the fact that I truly didn't care and I wasn't really interested in grades, and I was put in the special education classes before I was even in the first grade. This was fine. I made many friends. I was able to sit back and avoid learning much of anything, and I was able to feel as though I belonged. This was all good, but in the second grade, Holy Name decided to cut these programs in order to save money, so I was eventually transferred to Grand Avenue Elementary School and I continued my less than stellar performance there. After less than two years, I was once again sent to the Special Education classes where I would once again be in a small group of people who would again try to learn what the other class couldn't teach. The only thing was that this time I was miserable. I hated being in this school, I hated how they put me in these classes again, and I hated how someone kept telling me how I wasn't where I should be and that I needed the help from people I never even asked to help me.

This went on through the rest of elementary school. I was with the "special" people and after a while I started to believe I was one of those people and I once again started to make friends and have a normal life. But, in the sixth grade, one of my teachers felt that I was smarter than I let anyone believe when she noticed how I managed to fit the class system into a simple drawing of the Middle Ages. As a result, she started keeping me in her sixth grade class. All I can really remember is I hated going to her class since I did twice as much work, I felt like I was forced into something against my own will, and I was alone. My Special Education teacher did not approve of her abducting me into her class day after day, refusing to let me return. I still remember being called into all sorts of meetings around this time. On a near daily basis, I saw my parents in the halls. I was constantly being told what was best for me. I was constantly being given different answers for what was best, and around this time I starting to feel like none of these people really did know what was best for me. The school system wasn't able to define what I was, and I was completely overwhelmed when it came to deciding my fate. My whole life I had been told I was 'slower' than my peers and that I should blindly do as I'm told. It was around this point that I stopped trusting adults. They sent me to one school to do good, and that school said I wasn't good enough and sent me someplace else. One place told me I wasn't smart enough and sent me to the remedial classes and then I would be sent back because that was where I belonged. Eventually Junior High came in the seventh grade, and the issue was solved by default since there were no remedial classes. And, despite what I had been told would happen all of my life, academically I started to flourish. I did my homework, I did the class work, passed the test, and everything was starting to be great in my life. However, this improvement in my life only went as far as academia. Socially my world had become smaller than ever with my former friends from Special Education being left behind in their courses. I was overwhelmed by all of these new people around me. All the teachers in my Junior High knew I was the "special" one and I was treated like it and they held my way though all of my classes.

My classmates hadn't grown up with me since I was in Special Education and treated me as a new student to the area, and my friends from Special Education were being taken away against my will. So, like any living thing, I tried to adapt. I tried to make new friends and live my new found life. But, life threw me a few curve balls, and this new found life just never sat well with me. I tried to grow and to be normal like everyone else. But the fact of the matter was that I never really spent enough time around one group of people to ever really know what cliché I was supposed to gravitate toward. I had spent nearly my whole life in small group settings and it was fairly overwhelming to be placed in that situation, especially since I was never even told why this was happening to me at the time. Once more, the videogames, television shows, activates, and most other aspects of my self had been left behind. I was still thinking and behaving as a child since I never knew what to grow into. And I've never been a good pretender or poser, so everything I didn't know was blatantly obvious. So, as if all these other forces overwhelming me in my own life weren't bad enough, this also happened to be the time in my life that I started to question my own sexuality and came up with the answer every teenage boy fears. And this was yet another way that I could never be "normal," that I could never do what society expected of me. I was gay and I was alone. It was also around this point that people saw me as an easy target because of it.

Junior High became a dark time for my life. I had lost my friends and I had lost the comfort zone of Special Education that I had come to rely on over the years. Once more, I didn't have "normal" feelings about sex, I didn't have friends to rely on, I didn't understand the lifestyles of my peers, and I truly didn't know what I was supposed to do anymore. And it was around this time that the fights started as well.

The constant name calling started, the random jabs in the halls, the lies to the teachers, the empty promises of acceptance and friendship, all of it just kept coming and I truly felt helpless. And I fell for it every time. I just wanted it all to end and I just wanted to stop crying, to finally find a place and to be where I could belong. My own feelings seem to mirror Kristy Canfield's words from her article, "Repairing the Soul: Matching Inner with Outer Beauty":

> Low self-esteem was a direct result of being ridiculed and shunned by numerous peer groups, who viewed my difference as weird. The devastation continued as the ongoing process of cruel comments persevered. I felt as if I was fighting to stay afloat and each cruel word was a current desperately trying to pull me under. How long would I endure this pain before someone would throw me a lifeline? (20)

I fought, I laughed, I cried, I pleaded, I hid, I screamed, I did everything I could and at some point I decided that I wasn't going to be the victim anymore. And then my parents moved me to a new town.

My parents were scared for my life. Although to this day they try to remain oblivious to the personal affairs of my life, they knew things were bad at school, that I just spent my nights dreading going back there and hating myself for always screwing it all up. I talked about suicide, I talked about revenge, and I was basically creepy and bitter about living. So they did the only thing they felt they ever do: make the problem go away. They dragged me away from the problem and moved me to a new town called Merrick to begin a new life. There was nothing wrong with this new place; it was yet another Long Island suburb, it had tons of trees, and the usual assortment of anti-social neighbors. But even so, I hated it. In my eyes, I felt like I ran away from the problem, that I failed at living my life and now I was sent someplace else to repeat the same mistakes. So, I did the only thing I could do, I withdrew from all of it. I'm far from proud of this, but I threw in the towel, because it seemed like all the struggling was for nothing. So, this time I didn't want anyone to get close to me, I didn't want a friend and I didn't need anyone to get to know me. I believed it would just be easier to distance myself from the whole thing. And for three years it worked; I was alone, I avoided those around me, and I was ignored because of it. But, I still wasn't happy when I pushed everyone away either. As Peter Dai put it in his paper, "Why is P Afraid to Love a Woman," "…some self, some subconsciously seated demon, keeps him silent" (22). In the same way Pete could never really identify what held him back from his dreams, I could never explain why I would always feel like I didn't belong in the world and that I didn't have a place I could ever call my own. I didn't want to be hurt anymore but I couldn't find happiness on my own either. So I just sunk into a depression and kept all my pain, all my discontent, and all my anger all to myself. Eventually, I felt like I woke up:

> You're here because you know something. What you know you can't explain—but you feel it. You've felt it your entire life; that there's something wrong with the world; you don't know what it is, but it's there, like a splinter in your mind, driving you mad. [This is the Matrix.] The Matrix is everywhere, it is all around us. Even in this very room. You can see it when you look out your window or when you turn on your television. You can feel it when you go to work, when you go to church, when you pay your taxes; it is the world that has been pulled over your eyes to blind you from the truth… that you are a slave Neo, like everyone else, you were born into bondage; born into a prison that you cannot smell or taste or touch; a prison for your mind. Unfortunately, no one can be told what the Matrix is. You have to experience it for yourself.

In the film *The Matrix*, the character Morpheus gives this speech to the unawakened protagonist Neo. This speech illustrates that there is always a nagging feeling in our lives that there is more to life than meets the eye as symbolized by the Matrix itself, and how people are given the choice of whether or not they are willing to step into the world they have been denied up to that point in their lives. However, unlike in the film, no single pill is the immediate release into living the world. Rather, a series of events is always responsible for any type of meaningful awakening to take place in our lives. For me, that was in the Merrick library. Jobs weren't anything new to me but this time a job had led to my meeting a small group of friends, and from that I expanded and joined clubs in my school and made yet more small groups of friends there. And as I gradually moved ahead, as I stopped feeling apathetic towards the world around me, I was finally closer to people than I had ever been before. In a sense, it was when I finally started to accept myself that I had finally learned to be a person, I stopped trying to fit in and do as I was told and finally I learned to stand on my own two feet.

"You're focusing on the problem. If you focus on the problem, you can't see the solution. Never focus on the problem!" Arthur Mendelson was able to do more for Hunter 'Patch' Adams's life than any other doctor when he explained this point of view to him in the film *Patch Adams*. By living his life in the dynamic way Arthur wanted to, Patch was able to help out his fellow men and women more than any doctor, any agent, any weekend retreat—more than any other institutionalized method of healing—was able to accomplish for Patch. As an individual, my life was no different from Patch's in the sense that I was finally able to find happiness when I stopped looking in the traditional places I was recommended to by the people in my life. My life is something I wouldn't trade for anything in the world nowadays. And as the preceding few pages indicate, I didn't feel that way in the past. I feel Elizabeth Kubler-Ross's theory of the five stages, as presented in her classic *On Death and Dying*, helps one to deal with acceptance and death and how that applies to the patterns of my own life and to the acceptance of who I really am in the end.

STAGE ONE: DENIAL/ISOLATION

> Homer: Kids, Kids! I'm not gonna die! That only happens to bad people!
>
> Bart: What about Abraham Lincoln?
>
> Homer: Err... He sold poisoned milk to school children.

The character Homer Simpson from *The Simpson's* has a history of living in denial about the facts of life and I have done the same with my life in many ways. I feel that my problems really began when I was taken away from Holy Name of Mary elementary in the second grade. I didn't want my life to change, so I simply refused to accept that it had. I didn't try to fit in and I didn't try to make anyone happy. I was alone there and I wanted to go back to the way my life used to be. And when I was refused, I hid from those around me and isolated myself by pretending that I couldn't handle work and that I needed to be treated differently if any good was going to come to me. So, I was treated differently, and for a while everything was good.

STAGE TWO: ANGER

> "Somebody out there just doesn't want me to be happy," as said Max in the series *Dark Angel* and it sums up how I felt at this time in my life. This was about the time of Junior High when I stopped trusting those around me. I felt like they just kept screwing my life every time I let them control it, so I was going to prove them all wrong by doing what they felt I never could do, as in doing well in school. However, it was rage and anger that fueled my academics and not my own desire. And eventually, being alone and angry will cause anyone to burn out which led to my next stage.

STAGE THREE: BARGAINING

> Sean: Do you have a soul mate?
>
> Will: Define that.
>
> Sean: Someone you can relate to, someone who opens things up for you.
>
> Will: Sure, I got plenty.
>
> Sean: Well, name them.
>
> Will: Shakespeare, Nietzsche, Frost, O'Conner...
>
> Sean: Well that's great. They're all dead.
>
> Will: Not to me, they're not.
>
> Sean: You can't have a lot of dialogue with them.
>
> *Will: Not without a heater and some serious smelling salts.*

In the film *Good Will Hunting*, Sean Maguire points out this rather clear inability of Will Hunting to accept his loneliness in the world by pointing out that Will uses the works of the dead to superficially fill the holes in his life. Will wants to live oblivious to his intellectual gifts and he wants to just let his life behind, or at least that is what he convinces himself of. But, just as Will says one thing, but secretly wants another, the same could be said of my own life and how I chose to be with people. I felt I could still hold people in disdain and become friends with them. I was still mad about all the changes and screw ups that happened in my life but I also wanted to fit in, to be part of the group and live my life as happily as everyone on TV. So I tried to do both, I tried to be angry with those around me but I also wanted them to like me and treat me as one of their own. Obviously, there is a rather large flaw in this arrangement. Ultimately, this stage really didn't last for long and soon led to the next stage.

FOURTH STAGE: DEPRESSION

"Inochi nante yasui mon sa... toku ni ore no wa na (Life is cheap... especially mine)" said Heero Yuy in the anime series "Gundam Wing." This was the longest stage. In my depression, the anger I once felt for all those around me started to turn inward; I started to hate myself for being different and failing to be just like everyone else. Toward the end of Junior High, people harassed me more than ever and the anger I once felt was now being inflicted on me. The combined hatred broke me. I just stopped trying to win and just accepted that I would never be much of anything and I just wanted all the pain to stop. It was around this time that I moved to Merrick to begin my new life, but I spent it feeling bad for myself and trying to just feel like I would never belong and that I could never be as good as those around me. I still faced my fear of being alone. Samara Cohen expresses similar views in her paper, "I Only Thought I Knew It All," when she said "One of my biggest excitements, and biggest fears… was the idea that I was going to be completely independent" (15). I always wanted to belong, but I never could because I feared being alone. But I also feared what people could do to me. However, it was in the act of stopping that fear that I finally was able to start to come to terms with myself. I started to learn that while I was alone, I could deal with that and that no one could ever tell me how to live my life and that I could be myself even if no one would like it. In a way I had to lose everything in order to gain anything.

ACCEPTANCE: FINAL STAGE

Finally, Whistler from "Buffy the Vampire Slayer" most clearly represents this time in my life when he says,

> Bottom line is, even if you see 'em coming, you're not ready for the big moments. No one asks for their life to change, not really. But it does. So what are we, helpless? Puppets? No. The big moments are gonna come. You can't help that. It's what you do afterwards that counts. That's when you find out who you are. You'll see what I mean.

In my life, the moment came toward the end of my junior year in High School. I stopped eating alone and I stopped spending my days in my room feeling sorry for myself. It was now that I could finally see that I had myself and that I didn't need to measure myself up to everyone around me to be a good person. In reality, I had to completely abandon society in order to gain society. I had to stop trying to be something and actually be something in order to have self-worth.

"I still don't know where my happiness lies. I'll still think about why I am here and whether or not it was good to come back.

But that's just stating the obvious over and over again. I am myself." The character Shinji Ikari said these words near the end of the film *The End of Evangelion* and I feel that these words also express how I feel at this stage in my life. In the scheme of things, the problems I faced in my life amount to very little. I never lived in the gutters, I always had food, and I always had good health. But it's my philosophy that it isn't the problems you face that make you, it's how you handle the problems that make you. Everyone is allowed to make a better life for themselves as long as they continue breathing, but the only way that can happen is if you are willing to accept that you have nothing but yourself in the scheme of things. That is the best way to be a part of society if you want to be something more than the cultural norms lap dog. You must be yourself in order to be a member of society; it's that contradiction that makes life worth living.

To leave off, the character Lester Burnham sums up life in this world in the end of the feature film *American Beauty* after he is killed.

> I guess I could be pretty pissed off about what happened to me. But it's hard to stay mad when there's so much beauty in the world. Sometimes I feel like I'm seeing it all at once... and it's too much. My heart fills up like a balloon that's about to burst. And then I remember... to relax, and not try to hold on to it. And then it flows through me like rain. And I can't feel anything but gratitude for every single moment of my stupid little life. You have no idea what I'm talking about, I'm sure. Don't worry... you will someday.

Lester was just one of countless discontented people in the world, but in the end he was able to do what so many people have been unable to do with their entire lives, and in the end he looked back and smiled. The hardest thing in this world is to live in it, but it's also one of the most rewarding things to do in this world. The important thing is that you live for yourself, no one has the right to make you live for anyone but yourself, and you don't have the right to give up on the life you've received.

When you can look in the mirror and smile, that's when you've won the right to call yourself 'I.'

References

Canfield, Kristy. (2002). "Repairing the Soul: Matching Inner with Outer Beauty" in *Human Architecture: Journal of the Sociology of Self-Knowledge*, I, 2, Fall, pp. 20-26.

Cohen, Samara. (2002). "I Only *Thought* I Knew It All" in *Human Architecture: Journal of the Sociology of Self-Knowledge*, I, 1, Spring, pp. 8-17.

Dai, Peter. (2002). 'Why is P Afraid to Love a Woman" in *Human Architecture: Journal of the Sociology of Self-Knowledge*, I, 1, Spring, pp. 18-25.

Kubler-Ross, Elizabeth. (1969). *On Death and Dying*. Macmillan.

Newman, David. (2002). *Sociology; Exploring the Architecture of Everyday Life*. Thousand Oaks, California. Pine Forge Press.

Films:

"American Beauty." (1999). Dir. Sam Mendes. DVD. DreamWorks.

"Buffy the Vampire Slayer." (1997-2003). Dir. Joss Whedon. Warner Brothers.

"Dark Angel." (2000-2001). Pro. James Cameron. Fox Network.

"End of Evangelion." (2002). Dir. Hideaki Anno. Videocassette. Manga Entertainment.

"Good Will Hunting." (1997). Dir. Gus Van Sant. Videocassette. Miramax films.

"Gundam Wing." (2000). Dir. Gordon Hunt (III). Bandai Entertainment.

"The Matrix." (1999). Warner Brothers.

"Neon Genesis Evangelion." (1998). Dir. Hideaki Anno. ADV films.

My Image Struggles in Capitalist Society

Anna Schlosser

In our culture, women try so hard to be the ideal congenial beauty queen. We believe that there is only one standard of beauty and if we don't look that way then we are ugly. We compare ourselves to each other and especially to the size 0 models in the magazines. I have struggled with this since elementary school when girls start learning that they have to appear attractive to the opposite sex. Even in my fourth year of college I continue to stress over what image I want to portray.

When I was younger I was not aware of the constant effort I put towards achieving the perfect image. As I matured, I realized the impact it had on my life. I allowed people and culture around me to categorize me into groups according to my popularity and choice in clothes and friends. Any distress I experience because I am unable to achieve the ideal image can be somewhat blamed on society. Our culture has created this unattainable ideal which the majority of women do not resemble at all. I also see that society has shaped me and influenced the way I perceive myself. In order to better understand my experience, therefore, I need to explore the impact society has had on my life. Sociologist C. Wright Mills calls this mode of inquiry the **sociological imagination** (Newman 8).

A few months ago I became acquainted with a new girl who seemed like a potential friend. When you first meet somebody that you like you try to put your best self forward. I tried to be pleasant, talkative, and fun; in other words, the kind of person other people want to be around. I tried to figure out and read this girl in order to present myself as a person she would want to be friends with. Even at this early stage, I was performing **impression management**, a concept used by the sociologist Ervin Goffman (Newman 134, 138). Several months have passed since our first encounter and we are both learning new things about each other which may or may not coincide with our original impressions of one another. As time elapses we have remained friends and are much more comfortable with one another. However, I still find myself concealing information about my identity that may not necessarily fit into the person I want her to think I am. I have also had to decide how to handle some news I received about her that has conflicted with the image she had conveyed to me. I chose to accept the surprising information and not judge her. Knowing where this girl worked and looking at her clothes caused me to judge her in a certain way. Since she was attractive, I believed she was popular, confident, and sociable. To some degree, most of this was true but I automatically assumed it because she was attractive. I am happy to say that we've begun to let our guards down and we continue to be friends.

Through impression management, we expose certain characteristics to people in order to get a desired reaction. Certain identities are used in appropriate situations to whatever audience is present. There is usually an identity that an individual works on presenting the most in a given situation. In addition to changes in behavior, we tend to change our appearance to make ourselves feel worthy and to have other people think we are worthy enough to get their attention. This is where my struggle with image comes in. I buy clothes that fit an image that I believe people will be impressed with. On a larger scale, fashion is fed to us by designers who want to sell their products. If we weren't up on the trends we become fashion victims. I am programmed to believe that if I wear clothes everyone else is wearing I will be liked.

One relationship that has ended but is fresh in my mind is a romantic one. Just like any new relationship, we try to appear desirable depending on what we think the other person is looking for. The male person was under the impression, maybe because of my physical appearance or demeanor, that I was a sweet, innocent, pure, angel. He put me up on a pedestal and believed that I could do no wrong. I tried my best to act the way this "angel" should act and played along for a while. I pretended that I had never sinned in my life and I always acted like a lady. Goffman would describe me as an actor on a stage (Newman 144). The study of social interaction as theater is called **dramaturgy**, also a term invented by Goffman. When I was in his presence and portrayed myself to have particular characteristics, I was acting on the **front stage**. Here I tried not to say or do anything to jeopardize the favorable image he constructed of me. **Back stage**, though, when I was around my closer friends or family, I could act any way I pleased even if it were the opposite of the good girl image presented to him.

Eventually the person I was dating realized that I wasn't an angel especially after he had heard some gossip. He wasn't too happy with what he was told because it dramatically conflicted with the angel image he had of me. He felt betrayed and foolish for believing the false ideas about the person he thought I was. In contrast to the new friendship I have previously described, the information that I attempted to conceal caused deterioration in the relationship. One of the reasons this relationship ended was due to my, what Goffman calls, **spoiled identity** (Newman 151).

Newman writes in *Sociology: Exploring the Architecture of Everyday Life*, "Even those of us who pride ourselves on our individualism follow most of the time a pattern not of our own making" (80). As a college student, as much as I try to be myself and dress in my own style, I find myself wishing I looked like one of the perfect girls around me. I start to feel that I have to act like them to attract friends or the opposite sex. The party girl persona emerges when the social setting requires it while the quieter, sweet persona is used when the time is right.

Through our **nonmaterial culture**—anything nonphysical such as customs, values, beliefs—we learn what is considered appropriate behavior and end up being products of our society. We are expected to go along with this master plan and the better someone can do this the higher the status they receive. Clothing, music, and literature are part of our **material culture** and have had a large impact on my life. Since a young age material items were very important especially clothes and music. The choices you made about your appearance would make or break you in social circles. I remember rebelling against my surrounding norms of dressing. I was stared at and ridiculed by my peers. My mother almost broke down in tears begging me to dress like a normal girl. It's tough swimming upstream. **Subculturally**, college, especially one where most of the students dorm, has its own unwritten rules and regulations. From my own experience, partying, having an outgoing personality, and dressing in proper bar attire are a must if you want to have friends and be known. My concern with material things and popularity contradicts the values that my parents taught me. According to them these concerns were trivial. My struggle deciphering priorities probably has a lot to do with what I was taught.

We have acquired information concerning how to behave in a given situation. Cultural expectations and keeping **social**

order may explain why I portray myself as a person with, what I believe are, preferred attributes. Even though I personally worry about living up to personality and appearance expectations, this is a manifestation of society's values instilled in me. Culture tells us how to behave in public and how to behave in front of elders. Every group is **stereotyped**. Teenagers have to be rebellious and head-strong and college students party and drink. I deal with trying to live up to the image and everything that goes along with it. The pretty, outgoing girl image that I'm expected to strive for and keep up is something my subculture has shown me is the suitable way for a woman my age to act.

An academic version of **ethnocentrism** has become rampant on our campuses. Essentially, ethnocentrism means a group feels that their beliefs and values are the best and superior to others (Newman 91). Similarly, fraternities and sororities largely control the popularity and norms of the students. They create rigid sets of standards and do not allow much leeway. Involuntarily, I have internalized their standards even though I am not a part of their organization, and when I don't measure up I feel inferior.

Socialization is the process through which society's values and norms are internalized by the individual (Newman 106). The ultimate goal for a society is to produce a member who follows its guidelines. A person needs to become familiar with how things are done and this allows them to function well in society. My decisions and feelings are affected by society's goals as a whole. My decision to follow the crowd or to feel inferior when I don't is a result of society's shaping my identity.

Perhaps my sense of not measuring up to the perfect image began during my **acquisition and differentiation of self** (Newman 107). Our special personalities and characteristics create a self which develop as we grow up. Maybe I did not develop a strong sense of my own identity and that's why I try so hard to be like other people I view as more desirable. I am not confident in my own identity or doubt it is acceptable enough, so I look to others for approval and ways to improve myself.

Friends, after a day of shopping, will tell me that they saw an item of clothing that made them think of me. I always ask how it reflected me and they reply by saying that I have my own style and that particular piece screamed "Anna." Occurrences like this fuel my perception of myself as the "different one." Sociologist C. H. Cooley calls this process of how our self-perception are shaped through our interpretation of others' views towards us, the **looking-glass self** (Newman 109). My interpretation of a peer's opinion of me affects my own self-feeling and perception. Peter Dai also uses this concept in his article "Why is P Afraid to Love a Woman?" (2002), where he explores how his social anxiety towards women was a result of his perception (due to certain earlier events in his life) of how girls viewed him. Our anxieties towards achieving the perfect image makes us vulnerable to internalizing others' opinions, according to Dai.

Recently, while in the presence of a group of twenty-something year old men, I was dribbling a basketball. One of them, a sexist pig in my eyes, told me the action of bouncing the ball was unattractive. I was stunned and stopped playing with the ball. Sports were a big part of my life since the second grade and no one had ever put me down for it. In fact I was praised. Yet in the year 2003, from a supposedly young adult, I internalized a self-perception that I was unattractive over something I thought had nothing to do with image. In another instance, again involving a twenty-something male, he observed that I wasn't wearing earrings and my fingernails weren't painted. Thinking this was so out of the ordinary and unacceptable, he asked me why I didn't have these things done. I became defensive and answered, "I'm sorry I'm not girly enough for you." I was angry and thought up a few good names for the person; however, what he said got under my skin. I internalized his view of what my **gender** was supposed to look like. Similar to the expectations that boy placed on me, society allows only two genders and variations are discouraged. Showing athletic talent strays from the typical and accepted behavior of a woman. Society paints a specific picture of both a male and a female and each must portray this distinct image.

Human nature forces us to live in groups. Group connections are assumed to be the best guarantee for an individual's well-being (Newman 198). I am torn between being an individual and following the crowd to avoid alienation. In "I Only *Thought* I Knew It All: Society and the Individual" (2002), Samara Cohen discusses her plight with alienation due to her battle with Hepatitis. People avoided her because of her illness. She links the problem of alienation with the movie *Patch Adams* and draws up a good lesson. Patch went against the grain and had different views on how medicine should be practiced. Many of his peers didn't agree with his methods and as a result he was not welcomed among the other doctors and students. But when he persisted and people finally accepted his style, he was no longer detached from the group.

One way to deal with social pressures is to develop alternative selves. In the film *Multiple Personalities,* the people who suffer from this disorder create alternative personalities as a way to deal with their inner demons and issues that were never resolved. Many people including myself use different personalities in separate setting. It may not be as severe as the disorder but we feel the need to bring out specific traits at certain times. My personality in front of a boyfriend is not the same as that in front of a roommate.

As long as I continue to live society will affect my actions and the opinion I have of myself. I have to learn how to be comfortable with my real self and to be aware when I am acting different to please others. I'm sure there are people who are still dealing with these problems at the age of fifty but I'm hoping to work through it by then. On the other hand, different identities and personalities are needed in life especially in the workplace. Switching personalities is probably inevitable but I am going to try to be as true to myself as possible.

Newman discusses the idea of **bureaucracy** which occurs on many levels. Usually it is seen on the broader social level, but I think it can also occur on a smaller scale such as among a group of friends or a clique. Members of a clique, for instance, are also usually ranked in a **hierarchy of authority** (Newman 246). I have encountered various groups where there were one or two leaders and the rest were followers. I would have to categorize myself as a follower since I went with the flow of the group. Depending on rank your opinion may or may not have mattered. As I recall my opinion was taken into consideration but I rarely expressed it because I was afraid to say the wrong thing. Being judged as weird or different was a big fear of mine. Important information or gossip trickled down the hierarchy. I was always a little jealous of the leaders because I thought they were more popular for specific reasons. I viewed them as prettier and funnier than I when in actuality they were just outgoing and I wasn't.

When dealing with people or problems a bureaucracy can be very **impersonal** (Newman 245). For instance if a new student enrolled at school or a new person was trying to get included in the clique, their presence were not welcomed. They were talked about in a negative way both to their face and behind their back. Their imperfections and mistakes had to be brought to everybody's attention. They were harshly criticized and I sometimes wondered if the girls doing the talking had a conscience. As I grew older and more secure in myself, I learned to talk back and stand up for the victims. I regret not doing this sooner but I was too fearful of being kicked out of the group. It was hard for me to imagine not having friends and being labeled as a loser.

People in lower level positions try to find ways to succeed in social circles. In a sense this is related to **institutional pressures toward similarity**. On a larger scale organizations attempt to improve their productivity by following similar patterns initiated by the more successful organizations. They will not try to accomplish this through finding better methods but by imitating another company's ideas. Similarly, on a micro scale, if a person is not happy with their lower status they may begin to mimic the behavior of a higher ranked individual. Most of the time, in the same circle of friends, this will not work. Other members will notice the change in behavior and most likely will not accept it. This imbalance can cause others to ridicule the new characteristics of that person. They will probably even be seen as a copycat and no one will appreciate her or him anymore. Blinded by the urge to reach the top, people don't realize that a real relationship shouldn't be a struggle. The friends you surround yourself with should appreciate your true personality. Competition is not part of a healthy relationship.

By experience I have seen, even though it is a small sample, young Americans focusing entirely too much of their energy on popularity and the acceptable image. Other cultures and societies place much more emphasis on education. I think we need to do the same so our youth worry more about learning and less about which car they rather be driving. A friend of mine is a kindergarten teacher who had her kids draw pictures of whatever they wanted. A few of her students drew symbols of various car brands. Children as young as five years old are already preoccupied with material things. We need to put more emphasis on schooling and education. Perhaps, then having certain clothes and expensive cars won't be such a big priority.

Diverse **Stratification systems** still exist in the world today, including the American society (Newman 278). They may not be as extreme as slavery, the caste system, or the feudal system but equivalents are evident in the present world in open or subtler ways. Our **social class** depends partly on how much money we earn (Newman 280). When you are born into a family you become part of the same social class. This can change if you are disowned by the family, they become untimely deceased, or you decide to lead your own life and earn your own income. The link between social and economic status is so strong they are inseparable. The more money you make the more prestige you obtain. Many people will not socialize with anyone outside their own socioeconomic class, especially if they are from a very wealthy, powerful family. The mere association with a person of a lower status can damage their reputation.

I consider my family and myself to be a part of the working class. In the neighborhood where I grew up, there were many families that were middle to upper class. I attended school with their children and I am still friends with a few of them. Being around richer, popular peers was not always a fun experience. They owned more material things than I did and I always envied them for it. I learned to live with it because my parents couldn't afford to give me all the same things. At first I felt deprived but I learned to appreciate I do have things that many people don't. When I find myself comparing my life to other people's I try to remember how comfortable I am and all the things I have that can't be bought with money. It is hard not to get caught up in the cycle. My parents worked hard to send me to two private schools and college. Their hard work is what for exactly? It's for my education so I can earn more money and buy more things. We are just playing into the American Dream of owning a big, beautiful house and a big, expensive car. The struggle to have everything is passed down from generation to generation.

Since I always wanted to display the perfect image to my peers, my parents worried about me. They have lower status jobs than other parents and I didn't want them embarrass me. The **media** does not show favorable **images of the working class** (Newman 283). Al Bundy, the character from *Married with Children*, and Homer, the character from the *Simpsons*, are just two examples of how badly the working class male is portrayed. I was afraid my friends were going to see my parents as stupid people who couldn't afford to buy me better things. I rarely brought people home to spend time with my parents but now I realize that you shouldn't judge people by their financial earnings and job status. A person's opinion of your parents shouldn't affect your relations with them and if it does that person is not worth having as a friend.

Inequality in the United States causes individuals in the lower classes to have less access to opportunities due to their socioeconomic status (Newman 290). Parents who have upper class status are able to indulge their children. My parents have indulged me to an extent but I was never as privileged as my peers. My parents worked very hard to give me all the opportunities available. They were able to do this but many children aren't given the same opportunities. Newman uses the example of SATs. A family with higher income would live in better neighborhoods therefore their children attend better schools that offer SAT preparation courses. Those children will have a higher score on the SAT just because they were privileged enough to be better prepared.

My father has Irish and German heritage. Most ethnic groups have been **oppressed** and treated **unequally** at one time or another in history (Newman 334). Stereotypes usually develop about a racial group and we become very aware of them (Newman 339). For example, "All black men are illiterate and bound for prison," "All Chinese people are bad drivers" and "All Spanish women have children at a young age and out of wedlock." The Irish were seen as drunkards who spent all their time at the bar. In addition to other factors, I believe my father internalized this stereotype. Stereotypes are meant to oppress people by making them believe that it's all that they are. The opportunity for jobs and wealth is threatened by any new group that comes along. The United States was founded on the idea that everyone is welcome to make a better life for herself or himself, but when a person from another culture tries to do this Americans resent it. We are not comfortable with anyone that is different from us and we feel that they are just more people to compete with. We are threatened by the idea that a person of another race has the potential to gain wealth and success that supposedly belongs to us. The intense effort to constantly gain more comes from beliefs in this country such as **competitive individualism** (Newman 308). The sign of success is money and the goal is to make as much of it as possible. The more material things we own the more successful we are and it doesn't matter who we have to trample on to achieve it. We have become so greedy that we forget about those less fortunate than us. We also forget that there are more important things in life. Our society depends on money to be happy. I know my parents feel guilty that they can't afford to buy me a car and sometimes I think I would be happier if I had one.

Prejudice and discrimination can come in many forms (Newman 341). Racism and sexism are two examples but for now I am concerned with these issues in terms of socioeconomic class. We know that you can be judged by the color of your skin but we are also judged by how much money we have. There are other aspects of a person than what tangible and visible objects they have acquired. We assume things about someone's personality or life from what clothes they are wearing. I'm sure there have been times when people didn't get a job because they couldn't afford to buy a nice suit for the interview but were otherwise qualified. A male peer saw me on two occasions. One time I was dressed in sweatpants and a t-shirt with no make-up on. The next time I had nicer, more expensive clothes on and I was wearing jewelry. Which occasion do you think he was more receptive towards me? He didn't want to be associated with and wasn't interested in a girl who didn't possess a high socioeconomic status.

Women struggle harder than men to achieve the perfect image. We have to endure **sexism** in all stages and aspects of our lives (Newman 374). Since we live in a **patriarchal** society, women are not valued as much as men (Newman 374). We work twice as hard to prove ourselves and don't enjoy the same rewards. We have to live up to high standards which include being skinny, beautiful at all times, intelligent, kind, and domestic just to name a few. There are many contradicting characteristics we have to possess—which gets very confusing. For example, women should be virgin-like and virtuous but at the same time men want us to be sexual creatures. I was dating a boy who implied in many ways that girls who sleep around or talk to a few guys at one time are slutty. Ironically, I found out later that he was having sexual relations with more than one girl. This was acceptable because he is a young male. If I had done the same thing I would have been labeled as a slut.

Newman cites Laura Miller's work (1997) exploring the issue of females in the military (Newman 377). According to Miller and Newman, the reason this is such a controversial issue is because a woman in the military doesn't portray the normal image of a feminine woman. It portrays the image of a strong, disciplined woman who is capable of representing and fighting for her own country. The idea of a woman being equal to a man intellectually and physically is threatening to many people.

Women try to look feminine to attract a mate. We wear jewelry, make-up, and tight clothes but when we are raped it's our fault. **Rape as a means of social control** is another way women are oppressed. I have never experienced sexual assault first-hand but a friend of mine was pulled into a van and raped repeatedly. Once this happens we feel our image is tarnished. We feel dirty and see ourselves as damaged goods. The woman is blamed for the attack. She asked for it. She was dressed like a slut. These are common responses but she was probably dressed to attain a potential romantic relationship. Rape shows women they are sexual objects who can be controlled by men.

Depending on the culture you live in, women are forced to live up to certain expectations. A woman's role varies across race and class. The **global devaluation of women** is apparent and when women fail to express themselves as the correct image they are ostracized or even killed (Newman 401). Indian women who commit adultery are killed by their own family members because they are disgraced. In the U.S., it is difficult for women to live up to a desirable image because we are given mixed messages as to what that is. You can't be too powerful or else you're a bitch. If you wear certain clothes and make-up to make yourself appear attractive you're a slut. It seems to be a lose/lose situation.

Cohort and period effects can have major impacts on what is expected of us throughout our lives (Newman 416). During the 1990s the economy was doing relatively well. My peers and I were attending college and working to educate ourselves in order to have a better life. My role as a student is to study, do well in school, and eventually take advantage of the opportunities to come. Now, since the economy is being harmed by the war on top of recession, opportunities that were once available will no longer be. When I graduate, there are even more factors against me. What will I have to come up with to make myself a desirable candidate? My college degree is not going to be enough now that jobs are scarce. What additional qualities do I have to acquire to find a decent job? Conforming to the image the employer wants is more important these days. When my sister first entered the workforce these extra obstacles didn't exist. She was hired out of necessity and because of her education and experience. She had it a little easier because she didn't have to prove herself so much.

The consumption epidemic portrayed in the documentary *Affluenza* is another perfect example of how the obsession with having it all has affected me and my generation. My struggle with image is the result of our society never being happy with what they have and the insatiable need to always want more. Happiness lies in the newest trend and the obsession with material things is an epidemic. I have come to realize that possessions aren't the source of happiness. I haven't figured out exactly what is, but I know I need to focus on other things that don't have to do with money. I have learned not to care so much about what other people think of me. I likewise try not to base my opinions of others on the clothes they wear.

There is a saying, which is a statement of fact, "The rich get richer and the poor get poorer." The documentary *The Big One*, by Michael Moore, shows just how obsessed we are with wealth. The owners of companies like Nike will have their products made in other countries by people who are all being exploited to make a bigger profit—not to mention taking jobs away from Americans. The image of power and wealth is so important that the exploitation of other humans is not a problem. We will step on anyone to get to the top.

In the movie ***Good Will Hunting***, the professor discovers a genius who surpasses most intellectuals but seems to have an attitude problem. The professor doesn't understand why Will won't use his knowledge to acquire fame and fortune. It's not a priority to Will to gain from his intelligence. Cashing in and reaping the benefits shouldn't always be important. Pursuing love was more important to Will.

It seems that society creates its own reality. It dictates what is right and wrong and how people should live. In the movie ***The Matrix***, Keanu Reeves' character Neo believes he is living in reality until he is shown otherwise. We are born into a way of life and everything we hear and see is taken as the truth. How many times have we heard, "That's just the way things are"? There is a world outside of our own and even though different ideas seem strange we shouldn't be so quick to dismiss them. We can change the things we don't like. We don't have to live the way we are told to live.

References

Cohen, Samara. (2002). "I Only *Thought* I Knew It All: Society and the Individual." *Human Architecture: Journal of the Sociology of Self-Knowledge*, I, 1, Spring, 9-17.

Dai, Peter. (2002). "Why P is Afraid to Love a Woman?" *Human Architecture: Journal of the Sociology of Self-Knowledge*, I, 1, Sp., 18-25.

Miller, Laura. (1997). "Not just weapons of the weak: Gender harassment as a form of protest for army men," *Social Psychology Quarterly*, 60, 32-51.

Newman, David M. (2002). *Sociology: Exploring the Architecture of Everyday Life*. 4th ed, California: Pine Forge Press.

Films:

"Affluenza." (1997). Bullfrog Films.

"The Big One." (1999). Miramax Home Entertainment.

"Good Will Hunting." (1997). Miramax Home Entertainment.

"The Matrix." (1999). Warner Brothers.

"Multiple Personalities: The Search for Deadly Memories." (1994). Home Box Office.

"Patch Adams." (1998). Universal Studios.

"It's Not My Fault":
Overcoming Social Anxiety through Sociological Imagination

Charles

"A wise man speaks because he has something to say; a fool because he has to say something."—Plato

My name is Charles. I am a twenty year old, white male. My parents were and are middle class. For as long as I can remember I have felt a certain anxiety toward social situations and people as a whole. I have never actually enjoyed personal attention whether positive or negative. For years I simply accepted this as part of who I was. I am a shy, introverted, anti-social person. I don't like people, nor do I need them. I have trudged through twenty years of life with this attitude leading the way. I will attempt to explain the process of socialization through which I acquired these views.

Social structure is a human construct that organizes and guides our lives. I will show the ways in which social structure has shaped my life. I will employ the **sociological imagination** as a tool to explore my self. "Sociological imagination enables us to understand the larger historical picture and its meaning in our own lives" (Newman 9). I will explain the reasoning behind the views I hold and have held in the past. Furthermore, I will explain the progress made to date in resolving the dominant issues in my life.

Being the youngest member of a military family (sometimes referred to as a "military brat"), I have faced a different path of socialization. The military "stations" its members where it feels they would be most useful. As it happens, my family and I were "stationed" in Germany for a large portion of my childhood. The military provides amenities and Americanisms through bases that are maintained where people are stationed. These bases are virtual societies in their own right. While on the base, the culture doesn't differ greatly from that of the United States. Were you to venture off of the base, though, there would be no mistaking the absence of familiarity. Despite the age of **globalization**, one cannot help but feel isolated on the base. This could be compared to an island surrounded by an ocean of uncertainty.

Although one could seek refuge on the base, it was not wise to become too attached to it. This applies to the people that reside on the base as well. Army tours of duty are three years long. After your three-year tour is done, you will most likely have to relocate to a different base, state, or country. This requires saying good-bye to any friends you may have made, and meeting new friends when you arrive at your destination. Needless to say, this can be a very stressful endeavor. One may think relocating often would provide exceptional resocialization skills. In my situation, the contrary took place. It seemed as though meeting new people was too much work, and the benefits were short lived. I had my immediate family, and that was enough for me. Because we live in a **postindustrial society**, I was able to entertain myself for the most part. I was able to take advantage of our information and high-tech based society to the fullest extent. Watching television and playing video games for hours on end were my two favorite ways to pass the time. I also had a basketball hoop that could occupy my attention for the better part of a day. All this diminished the need or desire for friends. Over time, I became unconcerned and complacent when it came to meeting new people. This in turn would develop into an unbiased fear of people and loathing of social situations.

As I mentioned earlier, I have never desired any variety of attention directed toward myself. It always made me feel as though someone was passing judgment on me. The **looking glass self** has been an ever present element in my life. While referring to this concept in her essay Emily Margulies stated, "Whether taking a seat in class or getting ready to go out on a Friday night we are all constantly aware of how we may appear to those around us" (Margulies 7). This has been, at times, a debilitating affair for me. In an attempt to minimize this potential **embarrassment** (usually just a byproduct of my situational assessment), I would employ **role taking**—that is, evaluating myself from the perspective of others and behaving accordingly. Through constant role taking I could embark on **impression management** (acting in a way such that others will approve of oneself). This has made a difference in some situations. However, it is not an all-encompassing solution. Despite my amateurish **dramaturgy**, that is, treating everyday social life as a theater, the uncomfortable situations still far outnumbered the comfortable.

I was never the popular, outgoing person that I desired to be. What's more, in my own mind I perceived everyone else to be as Hunter "Patch" Adams was portrayed in the film *Patch Adams*. As far as I was concerned, everyone else was confident, outgoing, secure, and content with himself or herself. I took a number of messages from this movie. Perhaps the most relevant is to be yourself no matter what the cost. When the movie starts, Patch is depressed and is admitted to a psychiatric clinic. While in the clinic he finds his passion: helping people. Patch checks himself out of the clinic and begins medical school. While he was attending school, he began to let the real, uncensored Patch surface. Throughout the movie Patch is repeatedly attacked for his outgoing, "be yourself no matter what" attitude. He doesn't let this stop him though. He continues to be himself. At the end of the movie, Patch has his own clinic where he heals people using humor. This came as a result of uncompromisingly remaining himself. For me, being myself has been hard at times. This reminds me of the song lyrics: "I find, sometimes it's easy to be myself. Sometimes, I find it's better to be somebody else" (Matthews 1994).

In her article, "Alien Nation," P. Heim states, "…we compare ourselves to others and determine our self-worth" (Heim 41). Such comparisons also often led me to feel as though I was less of a person than everyone else. Consequently, I felt alienated. Most of this originated from the group with which I attended school. These individuals were part of my **secondary group**, that is, they were as close to me as my immediate family. They were merely in the school to be educated, as was I. Thus, they were more or less strangers to me. Nonetheless, nothing frightened me more than their opinions of me. Being a negative person, my role taking with this group resulted in an incongruent, negative self-concept. As human beings, we tend to like people that like us, and vice versa. Due to the evaluation of others' opinions of myself, I believed that most people did not like me. Hence, I did not like most people. This cycle of fear, dislike, and hatred would fuel my opinions of the world for years to come.

Another "vicious cycle" is that of the stereotypical view pertaining to sex. In our **patriarchal society**, the division of labor places men as the primary "bread winner." Along with the expectation that a man should be capable and talented enough for this task, is the implication that he would need to be outgoing and confident with himself. For how would a man satisfactorily perform the task of taking care of his family if he were not secure and outgoing? Secure and outgoing I was not. This lack of seemingly essential characteristics was to cause much doubt in my later years. People of authority would greet me with this stereotypical view in their minds (perhaps unconsciously) only to find me to be the exact opposite. Thus many times it was assumed that I was incapable of or not willing to perform required tasks.

According to David Newman (2002), being a white person I may hold **racially transparent** attitudes. He writes, "Whiteness is unmarkable and unexamined. It is so obvious and normative that white people's racial identity is, for all intents and purposes, invisible" (Newman 344). However, being that I spent a lot of time in Germany, things were different for me than for children who were socialized in the U.S. suburbs. On most of the military bases that I called home, white people were the minority. I can remember standing in the courtyard at W.A.M.S. (Wuerzburg American Middle School) with two or three of my white friends, waiting for the doors to open. As I looked around, I began to realize that we were the only white people in the courtyard (there were probably around fifty to one hundred people outside at that point). This was quite a surprise to me because it was incongruent with my inherent assumption that white people were the majority. I did not feel threatened or defensive; however, this incident did amplify the feeling that I did not belong.

On the issue of not fitting in, the movie *The Matrix* has some interesting parallels to my life. In the movie, the matrix is described as "a prison for your mind." Essentially what happens is that the human race creates artificial intelligence (A.I.). Because A.I. is able to think, it goes to war with the human race. Because A.I. uses solar energy, humanity "scorched the sky." For this reason, A.I. needs an alternative source of energy. It utilizes the human race for this energy. Humans are enslaved and used solely for the energy they provide. In the movie, this is depicted by endless cocoons that house the seemingly unconscious bodies of humans. The matrix is essentially an artificial reality that looks, smells, sounds, tastes, and feels like the real world. Your mind controls what happens in the matrix. This includes your perception of how you look, how you interact with other people in the matrix, and so on. If we boil all this down, we can say that essentially, in the matrix, "reality" is all in your mind. This is not unlike the world you and I live in. In my reality, I was not up to everyone else's standards. I could not fit in anywhere, or feel comfortable attempting to fit in somewhere. As mentioned earlier, this was merely my perception of reality. In fact, I could have fit in almost anywhere I desired to fit in. I was not terribly defective, and people would more than likely have accepted me if I gave them the chance.

Constant fear, awkwardness, dislike, and uncertainty are quite obviously not desirable states in which to exist. The way I found to escape these ailments was solitude. Although the next best thing to solitude was being with my family, their company still required a minimal amount of self-consciousness and acting on my part. Being that solitude provided relief from the pressure of social life, I sought it often. I remember faking illness frequently to avoid attending school. After the first semester of third grade, my teacher sent a letter home along with my "straight A" report card that stated I had missed, on average, about one and a half days of school a week. Of course, parental obligation tends to take precedence over constant illness. Most days I would make it to school on time, ready to grit my teeth through the agony. I vividly remember one morning during my second grade year. I had had enough of the people at school. I was not going. My mother had to literally drag me to school, kicking and screaming. She brought me to my class, but I was not going in. Eventually, the principal became involved. I remember watching my mother walk down the hallway as the principal stood soccer-goalie style in the middle of the hallway to prevent me from following my mother. Finally after what seemed like hours of trying to get past my principal, I was accosted. She gave me a minute or two to clean the slime and moisture off of my face, and then shoved me in the door to my classroom.

Sometime in my fifth grade year, I began to receive migraine headaches quite regularly. In fact, I had prescription medication due to the severity and frequency of occurrence. This affliction was undoubtedly due to the stresses associated with social situations and the like. My prescription required that I visit the school nurse when I began to get a migraine. A good majority of the times that I had visited the nurse's office, I was sent home from school. I never had the need to fake a migraine due to the frequency with which they occurred. However, I had discovered an "out" if you will. The school nurse and I became quite familiar with each other. **Sick role** is basically the way people expect you to act when sick. I became master of the sick role. If I were having a particularly troublesome day, I would ask for a hall pass and invoke the sick role without hesitation or remorse.

Sick role was simply the means to an end. The reasons behind my desire to invoke sick role have to do with my character type. While discussing character types in relation to drug addiction, Chanan Rapaport quotes Horney as saying, "…and the third is moving away from people, detaching oneself from others and building up a more or less independent existence, with the effect of avoiding whatever threat may be contained in human relationships" (Horney, cited in Rapaport 14). I believe that Horney was right on in this categorization. I fit into this mold very well. The "threat" that is referred to is either a defensive or an adaptive threat. That is, either a built-in defense mechanism (resulting from natural threats to a person, i.e. assault, murder, etc.…), or something that the individual or society has evolved to include as threatening to a person. In my case, I acquired an adaptive threat pertaining to social situations and most of the people in life. Though not grounded in reality, this threat was no doubt figured into my everyday life. In her journal article "Alien Nation," P. Heim tells the story of how she became bitter and sarcastic. She and her mother did not get along. Every time they spoke, it would result in an argument. She wrote about her dance instructor who would yell anytime the opportunity presented itself and would point out anything she had done incorrectly. This experience contributed to her development of sarcasm as a defense mechanism. I too developed sarcasm as well as the desire to isolate myself from others (both of these help to form my character type). These features enabled me to deal with the perceived shortcomings I possessed.

The main idea in the movie *The Big One* is corporate greed. Michael Moore is on a book tour. While he's touring, he stops at various corporations to ask them questions. He stops at the Nike headquarters and speaks to Phil Knight. Michael asks Phil why he doesn't have shoe factories in the United States. Phil's answer is, "American people don't want to make shoes." I personally can't tell you if Mr. Knight has used this answer before. However, I would venture to guess that this is his standard answer to this question. Though in my opinion this explanation doesn't have much integrity, it serves Mr. Knight's purpose— that is, to satisfy the immediate situation. I think the real reason Mr. Knight doesn't have factories in the U.S. is that he simply doesn't want to. It's much easier and more economical to have his factories in other countries. When I look to the past, I can compare my thought that "nobody is going to accept or enjoy my company," to Phil Knight's statement. Perhaps, I knew this attitude to be unrealistic, but it was just easier that way. For me, it was a satisfactory way to satisfy the immediate situation I was in.

While reflecting on my life to this point, I came to the realization that I may, in a way, comfort myself with material things. The film *Affluenza* is about the American people's excessive consumerism. One of the definitions provided for affluenza in the film is, "The bloated, sluggish and unfulfilled feeling that results from efforts to keep up with the Jones's." I myself have and still do, to some degree, suffer from affluenza. In the past, in order to facilitate a feeling of security with the way I looked, I would coerce my parents into feeding my affluenza. In my perception, my **birth cohort** had new clothes, shoes, and the like. Thus, my desire to be the popular one reinforced the need to have the same things everyone else had. This could perhaps be viewed as a **cohort effect**, or even a **period effect**, due to the overwhelming commercialism that tells the people of my generation they need certain things in order to fit in or be "cool."

Despite the fact that I didn't consider myself to be "cool," my life continued to be the same in my high school years. The only difference in my progression to high school was that I had access to automobiles. This eliminated the need for the school nurse. It was now much easier to find comfort and solitude by my own abilities. However, when I invoked the sick role without an authority figure's permission, neither my parents nor my principal thought it was good. High school, being part of the **social institution** of education expects certain social behavior and cooperation. I had been going against the culturally defined **norm** (expected behavior) that people socialize, smile, and are generally polite to each other. Furthermore I had violated the institutionalized norm of education systems that requires class and school attendance. This tug of war match was concluded during my junior year in high school. I dropped out of school and promptly acquired my GED.

I had realized that my behavior was abnormal before I dropped out of high school. However, I hadn't dedicated much reflection to it. I suppose it was easier to forget what happened (or didn't happen) and keep pushing on. It was about this time that I began to analyze my behavior. I came to a conclusion similar to that of Peter Dai. While discussing "P's" anxiety in his essay, he states, "As individuals, we have the right to solve our problems and end our discontentment" (Dai 19). I was absolutely not content with my situation. So, with the influence of my father, I made a step in the right direction by getting technical training. After a few months of living in my parents' home without a job, my father required that I get a job or get an education. I chose education. Within a month of this decision, I was in St. Louis attending my first A+ (computer hardware and software) class. This gave me more confidence than I had prior to attending the class. I stayed in a hotel by myself. I had never been alone in a city the size of St. Louis. I fed myself, made it to class without insult or injury, and overall did a good job in the class.

The movie *Good Will Hunting* has some interesting content that can be compared to my situation. In the movie, the main character, Will, is a janitor at M.I.T. One night, he proves a mathematical equation that's written on a blackboard in the hallway. The professor that wrote the problem sees Will and seeks him out. The professor finds Will at a hearing for assault. Will is sentenced to prison for assault. The professor talks to the judge and takes Will out of jail on two conditions: that he should practice mathematics with the professor, and go to a psychiatrist once a week. Psychiatrists repeatedly dismiss Will until the professor contacts one of his old friends from college named Sean. Sean takes Will's standoffish behavior with a grain of salt. Eventually, with patience, Sean is able to get to the real Will. It seems Will was abused as a child. This led Will to put on a front that prevented society from seeing the real Will. Sean begins to tell Will that it (the abuse) was not his fault. Sean repeatedly states that it is not his fault, until the real Will surfaces and hears the message. This process is not too different from the events that led to my decision to move to New York. All the situations in which I felt an ungrounded feeling of insecurity and fear could be compared to Sean's repeated words to Will. In essence, every uncomfortable situation in my life could be summed up in one statement; "it's not my fault." After the right self heard this message, I decided to make a change. I concluded that a move was in order. It would be a fresh start, a new beginning. I would move to New York by myself.

I decided it was time to rethink my career choice about eight months into my first job in the information technology field. I was not happy with the job I was performing. Furthermore, I had been used to existing in the social class that my parents belonged to. Due to **deskilling**, the career field I had chosen was not the most lucrative. I came to the conclusion that SUNY Oneonta would be a good place to facilitate my career change. This in itself was a titanic leap toward my further socialization. To knowingly make the decision to attend classes with my peers, who I had despised at one time in my life, was quite an accomplishment. The concept that I was "by myself" is an interesting one. Although solitude had been a refuge for many years prior to this point, this experience proved to be different. It was easy to avoid contact with people while living in my parents' home. But by living on my own, I was suddenly forced to put myself in situations that had terrified me for years. Such things as grocery shopping and speaking to an interviewer about a job served as a bit of a crash course in social behavior. Still being a quiet, shy, and an ultimately insecure young man, I put my head down and did what I had to do. After a while I obtained a job in Albany, New York. I came in as a worker, one of the lower levels on the hierarchy of authority. This exposed me to corporate **bureaucracy** at its finest. Furthermore, I spoke to people on the telephone for forty hours per week. I was quite hesitant and worried when I began. Yet, a few months after I began working there, I could speak to people on the telephone quite easily. I suppose this was a "baby step" toward functioning as a "normal person."

I mentioned earlier that the concept that I was "by myself" was an interesting one. There is a theory that proposes we all have multiple "selves." To go further, we all have many different personalities equipped with different qualities that we can employ when most appropriate. I can subscribe to this theory. In my case, for example, there is the self that is employed when in a social situation and impression management is required. There is the self that surfaces when comfort is possible, but awareness is still required; this self may surface in the presence of extended family. There may also be the self that enjoys only its own company. These selves are not immutable however. As my life progresses, so too do the selves I possess. When things change in my life, so do the means of coping with them. Different selves, in this case, possess these means. Yet, some linger on despite my lack of need for them. *Multiple Personalities* is a documentary on multiple personality disorder. A male police officer is one of the three people featured in this film. This man has scores of different personalities that, by his account, surface when they are needed. One of his personalities takes over when he drives because that personality is best equipped for the situation. A childlike personality takes control while sitting on the couch in the comfort of his home. Peter Dai's "P" was a child inside. To overcome his emotional disorder (he couldn't love a woman), he set out to reconnect to that child and convince him that "he has become a good man" (Dai 22). I too must find the child I have inside and convince him that the world is not a bad place. He is not deficient in any way, shape, or form, and not all people are evil.

I learned by writing this paper that I was not the only one who had a fear of social situations. Thomas Richards gives the following account of someone who has symptoms of social anxiety:

> A man finds it difficult to walk down the street because he's self-conscious and feels that people are watching him from their windows. Worse, he may run into a person on the sidewalk and be forced to say hello to them. He's not sure he can do that. His voice will catch, his "hello" will sound weak, and the other person will know he's frightened. More than anything else, he doesn't want anyone to know that he's afraid. He keeps his eyes safely away from anyone else's gaze and prays he can make it home without having to talk to anyone. (Richards 2003)

A case study featured on the Anxiety Network portrayed a middle-aged man named Jim. Jim had Social Anxiety Disorder. He is married and has children. He works at a local music store. He has known the owner for some time. Jim's wife performed any task involving a social situation for him. She would make appointments, go to parent teacher conferences, and so on. All of this was done because of Jim's debilitating ailment. He had no friends except for those shared mutually with his wife. When at work, he struggled when he had to call people to let them know that their order was in. He would begin to speak, and then his voice would shake and crack. He would freeze up, and then expel the rest of the sentence as fast as he could. Eventually, the music store was sold to a large corporation. Jim was offered a promotion. This is when he decided to get help. At first he was shy and avoided eye contact. Jim learned that "the world didn't revolve around him." He learned that everyone makes mistakes, and "it's ok" to make mistakes. He gradually made progress and eventually took the promotion at work. He now conducts weekly meetings at his job. His days are not free from anxiety; however, Jim's anxiety has become manageable and he is now able to overcome it.

It may be unnecessary to point out the fact that I have my fair share of problems. It may, however, be necessary to draw attention to the fact that I have made significant progress in the latter years. I am still exploring my identity, but I am making progress. I have explained the circumstances of my socialization. I have traced the formation of my views. I have also shown the progressive steps I have taken toward resolution of my issues. Though I have come a long way, I still have a long road ahead. Despite this, I have every confidence that, as Jim did, I will overcome my anxiety and distaste for social situations. Furthermore, my hope is that this paper serves others as a means to self-understanding so that they will become a better person.

REFERENCES

Dai, Peter. (2002). Why is P Afraid to Love a Woman? *Human Architecture*, I, 1, 18-25.

Heim, P. (2002). Alien Nation. *Human Architecture: Journal of the Sociology of Self-Knowledge*, I, 1, 36-44.

Margulies, Emily. (2002). Anti-man to Anti-patriarchy. *Human Architecture: Journal of the Sociology of Self-Knowledge*, I, 2, 1-8.

Matthews, D. (1994). *So Much To Say*. On *Crash* CD. RCA Records.

Newman, David M. (2002). *Sociology: Exploring the Architecture of Everyday Life* (4th ed.). Thousand Oaks, CA: Sage Publications Inc.

Rapaport, C. (1963). *Character, Anxiety, and Social Affiliation.* Ann Arbor, Michigan. University Microfilms, Inc.

Richards, Thomas A. (2003). *What is Social Anxiety/Phobia?.* Retrieved April 16, 2003, From http://www.anxietynetwork.com/spwhat.html#top

Social Phobia/Social Anxiety Case Studies. Retrieved April 17, 2003, From http://www.anxietynetwork.com/spcase.html#spcase1

Films:

"Affluenza." (1997). Bullfrog Films.

"The Big One." (1999). Miramax Home Entertainment.

"Good Will Hunting." (1997). Miramax Home Entertainment.

"Multiple Personalities: The Search for Deadly Memories." (1994). Home Box Office.

"Patch Adams." (1998). Universal Studios.

"The Matrix." (1999). Warner Brothers.

"Multiple Personalities: The Search for Deadly Memories." (1994). Home Box Office.

Treading Water:
Self-Reflections on Generalized Anxiety Disorder

Megan Murray

It has taken me twenty two years to face the fact that I am suffering needlessly from a debilitating problem, Generalized Anxiety Disorder (GAD). I suffered silently in fear that my peers, teachers, family, friends, and my boyfriend would discover my secret. I found it hard to hide my emotions and phobias in front of those I loved. I felt like I was a prisoner of my own emotions and fears. I managed to conceal my inner thoughts until recently, when I decided it was time to own up to what has plagued me for a lifetime. I decided it was time to free myself. The day I admitted I had an anxiety disorder was the first day of a new life for me. I am ready to free the emotions that lay trapped in my mind and have haunted me to this day as an adult.

In his essay titled "Why Is P Afraid to Love a Woman" (2002), Peter Dai reflects on a personal dilemma he faced while growing up. He describes how if no one knew he had anxiety they would think he was self-confident and self-assured. I also was able to conceal my fears and anxiety. Peter spoke of the surge of tension that went through his body when he was around girls. Similarly, there would be times when I would black out because situations became so difficult to handle. I just turned off. I would sweat in class dreading that a teacher might call on me and I would not be able to answer. I had a choking feeling when I took a test, and my grades reflected that stress. How can a person effectively take a test when they can not hold a pencil, can not breathe, and can not focus their eyes? It was impossible. All of these symptoms had become normal to me.

My anxiety peaked when I arrived at SUNY Oneonta. I felt the pressure of success and began to realize I strive to please others, not myself. I felt the need to fit into some niche on campus. There were sororities and fraternities all around campus. I felt uneasy when I walked around campus. The bar scene was an uncomfortable experience for me as well. I soon became afraid to go out to the bars for the fear something bad would happen. This led to my Agoraphobia which has lasted almost two years. My mother thought that it was awkward that a twenty-year old college student would stay home on Friday and Saturday nights.

I was terrified to leave my home or dorm room for the fear that something horrible would happen. I missed out of a lot of great experiences in college because I was afraid to tell anyone that I had anxiety attacks. I did a great job of hiding my anxiety in front of my friends. I always had an excuse for not going out; "I have a lot of work to do" or "I do not feel well" were most common. When I did agree to go out I would get excited thinking that everything was going to be great. But the excitement did not last long. I would become very agitated and soon a choking feeling would surround me. I was unable to swallow and I felt short of breath. The problem continued to the point where I dreaded going out to eat for the fear that I would have an anxiety attack in the middle of my dinner.

I have lived two lives. One is the confident Megan Murray who can handle anything that is thrown her way. The second is

---

Notice: Copyright of *Human Architecture: Journal of the Sociology of Self-Knowledge* is the property of Ahead Publishing House (imprint: Okcir Press) and its content may not be copied or emailed to multiple sites or posted to a listserv without the copyright holder's express written permission. However, users may print, download, or email articles for individual use.

the Megan Murray who was afraid of the world and broke down at the onset of stress. This has caused a chronic **front stage** and **back stage** behavioral dualism in my personality. When I was on the **front stage** I was a good student, friend, girlfriend, and daughter. I acted confidently and in control at all times, never allowing my true emotions to emerge. **Back stage** I was angry inside, always thinking of who I could blame for the latest crisis I was facing. I felt that my **identity** was missing. I was never confident of myself and who I was. Identity is the one thing that makes each of us unique and I was unable to establish that. I connected with the movie we watched in class on *Multiple Personalities* in that I felt like I was two different people. I was a child at heart who was afraid to be alone and make decisions; and yet, I had another self who could take over when things became difficult.

I was denied entrance to the Block Program for the spring semester. I was obsessed with proving myself to my family and SUNY Oneonta. I spent my week-ends working on projects and papers leaving no time for friends or family. I distanced myself from those I loved so I would have no distractions. I slowly pushed away the ones who meant the most to me. I knew I was different from my peers in that I was constantly stressed and anxious. I felt like I was on a treadmill running on the fastest speed. I was unable to accept what I had.

I had been able to disguise my anxiety until I received an email stating I got a C- in Economics, meaning that I was not eligible for the block program. I was overcome with emotion and collapsed on my dorm floor. I did not want to speak to anyone for days and I trembled so badly that I could barely hold a glass. I went to the doctor on Christmas Eve and I was told that I was having a nervous breakdown and I was suffering from Generalized Anxiety Disorder. I was put on anti-depressants and Xanax until my body could cope with the situation.

My doctor felt it was important that I begin taking Anti-depressants to get back to ground zero where I could cope with the situation at hand. In other words, they chose the route of **medicalization** to define and cure my problem. However, I was against any kind of intervention with medication. People who suffer from anxiety and depression are given drugs and then sent on their way. Anxiety is a deep-rooted emotional issue that stems from inner personal troubles but in a social context. Until I was able to take on the task of sociological self-exploration I could not combat my anxiety.

I believe that the **sick role** assigned to people with depression is misconstrued. Critics of anxiety and depression think that we stay in bed all day and do not function in our daily lives. However, many of us sufferers go about our daily routine disguising how we are truly feeling inside. I did not feel I was entitled to rest when I had my breakdown. I felt I had failed as a daughter and a student. I thought I should not be allowed to lay down and be pampered because I was a failure to my family. My mother told me she was proud of how I did under the pressure I was enduring. I was so relieved to hear that I had not been a disappointment and that in fact she was proud of me. It was difficult to understand how she could be proud of me for failing in such a huge way. I called my mother the day I found out I had failed Economics and I was hysterical. I thought for sure that she was going to be furious with me. Instead, she was understanding and supportive and convinced me that I had to see a doctor. I felt a love for my mother that day that I never felt before. It was the first time I ever felt the need to lean on my mother in my adult age. I never wanted to see or hug my mother as much as I did that day I came home. I had a new found respect and love for her that I never felt before.

Although my mother and I have become close in my college years I have battled with my relationship with her for years. All I ever wanted as a child was to appease her and make her happy. My childhood was happy but I was always seeking approval from those around me. I had a close **nuclear family** growing up despite that fact that I come from a divorced family in which I had minimal contact with my father.

I was raised by my grandmother and mother. I spent the majority of my childhood with my grandmother learning how to cook and do crafts. I was not an easy child to take care of; therefore, my mother was constantly stressed. She was a single mother of two small children and a full-time nurse. As I look back at my childhood I realize that my mother's stress was contagious. I often blame her for my anxiety today but I realize that she made do with a bad hand she was given. She played the role of mother, father, nurse, chauffeur, friend, and cook for twenty-two years. She raised two wonderful children and I would not be where I am today without her. For that I am eternally grateful!

As a child I was surrounded by a variety of social groups and organizations. We were involved in our church, girl scouts, and Irish Step Dancing. My mother felt it was important for us to be involved in a variety of organizations when we were in high school. I was involved in a variety of clubs. I was also a cheerleader. I never realized how all of this affected me until my therapy sessions began a month ago. I am still afraid to say that I suffered from depression at times. Depression still has a **stigma** attached to it nowadays; supposedly, those who are depressed do not go far in life. I already had a hard time facing the fact that I had anxiety; to add to the list my being depressed became overwhelming. I felt I would be an embarrassment to my family if I did not perform the expected student role task of going into the block program as scheduled this spring. I feared that I would fail at the one thing I love the most, teaching. I estimated my self-worth according to my grades and when I did not meet the grade I shut down.

The movie *Patch Adams* made me realize how depression can change a person's life in a positive way. Patch used his depression to help others. I have also often found myself reaching out to others who have admitted having anxiety. I want to make a difference in this world. I believe that teaching will help me with my goal to make a difference in someone's life.

While preparing my presentation in class on the first chapter of our textbook, *Sociology: Exploring the Architecture of Everyday Life* by David Newman, I learned about the **Sociological Imagination**. This concept is key to understanding my condition in that I realized that other forces have influenced me throughout my life. I alone am not the cause of my anxiety and phobias. Through therapy I have realized that anxiety is a culmination of diverse events and thoughts. The world around me influences my everyday behavior.

My not getting into block last semester led to my nervous breakdown. But looking at the big picture there were twenty-two years of emotions behind that breakdown. There were other forces that were working to decide that decision. My life involves millions of intersections with others I encounter each day. I feel that breakdown was the breaking of a barrier that existed in my family for years. The lines of communication opened and were filled with wonderful talks about what my life has been like the last two years. I felt comfort in each person in my family for they offered support and guidance.

I realize now that I need to change not just my personal characteristics but also the social institutions/roles I am involved in. My focus in life was always to live up to the expectations of my aspired **achieved status**. My social role in society has caused stress in my life. I have always wanted to be accepted by my peers and loved ones. My parents stressed the importance of education and being successful in life. It was an **institutional norm** for my sister and I to go to school and get good jobs. I worked diligently to ensure I received satisfactory grades for which I would be praised. When I did not receive the grade that would ensure me the spot in the block program I felt I had not lived up to my achieved status as a student and I felt like I had disappointed my family. I was a failure and a disappointment to my family. Although they reassured me that I made them proud in every way, deep in my heart I felt ashamed. It would now have taken me six years to finish a Bachelor's degree. I have often wondered why this has happened to me. All of my dreams seemed to fall to pieces over two grade points.

I can see how the person I am today has been shaped through a **looking glass self** process. I worry needlessly about what others perceive me to be. I look to others for encouragement and validation. I determine my self-worth according to what others think of me. For my whole life I looked to my mother for that comfort. I wanted to be praised by her and to please her with my accomplishments. In her article "Good Mother/Daughter Hunting: A Process of Self-Healing" (2002), L. Mlecz states that her mother picked her favorite color and eventually after a period of time she grew to love pink. This is how our gender and other identity features are often shaped. My mother is very controlling and has controlled almost every aspect of my life for twenty-two years. In the last two months I have realized I need to free myself from her and from the feeling that I need to please her. Ultimately, *I* can only do what is best for my future.

My mother enforced **impression management.** On weekends my sister Erin, my mother, and I would have a party or event to attend. On our way to the party we would fight and yell at each other. As soon as the house came in sight it was time to act as though we were the happy family. I became a better actor through each fight. No matter how bad the fight was no one ever knew how much pain was inside all of us. We looked great on the outside but inside I think we were all falling apart. We acted like we had a perfect family with no problems.

I often found myself in a **role conflict** with my family. I am an independent student at school. When I return home, though, I feel like I am a child. My mother tells me to pick up my room and make my bed. I feel like I still have to ask permission for what to wear to church. I forget that I am grown up and I don't need to be told what to do. This summer I taught seventh grade special education at the school next to my house. I again experienced a role conflict when I came home. I was the teacher in charge of 15 students, but when I returned home I was a six-year-old child being told what to do. I often found myself using the students' bathroom because I forgot I was an adult.

In her article "I only Thought I Knew It All: Society and the Individual" (2002), Samara Cohen asks two seemingly simple questions that made me stop reading to reflect critically on my own life. Samara asks:

How do I affect society? And how does society affect me?

How can I affect society? If I bring a positive outlook to life will someone take my lead and continue that trend? How is my anxiety affecting those around me? Can I be harming them without even knowing it, or helping them through dealing with my anxiety? These are all questions that still have to be answered. School is **resocializing** me to deal with society at large; through education, I want to set a new standard for myself in which I determine my self worth. But I can also make a difference through other institutions. I found refuge in the Catholic Church as a teenager. Church was one place I could be myself and I knew I would never be judged. I never felt anxiety when I was there. I became very involved in the youth ministry at our parish and went on a variety of religious retreats.

I have had the opportunity to join a new group this semester. I joined this therapy group for people with anxiety and I have learned a great deal about my disorder and myself. I have learned where my anxiety stems from and how I can help myself to overcome it. I believe that my **birth cohort** has experienced more pressure than those of other generations. My generation has faced new challenges and hurdles. College is now no longer an option but a way of life. College is now a requirement to get a job that will pay a decent salary. The State of New York has placed stiffer regulations on teachers than they have ever done before. For my profession, teaching, the standards have been raised and more is expected of us as professionals. The constant pressure on teachers, legislatures, colleges, and parents has led to a rise in anxiety for my generation in this profession. My do not live in an agricultural society where we would stay at home with our families on the farm. We live in a **post-industrial society**. As college graduates we are expected to be out in the work force using the technologies of today. The students that I have become friends with at SUNY Oneonta fall into the same cohort as I. I have been exposed to many **cohort effects** with my friends and fellow classmates. The War in Iraq and September 11th have caused many of us to bond together in a way that I don't think many generations have in the past. This is a result of a **period effect** our generation went through. We were all about the same age when the attacks happened in New York City. Many of us are now thinking differently about life, we take one day at a time and cherish what we have. On September 11th I had panic attacks just thinking about what it must have been like to be in those buildings. I knew I was not alone as many of my peers expressed their fears and anxiety.

I have come to realize through therapy that I worry too much about my **social status** in life. Reading our textbook by David Newman helped me realize that this is common. In high school **social class** determines how your four years would be. I was lucky to have friends who were in the higher social class. I was not made fun of as many of my fellow classmates were. I wanted to have nice clothes and be accepted by my peers. This did not seem to be a destructive way of life until I entered college. I realized that in life you are judged by who you are not what you wear. I met a great group of friends who taught me how to live without the fear of pleasing others.

In high school I was a cheerleader and secretary of our senate and a member of my class committee. I enjoyed school and was very involved. I was a "normal" student to others but inside I was different. I was diagnosed with a learning disability when I was in third grade. I did not want any of my fellow classmates to know where I was going when I went to the resource room. I was afraid that I would encounter the usual **stereotype** associated with learning disabled children. I learned from a young age that learning disabled students were frowned upon in the learning environment. I encountered **discrimination** in high school for being learning disabled. I was asked to leave the Regents Program for the fear that I would endanger the learning process of my fellow peers. I never told any of my teachers that I was learning disabled until testing approached and I asked for extended timing. I had one teacher tell me that my team of teachers were **prejudiced** against learning disabled students because they took up too much of their planning time for tutoring.

I thought that my battles were over when I entered college. Recently I found myself in a situation with a dean of a department on campus. This person said that learning disabled students do not always do well in the teaching curriculum. Another student and myself were asked to do tasks that were not asked of other students. I became defensive because I felt that I was being discriminated against simply for my disability. In our textbook Newman wrote about **symbolic racism,** which involves efforts to undermine institutions set up to deal with **institutional racism**. I feel now that I was also encountering a similar symbolic discrimination against those intended to benefit from learning disability programs. I firmly stood up for my rights and explained why I felt I would make an effective teacher.

Another student and myself stood against the department and in effect formed a **reform movement**. We formulated an **ideological** framework for how we thought academic matters should be handled. Rules should not be changed when the department is pressed to provide a service. All students should be equal regardless of their disability. The school is a great example of a **bureaucracy.** We went to several different academic offices asking how we could be receiving help with the department and no one was willing to comment. The school works as a **hierarchy of authority**. The pyramid is so large no employee wants to step on another employee's foot. In order to get to the top they have to go along with what the school tells them to do. If they want to advance they must not make any waves in the system.

Six years later I still struggle with being labeled as learning disabled. I don't feel that it has hindered my success but it can be frustrating to work so hard on a project and only receive a "B." My anxiety has hit a peak in the last few years due to an overcompensation for learning disability. I feel that I have to prove myself to others and my family. I want to overcome the label of being a learning disabled child. Although it is all a secret to many, I feel as though people can tell in my writing and performance.

I believe that much of it has to do with **competitive individualism.** I want to make my own way in life and to have a good job to show for it. I do not want to ride on the footsteps of anyone else. I have seen many students ride through the educational system on the tails of their classmates. There is a **free-rider problem** when you get to the college level. Group work in college is a great example of how the free rider problem can spread like a disease. Many students will sit back and watch as another student does all of the work. I tend to be the one who is a nervous wreck about getting the project done.

The movie *Good Will Hunting* reminded me of myself in the sense that Will was afraid to show who he really was. He appeared to have no true emotions when engaged in counseling. Appearances are not always what they seem to be. He was not dressed like a wealthy college student, but inside he was brilliant. I felt a connection to Will because he put up a great front for his friends and even for his counselor. Will was afraid to get close to anyone for the fear of being hurt. I was afraid to get too close to anyone and explain that I had an anxiety disorder. I pushed many of my friends away for the fear they would find out that I was having panic attacks.

I have also learned through therapy that I worry about my future and **Socioeconomic status.** I do not want to live check to check when I finish school. The future after college seems so open. There are so many opportunities in life and I want to make the right decisions for my life. I come from a **middle class** family with a college education and I want the same for my children and myself. I feel as though I have so much pressure from society to follow in the footsteps of my parents. I fear social **stratification.** I do not want to be on the low end of the stratification system. I did not grow up in a poor environment yet money is one of my biggest worries.

The movie *The Big One* by Michael

Moore opened my eyes to what is really happening to this county's work force. Many of my worries are embedded in the fear of losing my job when I have a family. This film showed just how this country does not protect families who are in the workforce. The factories **objectify** workers. The workers are objects who come to work and run the machines and go home. They do not think of the families they support and the bills they have to pay. Nike and other companies do not realize that moving their business to other countries forces Americans out of jobs and involves exploitation of foreign workers and children. This has become a **social dilemma**; Nike CEO and managers do not think how their actions impact their employees and their families in this country and in the world as a whole.

The PBS documentary *Affluenza* also hit home with me. I saw myself when I watched that movie. This generation is focused on working to get all of the things that we see in the commercials. People buy compulsively because we want to keep up with the new trends. I have fallen for the commercialization of society and I buy things that I will never use or want in months. But there are useful things one can buy. My sister bought me a book when I was diagnosed with GAD but I never read it until recently. The book is titled *The Things That Really Matter* and is authored by Jackson Brown (1999). This book has given me a new outlook on my anxiety and life. Brown also encourages self-exploration. He writes:

> Remember that when you take inventory of the things in life you treasure the most, you'll find that none of them was purchased with money.

I think that this statement really relates to all the movies we watched in class. I stress about having all the luxuries I want in life, yet I already have all of life's treasures. I have a devoted family, a loving boyfriend, and a great group of friends.

My boyfriend bought me a book titled *The Anxiety and Phobia Workbook* (2002) by Edmund Bourne soon after I was diagnosed with Generalized Anxiety Disorder. The book was recommended by my counselor. This book has proven to be a wonderful tool in overcoming my anxiety. While reading the book the following caught my eye:

> The four traits that perpetuate anxiety: perfectionism, excessive need for approval, tendency to ignore signs of stress, excessive need for control. (233)

I was reading these traits and I noticed that I possess all of them. These traits caused my anxiety for years over my performance in school. While writing this paper I realized that much of my anxieties about the future are due to my worries about how others think of me. I need to let go of how others perceive my performance on a daily basis and instead do the best I can. A person can only give so much to society. I have learned through writing this paper that I need also to sit back and let life happen. Life can not be perfectly planned, we will all get to our destination in time but we must go forward in order to get there.

References

Bourne, Edmund. (2000). *The Anxiety and Phobia Workbook*. Third edition. New Harbinger Publications.

Brown, Jackson. (1999). *The Things That Really Matter*. Jackson Brown.

Cohen, Samara. (2002). "I only *Thought* I Knew It All: Society and the Individual," *Human Architecture: Journal of the Sociology of Self-Knowledge*. Volume 1, No 1, Spring, pp. 9-17.

Dai, Peter. (2002). "Why Is P Afraid to Love a Woman," *Human Architecture: Journal of the Sociology of Self-Knowledge*. Volume 1, No 1, Spring, pp. 18-25.

Mlecz, L. (2002). "Good Mother/Daughter Hunting: A Process of Self-Healing," *Human Architecture: Journal of the Sociology of Self-Knowledge*. Volume 1, No 1, Spring, pp. 45-52.

Newman, David. (2002). *Sociology: Exploring the Architecture of Everyday Life*. Fourth Edition. Sage Books.

Films:

"Affluenza." (1997). Bullfrog Films.

"The Big One." (1999). Miramax Home Entertainment.

"Good Will Hunting." (1997). Miramax Home Entertainment.

"Multiple Personalities: The Search for Deadly Memories." (1994). Home Box Office.

"Patch Adams." (1998). Universal Studios.

Sociology of Shyness: A Self Introduction

Collin E. Campbell

Only the shy know the pain of shyness, the intense inability to interact in social situations.

The shy often rationalize their shyness by saying, "I don't know these people" or "These people make me uncomfortable"—thereby laying the blame on others rather than dealing with their own problem. Shyness carries with it a fear that makes many unable to, say, ask out that girl or to seek the job promotion. Surely these opportunities would benefit us, or at least allow us to grow and learn. Shy people who may even recognize this, however, allow their perceptions of their faults, real or imagined, to prevent them from taking the chances others routinely take throughout a normal day. Their shyness, often begun during the school age (approx. 5-18 years of age), can go on to take more serious forms later in life such as depression and social anxiety disorder, to say the least. Several of the patients documented in the video viewed in class on multiple personality disorder had shy, or introverted, personalities. To compensate for this, they also developed stronger confident personalities that could accomplish what the shy personalities could not. In some instances this gave way to extreme, violent personalities bent on the destruction of the weaker ones.

Growing up, I myself suffered from shyness. I projected negative qualities upon myself: I was too fat, too ugly, too smelly, too dumb, etc. Because of this I was unable to stick up for myself, usually falling prey to others who saw my lack of confidence as an exploitable weakness. I was unable to speak to girls for the longest time, and it has only been in my second semester as a Freshman in college that I have actually had a girlfriend. Shyness kept me isolated for much of my life, preventing me from creating meaningful interpersonal relationships throughout high school. To this day my "best friend" has never been to my house. Even today I find faults with myself. My nose is too crooked, or one eye is lower than the other, or I am too critical of others, etc. Ironically, I have even gone so far as to say I am too critical of myself. What I fear most is that I am inadequate in every way imaginable and other people know this but will not tell me. It is this sort of paranoia that disturbs me enough to make poor decisions, though fortunately I have so far manage not to.

In her essay "Honor thy Father and Mother" Nancy Chapin states, "Parents are transmitters of attitudes that the child adopts in forming a self image"(47). Of course it is true that many of our **values** are formed as children when we are most open to the experiences of the world, so it stands to reason that we would be most influenced by the people we come into contact with the most during this stage, our family being our '**primary group.**' If a child is the recipient of care from parents who have much time to spend with them, that child will most likely act in a kind and caring manner. However, if a child lived with parents who were unable to spend time with her or acted violently towards her, she would more than likely become introverted and push away people who attempted to become close to her. In "My Translucent Father" (2002) Katie J. Dubaj portrays how her father slowly removed herself from her family, first by getting a divorce and slowly by not visiting her and later withdrawing child support. In a situation like this the child would more than likely be unsuccessful at relationships, being fearful of abandonment, driving people away from him or her.

Shyness in itself is nearly the antithesis of social interaction as it prevents people from actually interacting with one another, instead relegating them to what they can experience in their own little secluded worlds. As Newman states in his textbook, *Sociology: Exploring the Architecture of Everyday Life* (2002), "The primary theme of sociology is that our every day thoughts and actions are the product of a complex interplay…"(Newman 15). As such, Newman says, who we are is partially determined by the people we interact with every day. As children we learn from others walking, speaking, going to the toilet, etc. To the day we die we are learning from other people. By using our **sociological imagination**, we can well imagine that not only large social forces but even the tiniest encounters with another person could affect us for the rest of our lives. However, a shy person does not experience many of these interactions, and may stagnate or, as a computer does, find himself in an endless data loop, the indefinite recirculation of information. This can corrupt a person to the level of a shut-in or a hermit, forsaking all interaction to preserve a preferred (and safe) way of life.

Newman also discusses how we humans, as social beings, require contact with other people to interpret situations so that we might know how to react or respond. The shy or introverted person, however, does not have this benefit. If confronted with a strange occurrence, he will not have the advantage of experience or the knowledge of what other people have done in similar events, so he will be prone to panic in times of crisis. Newman goes on to say, "Although society exists as an objective fact, it is also created, reaffirmed, and altered through the day to day interactions…"(Newman 37). Introverted people, by not interacting with other people, in turn do not add to society. When a person takes a chance and, say, wears a new style of clothing that catches on, he or she has influenced society. From the person who wore the clothes to the person who imitated him or her, they all had a self-assurance that an introverted person does not posses. A shy man is more likely to conform to the majority more easily than someone who is more at ease with himself, seeking ways to blend into the crowd so that no matter where he goes he leaves no impression, passing as invisibly as a ghost.

Society is made up of groups of individuals, be they nations, neighborhoods, or even as small as the simple interactions between lovers. Shy people do not interact in these groups and thus do not influence them. But despite this, the introvert themselves are not to blame for this. Games such as baseball, for instance, carry certain **latent functions** with them, preparing the individual to function in larger society. While these leisure activities promote the development of teamwork and leadership abilities, a child who is not very physically developed or does not possess the necessary skills to participate is excluded from learning those crucial skills when young. Because he was not allowed to be a functional part of the team, he will not develop the interpersonal skills needed to function properly at work with people in **authority** positions or with subordinates later in his/her life. The child will not learn the norms expected of him. For example, in my senior prom, instead of kissing my date at the end of the night, I merely dropped her off and drove away, much to my **embarrassment** the next day. That incident was due to my being uncomfortable in that situation because of my earlier limited interaction with girls.

"The social construction of reality is the process by which reality is discovered, made known, reinforced and changed by members of society" (Newman 76). What this means is that society is not just an objectively given but also a subjectively constructed reality resulting from our interactions with other people and conclusions drawn from those interactions. A shy person then will have a limited perception of reality without the presentation of new values or ideas that other people often force upon us to realize and ponder every day. We do not all have the same definition of reality and that is due to the different events each person experiences throughout their lives. For example, I had a great fear of heights resulting from a childhood accident. As a result for me heights became dangerous, while people such as window washers or acrobats may not feel as strongly as I do. A more timid person would perhaps not place himself in situations for fear of public scrutiny or of making himself appear foolish—so as a result of this he acquires a more limited view of reality. By not taking these chances an introvert's reality becomes mainly composed of what he or she has to deal with in the day-to-day events of their own little world. Because of this he or she may end up with a skewed vision of reality, as did the suicidal man in "Patch Adams" who murdered Patch's girlfriend. Since he had not been exposed to death outside of his books, he had no way of coping with the passing of his father and as a result ended up taking this out on himself and others.

Newman also discusses culture, the "language, values, beliefs, rules, behaviors and artifacts that characterize a society." He states "Culture provides members of a society with a common bond" (Newman 97). It is because shy people remove themselves from society that they do not feel this "common bond" with their fellow men and women. This in turn alienates them causing them to withdraw further. As some communities (on the local level) are made up of members of similar races and ethnicities, the shy people also are led to believe that their own culture may be the only one they can function in. This then perpetuates fears and **stereotypes** since shy people do not take the time or care to personally know others with whom they interact. Of course an introvert will have no evidence to counter these stereotypes so he and others will be unable to interact easily. I know this since my community at home consists primarily of white Catholics. In my entire school of nine hundred students there were only 3 African-American students who were actually bussed in from another school district. Cruel racist jokes were prevalent at lunchtime and some students even went so far as to verbally attack them. Arriving here at Oneonta I found myself confronted with a much larger body of students and faculty members, having a much larger range of ethnic backgrounds. Not having any experiences with people from different backgrounds, I was uncomfortable at first. But now, having spent time and learned from people of diverse backgrounds, the **prejudices** I had not even realized I had have been quickly dispelled. The hope is that in the future people will be able to learn to accept one another, but people must do their own part and overcome their own fears.

Newman goes on to discuss the importance of **socialization** with regards to the development of self. To do this we observe, mimic, and interact with other people (a behavior known as **role taking**). Children do this to understand and accomplish actions required for success later in life (such as walking). This continues through **resocialization**, leaving an old role for a new one. Shy people, though, do not or rarely socialize, stunting the growth of their sense of **self** or **identity**, delaying certain developmental stages necessary to create a fully functional member of society. As a child progresses through life to adulthood he must pass through several stages to reach his or her full potential. One such stage is the **game stage** where a child learns the ability to take the role of a group or community and obey the rules and meet the expectations of that group. I myself was rarely, if ever, encouraged to participate in group activities and lived with few other children so I had very little interaction with other people my age with the exception of the limited contacts I had while at school.

If a person who is more timid in personality does not participate in this stage of game activities he may find hard to get along with other people. He will be more prone to breaking the social rules and norms and thereby alienating themselves as "oddities." This in turn could stunt that person's personal growth even further. As society is a complex grouping, from humanity as a whole to the workings of romantic couples, someone who cannot abide by the norms of these groups will find himself to be a perpetual outsider.

Newman states, "A significant portion of life is influenced by the images we form of others and the images others form of us" (Newman 159). Someone who is shy will, by a sheer matter of low self-esteem, create a superior image of other people and to project a negative image of themselves. While someone "well-adjusted" and comfortable with herself and her place in society may stand up straight and present herself in a "loud" (noticeable) fashion and manner, someone of a shyer demeanor would be prone to slouching, dressing in neutral colors and fashions, and speaking quietly with little confidence. This could, and I regret to say has, allowed others to take charge over the timid person, exploiting his or her timid nature. People without the confidence to stand up for themselves could find themselves losing promotion opportunities at work, respect from their peers, and attention from the opposite sex. When we gather information about other people we are aware that they are doing the same to us. The shy person however becomes paranoid and uncomfortable, trying to cover or draw attention away from himself.

In the U.S. great importance is placed on relationships. When a celebrity begins to date somebody, more often than not it becomes a highly published affair with pictures on the news and articles in the newspaper. One's happiness is frequently calculated by the apparent happiness of their relationship with a significant other. But creating a deep meaningful relationship with another person is difficult even for someone versed in the ways of courting and love, let alone someone who has great difficulty talking to his or her own friends. Obviously the shy person fears relationships for the fear of loving and losing. He questions himself, "Who could love me?" or "Would she leave me once she really gets to know me?" He or she uses other people as a symbolic representative of what life should be like and finds himself or herself lacking. He or she becomes a **deviant** in his or her own mind, disobeying what society expects from him or her. So like Will in the film *Good Will Hunting* the shy person will not pursue that which he knows could potentially be a pivotal moment that would make him happy. Like Will, the shy person fears being alone since being without a significant other is a severe social stigma.

A fear contributing to the introvert's inability to have or maintain a successful relationship is the fear of being subjected to public scrutiny. More people, including myself, would be open to seeking romantic interests if they could remain a private affair; but the fear of being ridiculed overpowers this deep biological urge for companionship. The fear of being ridiculed can thus harm a person's sexuality, preventing him from exploring his needs for fear of being ostracized by his friends. As seen in the movie *Anger Management* the main character Dave, played by Adam Sandler, is unable to kiss or show affection for his girlfriend in public due to a traumatizing event that occurred when he was very young. Only by confronting that which caused this **stigma**, namely his feelings of inadequacy, is he able to have a full and deep relationship with the woman he loves.

Since social structure shapes social **norms**, those who cannot meet these norms can find themselves in a conflict with that society. Someone too shy to interact with people can find himself at the mercy of the system he lives in. He or she will be unable to deal with the many people he meets throughout the day. Unexpected events, such as a blown-out tire, could render that person helpless, as he would be too frightened to flag down a passing motorist to help him for fear of appearing foolish, even though this would be perfectly normal and acceptable behavior in our society.

Also, as national borders become more porous, allowing for the easy diffusion of peoples and cultures, societies will be prone to rapid cultural changes. Shy people will become increasingly unable to cope with this situation. Having limited exposure to their own cultures, introverts would be completely lost as the dynamics of their culture begin to change far too rapidly for them to follow, eventually leaving them completely lost and alienated in their own culture.

According to Newman, "Stratification is a ranking of entire groups of people, based on race, gender, or social class, that perpetuates unequal rewards and life chances in society" (Newman 320). This can be seen as early as grade school when the separation of "popular" from "unpopular" children, or the so-called "nerds" and "outcasts" from "normal" students, take place. Those who do not fit in the popular category are usually introverted youths who are apt to believe the disparaging comments others say to them. This causes the youths to introvert even more, hiding from the popular children who have harmed them, cutting them off from social interaction. Of course the popular children, who do not face the same hardships as the "outcasts," are exposed to many positive influences that the shy child would not seek, allowing them to advance faster in the world. So, most likely, those who were introverted as children will be found in lower paying positions with less responsibility due to their less developed interpersonal skills. In this way, shyness contributes to the stratification of everyday social structure into superior and inferior groupings, with the timid children being relegated to the underclass of the hierarchy.

In extreme cases, groups such as the Ku Klux Klan can be a "safe haven" for introverted people. This organization gives members a sense of belonging to something, but still keeps the members anonymous both physically and mentally. The hoods serve to keep the members anonymous and faceless to the general public, hiding those person's shortcomings in a sea of conformity. Also the members are able to "hide" among one another using the unifying fire of hate to keep members close, though they may differ quite a bit from one another in other aspects of their lives. Dr. Martin Luther King Jr. spoke of "a degenerating sense of nobodiness," that is, a sense of individual worthlessness that leads to the need to degrade other people to provide a sense of superiority and worth. An example of this cited in Newman's textbook is that of an American businessman meeting his company's counterparts in China. The businessman was fearful of having nothing to say and appearing foolish to his hosts. At a business dinner the man turned to the man closest to him and said, "Likee Soupee?" referring to the main course. The man nodded and said nothing. Later, the Chinese man rose and delivered a speech in perfect English. Seating himself again he turned to the man who had spoken to him earlier and said "Likee speechee?" Because the man had feared appearing foolish, he tried to appear superior in the eyes of the Chinese businessman and assumed he could not speak English.

Racism is a way of **social stratification**.

Racism is defined by Newman as the "belief that humans are subdivided into distinct groups that are different in their social behavior and innate capacities and that can be ranked as superior and inferior"(533). When one person practices **discrimination** based on another person's race it is often due to the fact that they do not actually know any members of the race they have tagged as inferior. This is partially due to **ethnocentrism**, i.e., the belief that one's culture is superior to another's. But another part of this problem is the fear of the targeted race. During the early 1900s, Jewish people were targeted, not only in Germany but also throughout the world, as being the cause of the world's ailments. Many feared the Jews were planning to conquer the world in a "Conspiracy of Zion." As a retaliatory response people, including Adolf Hitler, called the Jews an inferior and "impure" race that had to be removed from propagating their "ill-gotten seed." The minds of the time '**medicalized**' this and attempted 'gene-therapy' to turn different races into the European ideal. Hitler's so-called Aryan race had the **ascribed status** of savior of the pure race from the "dirty" races out to destroy it. This was largely due to a fear of something the people living in this era did not understand, that one's religion does not necessarily determine one's loyalties, and that they needed a scapegoat for the problems they were experiencing.

Similarly, **sexism** is also a major and prevalent problem in our society. Sexism is a "system of beliefs that asserts the inferiority of one sex and that justifies gender based inequality"(Newman 534). Similar is the need to place someone under you to promote a sense of power and superiority.

As earth's population grows at an astounding rate millions of people come into the world every year, a good percentage of whom are doubtlessly afflicted with varying levels of introvertedness. With more and more people unable to cope with the norms of society coupled with the faceless medium of the Internet—a **global** information network—we could find ourselves with an entire subculture of introverted people all acting according to the norms others have established. This would be, to a certain extent, a migration, not to another land, but to an invisible nation comprised of those who do not fit into the society of their birth. This may be seen as a positive move, allowing people who are unable to interact normally in society to meet and interact in a safe environment with other people who are similarly afflicted. However, this could also be seen as a negative move, allowing people to further withdraw into their own **virtual communities**, departing from mainstream society.

In the story *Ender's Game* by Orson Scott Card, the author deals with a young child growing up in a society where families are only allowed to have two children. Due to a special government grant Ender's family, the Wiggins, are allowed to have a third, Ender. Due to his 'special' **status** Ender is ostracized in his school and regularly beaten by his peers. Being selected for a special government project, Ender is then taken from his family, including his sister whom he loves deeply, and is forced to train at a 'battle school' to train for an upcoming war. At the end of the story Ender becomes a cold and emotionless killing machine unable to feel for his fellow man, even for his sister. Because all throughout his life he was not allowed to become friends with anybody he completely withdrew into himself unable to interact on any level except with those in positions of power over him.

Of course an important feature of any facet of life is change. How well one responds to change in the world is an important indicator of success. The developed adult should realize that all life is change. It is change that allows the child who is afraid of dogs to one day become an accomplished veterinarian. The shy person however will shy away from change to preserve the comfortable microcosm they have created for themselves.

In the movie *Good Will Hunting* we find Will becoming violent over the slightest provocation (beating up his childhood bully, screaming at his girlfriend, etc.). This was caused by several traumatizing events in his life related to his being orphaned at a young age, essentially being abandoned by the people who were supposed to love him and care for him the most at that age. He was also abused by one of his foster parents, so the violence he experienced as a child was transferred to his personality as an adult. As a result of his difficult upbringing, Will had a select group of friends whom he had known since childhood while he kept all other people at a distance, including his girlfriend whom he lied to on several occasions and drove away by screaming at her when she tried to become intimate with him. Thanks to the ability of his therapist (Sean played by Robin Williams) to identify and be honest with Will, he was able to confront the person he secretly held responsible for his problems: himself. Letting go of that which had kept him from knowing people he set off into the distance to seek his love and fortune.

The only way for a person to release himself from shyness is to realize that there is nothing wrong with him other than that which he himself creates. By confronting his fear of inadequacy and loss, as I have tried to do in this paper, he will realize that there was nothing to fear in the first place.

REFERENCES

Card, Orson Scott. (1994). *Ender's Game*. Tor Books; Reprint edition.
Chapin, Nancy. (2002). "Honor Thy Father and Mother." *Human Architecture: Journal of the Sociology of Self-Knowledge*. Vol. I, No. 2, pp. 47-54.
Dubaj, Katie J. (2002). "My Translucent Father." *Human Architecture: Journal of the Sociology of Self-Knowledge*. Vol. I, No. 2, pp. 55-61.
Newman, David M. (2002). *Sociology: Exploring the Architecture of Everyday Life*. 4th ed., California: Pine Forge Press.

Films:

"Anger Management." (2003). Theatrical release.
"Good Will Hunting." (1997). Miramax Home Entertainment.
"Multiple Personalities: The Search for Deadly Memories." (1994). Home Box Office.
"Patch Adams." (1998). Universal Studios.

"Let Me Introduce Myself":
My Struggle with Shyness and Conformity

Sherry Wilson

Hi, my name is Sherry.

I can't believe I just introduced myself! That's because we're not standing face to face. If we were, you can rule out my talking to you—unless we've already met. I have always been wary of approaching people that I do not know, whether it is out on a street or in a classroom. I have always wondered why I have a problem opening up, while others I know can talk to strangers as if they are lifelong friends. Also, when dealing with new people, I find myself conforming to their views, a practice that I do not like.

When I was little, I would rely on my sister to meet other kids so that we could play together, or I would sit and wait until someone approached me to play. At that time I was not aware of the dilemma I was creating for myself by believing that others were responsible for my social interactions. With respect to my sister I became a **free rider,** even though my actions did not affect society as a whole. I would stand back and watch as my sister approached other kids; she became my gateway to new friends. Once we started playing tag or catch I might begin to open up, but I was never as outgoing as my sister. She wanted everyone to do as she said, while I was always a follower.

This childhood problem has followed me throughout my life and has affected my **anticipatory socializations**. Today I have trouble establishing new relationships with others because I expect others to open the way. But I can no longer rely on my sister to talk to my classmates or the people who live down the hall. And I can also not expect others to approach me to begin a conversation, for they may also be shy themselves. I am thereby forced to begin the introduction act myself, a process that is so difficult for me to begin with.

Presently I am a junior in college and, of course, I have friends. I've allowed myself to open up to certain people. However, similar to Will in the movie *Good Will Hunting*, I am very selective about who those people are. Will was an intelligent person who chose not to maximize his potential by working simple jobs, such as in construction. Will went to jail as a result of a fight, but was released under the supervision of a Harvard professor. In probation, Will worked with the professor to solve complex math problems, but was also required to undergo therapy. During the therapy sessions, Will refused to allow the therapists to see his real self by joking and remaining silent. Eventually, Will related to one therapist and became comfortable enough to discuss his life. Like Will, I require time to become comfortable enough to share my life with someone. While I am first getting to know someone, I will occasionally censor myself to avoid saying something that I will regret. By censoring I mean that I will debate with myself whether to express a thought or simply let it remain as a thought. However, I find that I even censor myself when talking to my best friends and to my family.

After I get over my initial fear and begin new relationships with others, I often conform to their views. Rather than having to defend my own ideas, I tell people what

I think people expect to hear from me. I do this most often when I face people I have just met. Instead of expressing myself as an individual, I conform to society, whether it concerns clothes or opinions. In a way, I tend to be the opposite of Patch as portrayed in the movie *Patch Adams*. Patch often rejects conformity and shows how he will not be like everyone else. During one scene Patch conducts an experiment in which he walks down a street and says hello to anyone that he passes. While watching this, I envied Patch's carefree ways. To be able to even smile or say hello to a stranger would be a leap forward for me. At times I have trouble working up enough courage to acknowledge an acquaintance that I might have met the day before.

Exercising my **Sociological Imagination,** as proposed by C. Wright Mills, I intend to explore my personal troubles with shyness and conformity. The sociological imagination refers to the ability to examine the interaction between private lives and broader social forces (Newman 8). Some people believe that in order to be accepted they must share the views of society. So, to avoid being different they conform. This is where my inability to voice my own opinions occurs. Rather than being considered different and having to explain myself to people, I pretend I feel the same or I even change my views to fit those of others. As a result, I also rarely participate in class discussions. I have a fear of appearing foolish to my classmates so I will not answer a question, even if I know the answer. Instead, I use my notebook as a **prop** to indulge in the classroom drama so as to draw less attention to myself. I will act as if I am reading my notes, in hopes that the professor will not call on me. According to *shyandfree.com*, a website developed by Kevin Rhea that is devoted to overcoming shyness, shyness serves as a survival mechanism (Rhea sec. 2). A person will bring less attention to herself or himself, thereby eliminating any possible negative actions. As a result, he or she is able to live a better life without any negative interference.

In classroom, I often assume the **role** of a quiet student. At the beginning of a new semester, I rarely speak up during class. Later on, when I do have an idea, I still remain quiet because I believe that this is what the class expects; they would not expect me to voice an opinion or answer a question. I believe that, in a sense, they form a **stereotype** about me as being a quiet studious person, even though I am usually only that way in a formal setting like the classroom. I have occupied this role from the beginning of my education career as a student. My parents would attend teacher conferences and tell me that teachers thought I was "a very good student, but very quiet in class." This role has become so familiar to me that it is now hard for me to change to an outspoken student. I realize that volunteering and participating in class may be easy tasks, but having become habituated to being the same "type" of student since kindergarten I cannot fulfill my desire to participate.

My academic behavior has been shaped in relation to my teachers through the mechanism of what Cooley calls the **looking glass self**. I have respected the power of my teachers as **authority** figures. Therefore, as a student, I always did my homework and turned it in on time. I always followed rules, and I always gave teachers my attention. As a result, my teachers treated me with respect and encouraged my work habits. They made me feel like I was a good student, but I continued to keep quiet in class because I believed teachers respected and wanted this type of behavior from me, including my shyness and classroom conformity.

I tend to be serious in the classroom because I am concerned with maximizing my educational attainment to help me in the future. As David Newman states in *Sociology: Exploring the Architecture of Everyday Life*, educational competition is now a global process (Newman 263). I could be competing with not only Americans but also foreigners when I enter the workforce. As a result, I understand that I need to receive good grades so that I appeal to employers. It may appear to other students that I only concentrate on my studies, but most of my classmates observe me only in the classroom and not in other settings.

In addition, I have always been more withdrawn in groups in which males are present. I have never experienced **sexism** nor have I ever felt **objectified,** but males intimidate me because I am more worried about the impression that I make on them than females. Newman states that some females perform worse in classes that contain both males and females, rather than a class of only females (394). When I am placed in a group of all females I am more willing to share my voice, opinions and ideas. In a group of both males and females I am more apt to listen to others instead of offering my own views.

Considering that my classmates and I are **birth cohorts**, one would think that I should have many things to discuss with them. I suppose I could start a conversation about a current event involving a common **period effect** on our lives, such as the war against Iraq, but I can't. Maybe I could begin by discussing a **cohort effect**, like our common fears concerning graduation, but I won't. I have numerous subjects and events in common with my classmates yet I still cannot begin a conversation with anyone.

Newman is right when he points out that being a member to the Millennium Generation I am likely to be proficient with computers (419). I use my computer primarily for e-mail and instant messenger, though. Much like in person, I rarely call upon another person first; I usually wait until I receive a message to respond. However, I am much more open and talkative on instant messenger than in person. For example, when I receive a message from a new person I am more apt to be responsive than if I were to meet the individual in person. Perhaps it is because I am not aware of the facial expressions and reactions of the individual. Through the computer I cannot decipher how the individual really feels so I save myself embarrassment by not being aware.

Newman also explains how schools also serve as a bureaucracy consisting of rules that govern most aspects of a student's life (247). As students, we are told when to register, what classes to take, and when to graduate. These rules control a large part of our lives and create an environment of conformity as students become concerned with meeting requirements rather than keeping a sense of themselves. For me it becomes one more way in which I have to fit in; I have to abide by the rules without questioning the control college has over me. However, it also relieves stress because there are fewer decisions that I have to make for myself. It is easier for me to follow someone else's decision rather than make my own. In the movie *The Matrix*, Neo learns that he is not controlling his life; rather, he is serving as a pawn in a matrix. A larger force decides every move of the individuals in the matrix and is so dominating that the individuals do not realize they are being controlled. This is similar to the bureaucracy of the school, as the students do not realize that the standards we live by are controlling and shaping our lives.

Conformity was an important issue in my life growing up with peers, and it still remains in my mind today. Most of the friends I've had have all belonged to the same **social class** as myself, so I have not felt pressure directly from them in dressing and possessing things. However, I felt the urge to be the same as the rest of my peers in order to fit. Our **middle class** standing permitted my parents to appease me at times, but they also taught me the value of having nice things. The PBS documentary *Affluenza* discusses how we in society tend to seek happiness by buying more and more things but enjoying our possessions less and less. *Affluenza* also shows how our self-esteem are often based on what we own. I have felt better about myself when I was able to wear a new outfit or a new pair of sneakers to school.

I am also influenced by the stigmas attached to **gender** roles, which distinguish masculinity from femininity (Newman 119). Women were once repressed by society and discouraged from voicing their opinions. Unconsciously, I have also internalized the way women have been portrayed in the past. I believe I have to uphold the image of being withdrawn and not speaking to others. I do not support the way women were once treated, but I may have picked up on those behaviors without realizing it.

Newman also points to sexism and the media portraying an inaccurate interpretation of women (386). There are always pictures of women surrounding me, most of whom possess no physical flaws. I see these women and I feel that I have to look and act like them in order to be accepted by society. I suppress my actual desires concerning what to wear to conform to what is "popular" at the time to fit in. Even though I may not be overweight I constantly feel as if I could lose a few pounds so that I look like the celebrities portrayed in the media. **Cultural innovations** have influenced how we look. For instance, I started to wear glasses in tenth grade to correct my vision. I could not immediately wear contacts, so I selected a pair of glasses I liked at the time. By the summer I was ready to wear contacts because contacts were not visible, whereas everyone can see the glasses resting on my face. Today when I look at pictures of myself in the glasses it does not take long for me to threaten to get rid of the picture. What I liked in tenth grade no longer passes for my acceptance as I change to fit in with the changing times.

G.I. **Gurdjieff** believes that human liberation rests on developing one's master self (266). The biggest step in liberation is to become free of outside forces, through developing a strong and stable "I." I am greatly influenced by the forces that surround me, including the opinions of others and the media. I rely on other people to decide what is "popular" or "cool" so that I can follow their ways to fit in. I make sure that I am appropriately dressed when I go out in public, even though I may just feel like wearing sweats. I believe that I can never give others an opportunity to pick on me or say something degrading so I always try to be at my best. In order to overcome my fears of public scrutiny, I need to realize that the only opinion that matters is my own. I do not need to depend on others to tell me what to wear; I should wear what I am comfortable in. This liberation from the eyes of the public will be the biggest step for me to move forward, but knowing that I have people in my life who will support me no matter what I am wearing or saying will make the change easier.

As a daughter, friend, and student, I undertake many different roles. I behave differently towards my parents than towards my friends. By **role taking**, I try to lead my parents to believe that I do no wrong, while with my friends I act somewhat immature. As P. Heim writes in her article "Alien Nation," "With my friends I'm much more open, I tell them things that parents shouldn't know, I curse, and I participate in activities that normal teenagers do" (Heim 2002). I am not implying that my parents think I am a completely different person than my friends do, but there are things I tell my friends that I would never think of telling my parents.

In the documentary *Multiple Personalities: The Search for Deadly Memories*, the subjects of the movie deal with Multiple Personality Disorder. They are faced with housing many different personalities in one body that manifest themselves in different situations. Even though I do not suffer from multiple personalities, I can relate to the subjects, as I may appear to be a different person when confronted with different situations. I am a different person with people I know than when I am in an environment with strangers. People that I am not yet comfortable around will often ask my friends if I ever talk or laugh. This surprises my friends because I can be the loudest person in the group when I am with them. As Samara Cohen writes in her article "I only *Thought* I Knew It All: Society and the Individual," "We are different people in different situations because we have moods and behaviors that express who we are at the moment" (Cohen 2002). When I am with my friends there is rarely a serious moment, so most of our time is spent laughing and joking. On the other hand, class is a serious time for me to learn. As a result, during class I am goal-oriented and attentive to the professor.

This also relates to a topic discussed by Kevin Rhea on the "Shy and Free" website. Rhea claims that people who are shy consider themselves to be shy because that is the only part they allow themselves to see. Shy people are so consumed with being shy and trying to triumph over shyness that they do not realize there may be other parts of themselves that are open and outgoing. I relate to this theory as I realize when I am with certain people that I am outgoing without caring what people think of me. When I am around new people, I forget that I am capable of socializing well and I revert to my quiet self. This brings up the interesting question of whether in fact all of me is shy, or only some of my selves.

Gurdjieff recognizes that a person has many separate "I"s that together make up the whole person (240). The "I"s involving various parts of a personality, gravitate towards the three mental, emotional, and physical centers of the human organism. To know and change oneself may involve knowing and changing a particular self or aspect of a self in the person. In my own case, it may be that not all of my selves are shy, but only some, as I stated above with regards to how I behave differently among friends and family. I wish that I could react the same way to everyone, believing that I have known a person my entire life even though I might have just met him or her. I would like to freely talk to a stranger about anything that might cross my mind, if appropriate, instead of simply thinking about starting a simple conversation. I need to invoke and engage more with the "I" that interacts shyly with unfamiliar faces to open up so that I may interact with my whole person and selves. As Gurdjieff states, "Each day you put on a mask, and you must take it off little by little" (1991 240). Instead of veiling my real personality behind shy selves, I must try to uncover it in small steps.

This change in personalities can also be explained using Goffman's concept "**dramaturgy**" and its associated notions of **front stage** and **back stage**. Front stage is where people maintain appropriate appearances as they interact with others (Newman 144). Back stage is the area where people can knowingly violate their impression management performances (Newman 144). I act very differently towards people in public than I do with my friends in private. I am more outgoing and talkative when I am around only people that I know well. When strangers surround me I talk much less. I use **impression management** and keep quiet because I worry about the impression that I make on people when I meet them. I believe that I cannot be ridiculed or appear foolish if I am silent.

My shyness does not inhibit my personal life, but can also influence how I relate to society and social change. As a shy person, most likely I will never lead a **social movement** to change society, reformist or revolutionary. However, I admire people that can start one based on their views. For example, Michael Moore in *The Big One*, personally visits corporations to ask executives about their business practices. Corporations have been laying off employees even though they are reaping record profits. Moore even sarcastically presents the executives with "Downsizer of the Year" awards. After watching the film, I became intrigued by Moore's straightforwardness with the executives, even when they became visibly annoyed with him. If I am ever in a situation in which I feel I am offending someone I immediately cease discussion of the topic. As a result of my shy nature, it is difficult for me to obtain certain **achieved statuses**. I was accepted to college on my own efforts, but I rarely participate in clubs or groups now. It is difficult for me to join clubs on my own because it requires me to begin and to form relationships with the group members. I never find myself in the role of a club officer or as a group leader since I have trouble with **socialization**. Because I tend to avoid social situations, I occasionally have problems when I am placed in one. In college, it is difficult to know of another's background and characteristics because students are not from one distinct region. This makes it harder for me to join groups because I am unaware of their **social group memberships**. I do not know their views on topics, so I do not join groups or talk to others to protect myself from possibly being judged or ridiculed.

The **culture** surrounding me has shaped me into the person I am today. It has formed my **values**. The things that I value in life are very important to me. As a college student, I value the significance of good grades. Unlike some of my classmates, I do not go to parties every night of the week. As a result, at times I find it difficult to communicate with classmates who are very social. They talk in class about the parties or the bars they went to, while I do not have that social experience in common with them. Occasionally, I do go out with my friends, just not to the extreme that some others do. Given the reality of **institutional sexism**, I feel that I have to work hard in my endeavors because women have been discriminated against in the past. Therefore, in class I am more concerned with learning the material than socializing with all of my classmates. Good performance will give me an advantage after graduation because I will have to compete with others in the workforce.

When I do find myself at a party, my shyness overwhelms me and I am unable to approach people and begin conversations. I engage in what Robert Merton called **self-fulfilling prophecy**. I always choose not to talk to other students because I fear they would think I was weird; so, I keep to myself. In other words, my own perception of myself as a shy person makes me become and continue to be a shy person. One day, I decided to approach a classmate of mine for his opinion on a test after an Accounting class. He was very short with me, remained distant, and ultimately left. Immediately, I told myself that I knew it was a bad idea and I berated myself for making the attempt. To this day, I fear the same thing will happen if I were to try again. To save myself from further embarrassment, I do not participate in class discussions so that I cannot be ridiculed for my thoughts. When I do engage in conversation with others I will often deliver a **disclaimer**. I do this even if I feel strongly about an idea, just in case the other person might disagree with me. I might say "This may sound crazy, but..." before I say something offensive or simply to present myself better.

As a **primary group**, my family is an important part of my life, shaping my personality and behaviors. My immediate family consists of my mother, my father, my sister, and myself. Growing up, when I did not have friends to play with during the day, my sister was always there. Being younger, I usually succumbed to her ideas for activities and I rarely spoke up a different idea. This may account for my reactions today as I will "go with the flow" and join in even if I don't like the selected activity. I am usually never the one to suggest or begin an activity for fear that no one will want to join in, so I rely on others to start the process.

In her article "Banana or Bridge? How Capitalism Impacts My Racial Identity," YuhTyng Tsuei writes while comparing herself to her sister, "How did two sisters who grew up in the same house at the same time be so different?" (Tsuei 2002). The difference between my sister and I also forces me to think about the debates on **nature vs. nurture** as factors shaping human personality and behavior. Those who favor the nature argument state that genetics is responsible for a person being who he or she is, while those favoring nurture state that the social environment surrounding a person is responsible for her or his behavior (Newman 105). My sister and I were raised the same way by the same parents. Today, she is more outgoing and is more comfortable in front of a group of people, while public speaking is my worst nightmare. Before a presentation, I always tell myself that I have nothing to fear and that I am capable of a good job; I give myself a "pep" talk. However, once I am placed in front of a group, my words of wisdom fade. My voice becomes very soft and it is difficult for me to make eye contact with others as I am speaking.

It is hard for me to decide whether nature is more of a factor in personality than nurture, or vice versa, as my sister and I are different despite our upbringing. According to Goff (par. 7) shyness may not be determined by biology; shyness may just simply be based on a person's life experiences. Negative experiences during childhood may lead to a person's being more introverted when placed in a situation similar to the childhood event. My parents have not exhibited signs of the same shyness that I possess and they were both active in high school. Therefore, I tend to favor the nurture argument, emphasizing life experiences as the cause of my shyness.

Although I cannot recall one distinct experience that was so negative to cause me to feel the way I do, many small factors have accumulated to account for my shyness.

My parents have instilled a sense of **competitive individualism** in me. This also makes me want to work hard in school. Neither of my parents went to college right after high school, although my mother later went on to get an Associate's Degree. From kindergarten on, my parents have challenged me to succeed so that I could go on to college to establish a comfortable life for myself. Even though we always had sufficient funds growing up, they want me to take advantage of opportunities for **social mobility** so that I can be even better off financially. They have always taken great pride in the **socioeconomic status** they have achieved, starting out with very little and being able to live comfortably today. As a result, this makes me want to work hard so that I can make them proud.

After almost completing a semester in sociology and analyzing this issue that is present in my life, I finally see that an end of my shyness may be in sight. Although not immediately, small steps can change the ways in which I live and curb my fears of not being accepted because of what I think or the way I look. My inner dilemmas concerning whether to participate in class or start a conversation with a stranger can be tackled by realizing that I am not entirely shy; only certain parts of me are. If I can learn to adopt similar behaviors with strangers as I do with the people I know, I might be able to make a friend anywhere I go. My outer dilemmas have shown me that opinions formed by outside forces should not weigh as heavily on my mind as my own views. I need to relinquish the hold that others have on me in order to liberate my "real" self.

After much reflection on my issues of shyness and conformity, I know that they can be resolved, but for me it will take time. It will take some time for me to become more comfortable in social situations, to gain courage to share my thoughts with classmates, and to realize that being different is worth defending. I look forward to the day that I can stand in front of a group of people and give a presentation without wondering if I can make it through without a shaky voice and unsteady hand. I think time and practice in these situations are the keys to my issue.

Let me end by saying, "It was nice to meet you and I look forward to talking to you again."

REFERENCES

Cohen, Samara. (2002). "I only *Thought* I Knew IT All: Society and the Individual." *Human Architecture: Journal of the Sociology of Self-Knowledge*, 1, Fall, 9-17.

Goff, Karen Goldberg. (2001). "Shy Squared." *Insight on the News*. 11 June: 32.

Gurdjieff, G.I. (1950). "From the Author," in *All and Everything: Beelzebub's Tales to His Grandson.*, First Edition. New York: Harcourt, Brace and Company. pp. 1089-1135.

Gurdjieff, G.I. (1991). *Views from the Real World.* New York: Arkana.

Heim, P. (2002). "Alien Nation." *Human Architecture: Journal of the Sociology of Self-Knowledge*, 1, Fall, 36-44.

Newman, David. (2002). *Sociology: Exploring the Architecture of Everyday Life*. Ed. Douglas Harper. California: Pine Forge Press.

Rhea, Kevin. (2003). "Shy and Free." 20 April 2003 <http://www.shyandfree.com>.

Tsuei, YuhTyng. (2002). "Banana or Bridge? How Capitalism Impacts My Racial Identity." *Human Architecture: Journal of the Sociology of Self-Knowledge*, 1, Fall, 62-73.

Films:

"Affluenza." (1997). Bullfrog Films.

"The Big One." (1999). Miramax Home Entertainment.

"Good Will Hunting." (1997). Miramax Home Entertainment.

"The Matrix." (1999). Warner Brothers.

"Multiple Personalities: The Search for Deadly Memories." (1994). Home Box Office.

"Patch Adams." (1998). Universal Studios.

Religion in an Individualistic Society

Jillian E. Sloan

During my freshman year at SUNY Oneonta I took a class on world religions. I remember that my professor warned the class about entering a relationship without discussing religion. I thought at the time, "How can you discuss something so important and serious at the start of a relationship with another person?" It would be awkward, as if it was an interview for a future marital arrangement. It turns out that during the time I was taking the class, I started dating my boyfriend, Rudy. Rudy and I have very different beliefs about religion and now, two years later, it has brought up some very important issues. Would we raise our child with or without religion? Is it possible to raise a child without religion to become a moral adult? Can a child without religion want to practice religion when raised in such an individualistic culture as that in the U.S.? What circumstances lead to the development or the loss of beliefs?

Although personal characteristics and situations have a great impact on individual lives, it is also necessary to look at the bigger picture. Using my **sociological imagination** I intend to analyze the place of religion and religious beliefs in my relationships in a broader social and cultural context. This is because our beliefs are often affected by the relationships we have with others—such as the relationships of mother to daughter or husband to wife— and with society at large. In her essay "For the Love of Our Many Lives" (2002), Stephanie Roth stresses the same point when she explores how her relationships with her parents led her to make and then change important decisions about her choice of schools for higher education. This is also what I intend to explore in the context of my attitudes towards religion. What choices affect our lives and do we really make them ourselves or are we on a life course that nothing can change? Is religion relevant to our moral self and social identity?

I was raised as a Lutheran Protestant. I still practice this religion, professing:

> I believe in one God the Father Almighty, Maker of heaven and earth. And in Jesus Christ, His only Son, our Lord, who was conceived by the Holy Ghost, born of the Virgin Mary, suffered under Pontius Pilate, was crucified, dead, and buried; He descended into hell; the third day He rose again from the dead; He ascended into heaven and sitteth on the right hand of God the Father Almighty, from thence He shall come to judge the quick and the dead. I believe in the Holy Ghost; the holy catholic Church, the communion of saints; the forgiveness of sins; the resurrection of the body; and the life everlasting. Amen." (Apostle's Creed, Dr. Martin Luther: The Small Catechism).

Lutherans are not very strict or formal in their practice. In my experience I have had every opportunity to develop my own beliefs, both by my church and my mother. To me being a Lutheran is an **ascribed status**. I was born into it and even though I do have the power to leave this group, I will not.

Rudy was raised as a Catholic. As a child he went to a private Catholic school and believed in God, Jesus, the saints, the holy mother Mary and the pope's divine power. Rudy developed very different beliefs as he grew up. Today he does not believe in religion as a whole. He believes in spirituality, Karma, and the possibility of a higher being. Rudy's experience as a young Catholic was not as liberal as mine was as a Lutheran. The Catholic religion is very strict in its methods of practice and its beliefs. Rudy could also feel the fear and sadness from his mother if he decided not to believe in Catholicism but left it behind anyway. It is obvious that Rudy's new religion is an **achieved status**.

If a child is raised in a household by parents who do not have the same beliefs the child may become confused about her or his own **identity**. In her essay, "Honor Thy Father and Mother" (2002), Nancy Chapin states, "Parents are transmitters of attitudes that the child adopts in forming a self-image… Our parents are our primary means of socialization experience that provides the lens through which we perceive ourselves" (Chapin 47). This is important. Children learn and develop beliefs through experience and as infants they experience life mainly through interaction with their parents or guardians.

If my child is raised without religion, is it possible that he or she will still become a moral person in society? From a **Structural-Functionalist** point of view, religion has served many functions in the past. First, it provides communities with a meaning of life. Questions that cannot be answered through factual scientific evidence can be addressed through the Bible. Second, religion provides personal support and means to worship the lord (for those who believe). These functions can be considered the **manifest functions** of religion or functions that are intended. There are also unintended functions or **latent functions** of religion. Religion keeps every society under surveillance. There is no question about the difference between right and wrong. The Bible, the Koran, and the Torah all have specific rules for behavior and consequences for misbehavior. Through fear of eternal damnation because of "**deviant**" acts, individuals can be taught to become moral members of society. Another latent function of religion has to do with exerting domination and power. Religions, particularly the Catholic religion, exert power over their followers and they gain respect and glory from it. L. M. Damian critically addresses this issue in his essay "Conspicuous Conflict" (2002) by stating that "Large groups with special interests are always involved in a conspicuous conflict against each other, so they fool potential followers into thinking that membership will earn them power and prestige. The glory, however, is given to the existing ones" (Damian 11).

In spite of criticisms such as that by Damian, given the many functions of religion it seems to me impossible to raise a child without it. Religion has a structure that no other institution has. I believe that it would be most beneficial for a child to grow up with a set of beliefs and come to her or his own conclusions later. However, Aaron Witkowski would perhaps disagree with this method of child rearing. He discusses children's rights in the essay "Children: The Unheard Society" (2002). He states, "Our society was born for the reason that people wanted freedoms, and that a strict rule on how people live their lives was wrong" (Witkowski 113). Witkowski may argue that not allowing my child to have a choice on religion is wrong. Rudy has the same theory. He would rather see his child grow and come to an intellectual decision about his religion on his own without persuasion from parents. Although I see his point, I am more concerned with what is lost or not found during childhood religious experience. I want my child to come to her or his own reasoning but I do not know if childhood without moral instruction is the best method. In the Native American culture it is a custom to allow children to do as they please because most feel that this is the only true way to learn the best and most peaceful way of living (Aulette 178). The majority of Native Americans are considered to be very spiritual and peaceful, which could serve as support for Witkowski's perspective.

Both Rudy and I were born and raised in New York City, although we did not meet until I came to Oneonta. Being Americans and more specifically New Yorkers, we both tend to believe in individualism. Neither Rudy nor I ever wanted to follow the social trends. This seems a common trait in American children, adolescents, and even adults. Americans strive for individual fame and glory. In order to achieve success in the U.S., one must stand out from the group. Americans try to escape most forms of conformity. For individuals living in the U.S., conformity might be considered a frightening concept. My high school had suggested frequently that uniforms would be beneficial to the school. I remember that most students, I included, were outraged by the idea. No one wanted their privilege taken away to express their identity through dress. With these views, why do some people conform to social **norms** and why do others break free? (This last question involves my assumption that Americans support individualism because I have unconsciously referred to identity as a more positive idea than conformity, using the words "break free.")

How do Rudy's and my individualisms affect our beliefs? Perhaps I was destined to be more of a conformist due to aspects of my personality and the circumstances of my life. In his essay, "The Capitalist Cuckoo's Nest" (2002), R.F.A. discusses situations in his life that led to a "rebellious personality." R.F.A. believes that the more the world tried to constrain him, the more he rebelled. He also states that his love for Rock music had a significant impact on his life and his attitude. This seems to be very similar to Rudy's movement through life. Rudy majored in Music Industry, wants to be a famous musician, and avoids most of society's trends. I, on the other hand, am interested in social work, psychology, and jobs that usually require a suit and tie and an office. I never felt constrained as a child. I always felt that I had the right and freedom to choose. I have also felt that I am in somewhat of a competition with my siblings. I work harder and harder each day to attain approval and respect from my siblings and my parents. In the movie *Patch Adams*, the character Patch, played by Robin Williams, seemed to be extremely individualistic. He also had views much different than that of the woman he fell in love with. Patch had undergone many difficult situations that made him believe that the only way for happiness is through rebellion and non-conformist ideas. Patch's girlfriend was conservative and conformed to institutional norms of the medical establishment. She reveals late in the movie that she was molested as a child. These circumstances created an attitude that emphasized conformity. She wanted to achieve success the most respectful way possible. So, it seems that for each of the mentioned characters constraint or pressure to conform led to rebellion. Yet different circumstances led both Patch's girlfriend and me to feel a need to prove ourselves and therefore conform to more of society's norms. Referring back to Roth's view (2002) on personal relationships, both past and future relationships affect our judgment. My relationship with Rudy has led me to feel differently on the issue of marriage. I always believed it was the next step and I almost took it for granted. Now I feel that it is not a necessary step and that what really matters is our relationship. Patch changed his girlfriend's outlook on life in many ways. She freed herself from social constraints rooted in **social structure** which made her life predictable.

Role conflict refers to times when one or more **roles** are incompatible with each other and cause stress. Religion in an individualistic nation can cause role conflict. Specific demands of modern individualistic life make it difficult to always follow religious teachings. The Catholic religion has required that 10% of a person's or family's income be donated to the church. This percentage is called tithing. Ten percent of one's earnings are a great sacrifice that some cannot afford to make. When a person has to choose between a successful life and career and a religious sacrifice in a society that emphasizes individual success, the choice seems clear. It would take a devote martyr to choose the church over his own success. Perhaps this may seem wrong but when living in such a society a person's **values** are very different from that of a person living in a conformist nation.

Throughout the years, the Pope has placed many rules on Catholics using his "divine right." One such rule is that Catholics should not marry outside their religion. This would be considered blasphemous or a negative **sanction** at the least. In America today, religion in general has much less of an effect over society than years ago. It is not uncommon that people of two different religions engage in serious relationships, wedlock, and childbearing. In his *Sociology: Exploring the Architecture of Everyday Life* David M. Newman cites N. Glenn (1982) suggesting that in the U.S. "over one-quarter of all marriages occur between people of different religions" (Newman 213). This can also be directly correlated with the emphasis on individual identity. A person's identity is made up of traits, characteristics and social group memberships. **Deterrence theory** assumes that a person is considered to be fully capable of weighing costs and benefits in a rational manner. This theory is most often used in the context of sanctions for **deviance** but can also be used to relate to an individual's choice in following the norms of their religion or culture. The Catholic religion requires a strict dedication at great costs. Catholicism requires conformity and sacrifice. Individualism, which has often been equated with selfishness, has less such similar costs of being part of social groups, though it may encourage **ethnocentrism**, and bring about **social dilemmas**. When trying to incorporate both these cultural traits of religious commitment and individualism in one's life, conflict occurs and a decision must be made. If a person's religion is less rigid, there is less conflict with individualism. Lutherans are very casual in their beliefs and practices in comparison to Catholics. It would be much simpler to resolve the conflict between religion and culture with a more liberal religion. Each person has the power to decide her or his own identity.

Another issue that emerges from individualism is materialism. Individualism promotes materialism. According to the PBS documentary *Affluenza* "children are the fastest growing consumer segment of the population today." Materialism perpetuates social dilemmas inducing conflicts between individual interests and social commitments. Children growing up in a materialistic culture will continue to be a dominant feature of our nation. My youngest brother owns every game system ever created, from the first Nintendo to the, now ever-so-popular, Playstation 2. He would get upset and even angry if he could not own these systems and every accessory that is attached to them. My brother and I were both raised Lutheran, so why did he become so materialistic? I believe that religion often teaches the importance of quality, not quantity. I am more religious than my brother. Perhaps a person cannot live in an individualistic, materialistic society and be very religious. I also purchase more than needed, but I am much more frugal than my brother or Rudy. I for one have been happy with what I have (or do not have). I have always considered myself lucky. Rudy is also easily pleased but he is always looking for something better. He insists on having two televisions, a nice car and many gadgets (mp3 player, digital camera, road-runner, etc.). Perhaps if he believed in religion, he would be less materialistic.

The rise in materialism may correlate with the decrease in participation in religious activities. Decades ago, when communities predominantly grew their own food and made their own clothing, material possessions were more highly valued and considered a blessing. As time went by, the technological advances took their toll. The industrial and technological revolutions sparked massive mobilization of peoples and resulting social conflicts and movements, during which lifestyles were drastically changed. Today, material goods can be mass produced anywhere in the world. Most of us have never milked a cow, maybe never even seen a real one but before technology sprung up it would have been considered common knowledge to know the entire milking process. Technology breeds **anomie**. Every person's life is forever changed due to mechanization. This anomie has created a massive **free-rider** problem among Americans today. No one understands the value of a dollar. Mass production, materialism, and individualism have come about at the expense of moral values. This is something that religion has consistently tried to warn its followers. Anything in excess is wrong.

Gurdjieff (1950) shatters the deterrence theory with the idea that man is incapable of making any decision. Gurdjieff believes that in ordinary life individual life is completely a result of external influences such as social institutions, organizations, and culture. Therefore, no person really has a choice to weigh pros and cons in a metacognitive way, unless trained consciously to harmonize his/her inner selves and centers. Gurdjieff believes that there are "uncontrollable conditions which may not permit this liberation" from external conditions of ordinary life (1118). He refers to people as "victims of contemporary civilization." He does state, however, that it is possible to break away from the slavery of civilization and become an independently functioning individual. Despite some of Gurdjieff's valid points, it may appear to be contradictory to say that a man can be both a slave to but capable of becoming, as an individual, free from social constraints. If a person can be a slave to civilization, he or she can also be a slave to individualism. It is important to remember that our civilization promotes individualism. Our civilization being individualistic, one may argue that a person can be both individualistic and yet not able to escape society's standards. Individualism and rebellion have become trendy in U.S. culture, and Americans have become a slave to finding their unique identity.

Films like *The Matrix* or computer games like *Sim City* relate to the world as a predestined, systematic software machine. Perhaps the fate of my child's life is already written and the choices I make in raising her or him will not affect the outcome. Here issues such as **birth cohorts** and **cohort effects** come into play. It seems strange that groups of people carry out a similar course in life when born around the same time. For example, because of the recent war with Iraq and because of the terrorist attacks of 9/11, Rudy and I will both experience difficulty in gaining employment and in other financial areas. Someone in their sixties may not experience a significant change due to early retirement and pension. A child who does not have major financial worries may not realize a difference in the economy. When looked at this way the cohort effect does not seem that mystical or strange. Perhaps there are specific rules that determine our destiny. In *The Matrix*, Neo must choose between two pills. One pill is his ignorance and the other is enlightenment to reality. Even though Neo is given the choice between the pills, the move still defines the outcome. Later in the film, Neo seeks an oracle that knows all. If this oracle can see the future, then the future must be fixed. From such a fatalistic point of view, no matter what decisions I make the proper or destined outcome will arise and religion is just one factor that may lead to a predisposed end.

The important fact to remember is that two people, Rudy and I, have both been raised religiously yet have developed such different beliefs. This could be a result of globalization. According to L. R. Kurtz (1995 1) as cited in Newman (204), "Technological advances are making many of the world's religions even more international: 'Jews from around the world can now fax their prayers to the Wailing Wall in Jerusalem. Fortune-tellers in China provide computer-generated astrological charts... American television offers its viewers Christian preachers and Buddhist teachers." Through technology the world has become increasingly interconnected. Using telephone, television, and the Internet are a few ways in which the world has moved closer together. It would seem that these advances would promote religion and strengthen beliefs but it seems to have the opposite effect. "Exposure to competing worldviews challenges traditional beliefs" (Newman 264). This increase of information and the decline of Catholics' status are largely connected. Recently many Catholic priests have been accused of molesting children. This information could have been censored if Catholicism still had power and **authority**, and if the world's gossip was not so easily communicated and discussed. Many Catholics that I know personally have lost their faith due to the recent revelations. This **stigma** will be carried by the Catholic Church forever and I do not know how anyone could continue to respect the church as before, let alone raise their children in it. It is difficult not to acknowledge the **stereotype** of priests as molesters. The power of the Catholic church has truly been remarkable at times. It is a bureaucratic organization whose following expands across the globe and involves a **hierarchy of authority**, ranging from the Pope, to the clergy, and to the Catholic priests themselves. This hierarchy leaves no room for the expression of ideas from the people that are most involved. The Catholic Church's rein is similar in comparison to many large institutions. Whether a person should have freedom to choose one's beliefs and religion invites important philosophical debates. I believe an individual should have the ability to choose whether or not to make decisions for himself or herself rather than live his of her lives as a pawn in the world's chess game. The question of following social norms or seeking freedom from them provokes too much anxiety. Therefore the individual often decides, consciously or unconsciously, to avoid rebellion.

The documentary *Multiple Personalities* discusses the effects of extreme anxiety and stress resulting from childhood abuse. Gretchen, a woman with multiple personality disorder, cannot deal with horrible memories of her abuse. She has developed alternate personalities, inventing "ways of bearing the unbearable." This is something that every person does to a degree. Gretchen's alters are unhealthy and dangerous. An average person supposedly takes on one personality and lives with that, until that person decides otherwise. In the film *Good Will Hunting*, the protagonist Will has several personalities that are hidden underneath his social mask. Will unconsciously hid aspects of his personality that might render him vulnerable to pain resulting from childhood trauma. A person's personality and identity is drastically shaped by her or his childhood experiences. If Will had been raised by a stable, loving family he may have most certainly been as intelligent as he is as an adult, but many aspects of his identity would have certainly been different. He would be more open to establishing stable relationships. He would have found joy and motivation in being successful. There are many people who are raised in a religious home but are abused. Religion does not seem to be the deciding factor in moral development in these cases. Security and Love may come first.

In the political documentary *The Big One*, Michael Moore allows the viewer to get a glimpse of what greedy corporations will do to benefit themselves and no other, laying off **workers** from their jobs. These people end up not having enough money to raise and feed their families. Like economic enterprises such as greedy corporations, religious institutions begin to look very disturbing when they are put into the wrong hands. Such abuses of power is another factor that has led to loss of power in many churches. Besides, given the increasing stresses of life, today it is difficult to make time for religious practice. I, for one, used to attend church every Sunday. Since I have been away at school and away from my family, I have found it difficult to do this. Besides, due to constant layoffs and job relocations it is difficult for families to stay connected to the church. These survival measures come at the expense of meeting the traditional requirements of religion. For example, one major requirement of most religions is to interact with fellow members in the church. How can one feel connected when they are always moving around?

Moreover, there have been situations where religious people have acted in extremely immoral ways (e.g. molestation, terrorism, etc.) and these occur both at home and across the globe. Citing Juergensmeyer (1965) Newman writes, "The rise of religious nationalism around the world has created a threat to global security. The values and institutions of Western countries are frequently blamed for a society's moral decline. The possibility of violence by supporters of religious nationalist movements has brought down political regimes, changed the outcome of elections, strained international relations, and made some parts of the world a dangerous place for Western travelers" (Newman 265). Religion can be misused in the wrong hands.

I stated earlier how I agree with Chapin and her views on parenting. Children learn from their guardians. This is the only way a child can become a moral individual—by mirroring their loved ones. But perhaps religion is not the only factor that will raise a child to be moral. There are many factors that affect the development of a child. Religion is just one of them. Religion cannot and will not save everything, but I feel confident that when times are hard God will comfort me. God will show me the right and most moral way of living. However, religion and God are not the only factors that affect life. Rudy feels that the best lessons are learned through experience and although it is always helpful to believe in God to move things along smoothly, it is not necessary. If the child can relate to anything with comfort and confidence, the child will have all of what he or she needs. Perhaps all a child needs is security in life.

Rudy often seems confused about his beliefs and does not like to converse about concepts of eternity, infinity, or space. I have a specific belief through the Lutheran church that gives me courage to explore the areas that Rudy will not. I believe a child needs some sort of belief system to feel secure. According to Abraham Maslow's hierarchy of needs, the first step toward becoming a healthy individual is physical needs and safety (Engler 344). These needs must be met before a child can progress toward self identification and an accurate belief system. I believe that children do need these qualifications, along with some sort of **ideology** to reach self actualization. It is obvious at this point that the best way to raise a child is through providing security and love. Religion is an important factor, however not the only factor. World events, period effects, cohort effects, and relationships in everyday life all play a part in shaping our decisions as individuals in a society.

I am not certain that I answered the question with which I began this essay; perhaps I just made it more complex. Religion is a very important part of my life and I would like it to be a part of my child's life. However, through this exploration I have realized that it is not the most important factor.

REFERENCES

Aulette, Judy Root. (Ed.) (2002). *Changing American Families: A Custom*. Boston, MA: Pearson Custom Publishing.

Chapin, Nancy (2002). "Honor Thy Father and Mother," *Human Architecture: Journal of the Sociology of Self-Knowledge*. Volume I, Number 2, Spring.

Damian, L. M. (2002). "Conspicuous Conflict," *Human Architecture: Journal of the Sociology of Self-Knowledge*, Volume I, Number 2., Spring.

Engler, Barbara (1999). *Personality Theories*. New York City, Hougton Mifflin Company.

Glenn, N. (1982). "Interreligious marriage in the United States: Patterns and recent trends." *Journal of Marriage and the Family*, 44, 555-566.

Gurdjieff, G.I. (1950). "From the Author," in *All and Everything: Beelzebub's Tales to His Grandson.*, First Edition. New York: Harcourt, Brace and Company. pp. 1089-1135.

Juergensmeyer, M. (1996). ""Religious Nationalistm: A Global Threat?" *Current History*, Nov.

Kurtz, L.R., (1995). *Gods in the Global Village*. Thousand Oaks, CA: Pine Forge Press.

Newman, David M. (2002). *Exploring the Architecture of Everyday Life- Sociology*. London, Sage Publications.

R. F. A. (2002). "The Capitalist's Cuckoo's Nest," *Human Architecture: Journal of the Sociology of Self-Knowledge*. Volume I, Number 1, Fall.

Roth, Stephanie. (2002). "For the Love of Our Many Lives," *Human Architecture: Journal of the Sociology of Self-Knowledge*. Volume I, Number 1, Fall.

Witkowski, Aaron (2002). *Children: The Unheard Society*; Human Architecture- Journal of Self-Knowledge. Volume I, Number 1, Fall.

Films:

"Affluenza." (1997). Bullfrog Films.
"The Big One." (1999). Miramax Home Entertainment.
"Good Will Hunting." (1997). Miramax Home Entertainment.
"The Matrix." (1999). Warner Brothers.
"Multiple Personalities: The Search for Deadly Memories." (1994). Home Box Office.
"Patch Adams." (1998). Universal Studios.

A Precarious Balance:
Views of A Working Mother Walking the Tightrope

Jennifer S. Dutcher

"There is no slave out of heaven like a loving woman; and, of all loving women, there is no such slave as a mother."
—Henry Ward Beecher, Proverbs from Plymouth Pulpit (1887)

INTRODUCTION

A paramount issue that has recently emerged in my life is the balance between family and career. I refer to career instead of the more common label for work outside the home, as anyone who is a wife and mother knows parenting and marriage are also work. Also, a career implies some sort of significant investment on the employee's part beyond work at home. The issue of a mother working outside the home is not new to me, as I was the child of an employed mother; however, as I have become a mother myself the challenges of career pursuits while maintaining focus on family have taken on new meaning. Often throughout my college career I have had occasion to address this and related topics in research papers. I see this particular paper as the culmination of my past work combined with the exciting opportunity to reflect upon my own life in a very personal way.

As I begin to see that sociology really does pertain to real-life, I am increasingly interested in taking this analysis to the next level—to examine how larger societal and global forces affect, and in turn are affected by, my microsocial world. What might society do to make mothers' balancing act easier? What effects might improved day-care options and flexibility in the workplace have on women's capacity to work outside the home, whether for self-fulfillment or to help provide for their families? Why are women not adequately compensated, either extrinsically or intrinsically, for the most important social task there is, i.e., raising children? At what cost will these and other answers come?

Growing up in a small, rural town, I was an "A" student, athlete, officer in every school club, and prom queen. My community had seen my successes, and expected nothing less as I prepared for college. However, feeling that I was in love with a local boy, my choice to pass on the four-year private university and instead attend a local two-year college undoubtedly brought disappointment to everyone. Needless to say, the romance fizzled during my freshman year, and again my focus was on academics. Obtaining high grades in pursuit of an Associate's degree, I was offered a full scholarship by a prestigious four-year private college in the event I transfer and complete a Bachelor's degree. Seemingly not a quick study in affairs of the heart I would again choose to stay close to home, and to a special man, and turn down the scholarship to get a job and think about what I really wanted to do with my life. I must at this point interject the fact that while I felt I had again disappointed my family and community, I know this was the right decision; seven years of marriage and one child later, the man is still special to me and to my life.

Upon receiving my Associate's degree, I worked as a teller at a local bank, and then took my present job as an administrative assistant on the SUNY Oneonta campus. The people I would come to work with, the educational environment of the campus, a supportive husband, and a very personal drive to in effect "redeem" myself educationally, would combine to carry me into an exciting and challenging new phase of my life. As Georg Simmel has observed "…small town life … rests upon more deeply felt and emotional relationships" (Simmel 149). Being myself from a small rural community, I also believe such emotional ties makes me, consciously or not, particularly sensitive to what my community thinks of my achievements—especially since I now live in the same community as an adult. These have contributed to the development of a strong sense of **generalized other** (Mead 167) in my identity, shaping my life goals and plans.

After working hard to establish some success at work I decided to return to the classroom as a part-time college student. Working full-time, taking classes part-time, and still making time for my husband (and doing all well), was a balance I strove to achieve. Following the birth of my son, this balance became all the more delicate and difficult to accomplish. There has never been any question that my role as a mother was now the most important—but my sense of self-fulfillment to be gained through being a good wife and partner, having an enjoyable job, and my return to complete my college studies, remains important also. I have always believed that I owe myself something that is my own, and that a happy woman will be a better wife and mother. If necessary would I put my own dreams on hold for the benefit of my family? Without hesitation. Would I give them up altogether? Never.

Reflecting back, I see there are many forces that have shaped my drive to do well at everything, and in particular, at achieving the balance between career and family. One of the most influential people in my life has been my mother. For a time following her divorce from my father, when my younger brother and I were one and five years old respectively, she was a single mom struggling to keep the household afloat. After being an excellent student in high school, she too had decided against college to marry my father instead. Therefore, without a college degree she would always hold jobs with low pay and minimal benefits. She has finally been able to prove herself and work up to the respectable position she has today, but this effort has taken nearly thirty years. Growing up, my mother always stressed to us the importance of being independent and self-sufficient, and she never hid her regret at not going to college. So, I have worked to fulfill a dream that has been hers and mine, to finish college and ensure that I will be able to be my husband's partner and not his dependent. I mirror Emily Margulies's observations in "From Anti-man to Anti-patriarchy" that, "I am determined to be self sufficient in my life," and that "My need for self sufficiency relates to the fact that I never want to be the kind of woman who relies on a man to fulfill her" (Margulies 1).

Another prominent role model for me has been the woman I would work for when I first began my current job on the college campus. Having received her doctorate in education after having her first child, she espoused everything I pictured a professional woman to be. She was knowledgeable, professional, steadfast in her convictions, supportive of those around her, respected by her peers and support staff, and most importantly—a wife and mother. She saw my potential, rewarded it, and encouraged me to go back to school. Once my son was born, she continued to encourage my education while acknowledging my new focus on family. She has shown me what is attainable by women, yet never implied that the balance between family and career would be easily achieved. It is the attempt to find this balance that has become my greatest challenge.

Parsons's **Functionalist** theory, while to some extent outdated, does much to explain the role of women in the United States and the part they play in its social structure. Young girls are taught early in life that the **feminine role** is to serve the functions of wife, mother, and manager of the household, all of which serve as a **"pseudo"-occupation** (Parsons 240). When this **domestic** "job" within the home is partnered with an outside career, the entire structure of the family is altered (Parsons 242). In the film *Billy Elliot*, the lack of a mother role in the family structure does indeed result in the family being without a "nurturer," and when the father is consumed by a labor strike his focus is diverted from the household and everyone in it neglected. Even as a child Billy must take a major responsibility for the care of his elderly grandmother, and the hole left in his life by the death of his mother is evident. Billy goes so far as to imagine his mother in the kitchen telling him to get a glass and not drink milk straight from the bottle.

The importance of the mother within the family is also demonstrated in the film *Erin Brockovich*, which depicts the struggles of a single mother to obtain employment and balance professional responsibilities with those of her family. In one scene Brockovich's ten-year old son is upset when she has worked long hours and missed dinner, to which she offers, "Don't you want Mommy to be good at her job?" Her son is only aware of her role as his mother, not that she must also provide for the family. The mother's conflict is compounded when the job is satisfying and evolves into a career that earns her respect. This film also shows the possible effects of outside employment on the male/female relationship. After many months of long hours, Brockovich's boyfriend and day-care provider leaves her when he states he is receiving nothing out of the relationship. The woman portrayed in this film was obviously attempting to strike several balances and was seemingly failing for awhile, albeit for a good cause.

In their article "Women's Employment, Marital Happiness, and Divorce," Schoen et al. address the question of whether or not a woman's participation in the labor force destabilizes otherwise happy marriages (2002). Their study shows that rather than disrupting happy marriages, a wife's employment is instead an enabling factor in her ending an unhappy marriage. When a woman works outside the home, she will be less apt to remain part of an unhappy union and because of her employment has the means to end the marriage and support herself (Schoen et al. 2002).

Phenomenologically speaking, I have spent my lifetime observing and learning from my mother and other women, through which I have gained much **common-sense** knowledge in regards to women's roles in parenting, marriage, and the workplace. As described by Shutz, our commonsense knowledge and "all interpretation of this world is based on a stock of previous experiences of it, our own or those handed down to us by parents or teachers" (Shutz 315). Using this accumulated **knowledge at hand** and my personal **standpoint** as a woman, I form opinions, set standards, and weigh choices in how I will go about fulfilling my roles. In "Honor Thy Father and Mother" Nancy Chapin writes, "Our personal narratives are initially largely constructed through our relationship with our parents or other significant adults. The relationship that we form with our parents is elemental to the concept of self, forming the base of our identity" (47). In the film *Twelve Angry Men*, for instance, it becomes evident just how different individuals **interpret** the same events differently. The juror who had himself been raised in a slum showed much more understanding toward the defendant of the same upbringing than did the angry juror whose knowledge of slums was far removed and prejudiced. Each was clearly drawing upon his own experience and worldly education to understand the facts presented in the murder trial, and their interpretation would have serious consequences for others involved. This is a key point: how we **internalize** society has much to do with how we in turn affect our environment. My **predecessors**, being my parents as well as people who have lived throughout time, have affected the situation in which I live as a woman today—just as I and my **contemporaries** will affect the future of society for our **successors** by **externalizing** our own attitudes in society and the changes we make or fail to make in our own lifetime (Shutz 320; Wallace and Wolf 278-283).

Am I as good an employee as a man? Yes. However, my work on the college campus is not my only job. When I am at the office, that job is not the only thing on my mind. My attention is bifurcated between family and career, as Dorothy Smith has aptly characterized the experience:

> The bifurcation of consciousness becomes for us a daily chasm to be crossed, on the one side of which is this special conceptual activity of thought, research, teaching, and administration, and on the other the world of localized activities oriented toward particular others, keeping things clean, managing somehow the house and household and the children—a world in which the particularities of persons in their full organic immediacy (feeding, cleaning up vomit, changing the diapers) are inescapable. (Smith 375)

My husband is a great help; however, in our society **gender roles** still prevail. According to the **socialization theory** my husband's and my images of the roles of wife, husband, mother, and father, are rooted in what we have each been taught those roles to be, by our own parents and the larger society. When my son is ill, it is most often mommy who needs to take the day off and be home with him or who makes the trip to the doctor's office. Hence, upon return to work there are tasks to be completed in addition to my regular duties, in order to catch up for the time away. Also, responsibility for securing and maintaining quality day-care is primarily mine. Besides the everyday task of taking him to and from day-care (coat on, coat off, coat on....), I am the person who must keep track of when he needs clean clothes, diapers, and other provisions to re-supply the day-care provider. Each evening I return home to get my son settled, prepare dinner, do laundry, spend time with my son, ready him for bed, and then do course work before going to bed myself. Once in awhile my husband and I actually find time to spend together, watching a movie or having an adult conversation. Then we rise the next morning to do it all over again. The pace is often taxing, so my husband and I make an effort to keep weekends mainly for family time, with some opportunity for grocery shopping and my course work.

"THE IDEAL MOTHER, LIKE THE IDEAL MARRIAGE, IS A FICTION." —MILTON R. SAPIRSTEIN, PARADOXES OF EVERYDAY LIFE (1955)

Being a mother for me is not simply a struggle to find balance between career and family, as I interpret balance to mean each is getting the necessary attention. I want to do both and *do both well*. I do not simply want to be a mother to my children—I want to be a *great* mom, a role model, a source of comfort and strength, a teacher, and a friend. After all, my children will undoubtedly be the most significant product of my life. For my husband I want to be a great wife, a partner and friend, with time as a family and time as a couple. And in my education and career, which I see as my opportunity to do something for myself, I want to be the excellent student and prized employee. Therefore, it is not only an external balance of tasks and duties, but rather an internal organization of roles or **selves**. It is not possible to completely push all other selves aside for the prominent self of the moment. For instance, at the workplace I am not able to bury the mother self in order to be an employee—the **"me"** that is a mother remains and to some degree overlaps with other selves. There is a constant organization and reorganization of selves as appropriate for the situation at hand (Mead 161). In the film *Multiple Personalities*, several cases were illustrated where such an organization and overlap of selves was absent. The individuals who shared their painful stories often had completely separated selves to the extent that particular selves did not know what the body or other selves were doing, or would even attempt to injure the body or other selves, not being able to see all of the selves as part of the same person. I do not experience such extreme alienation of selves in my own situation; however, the task of balancing my many roles does involve the integration of multiple selfhoods.

Is achievement of my conflicting goals possible? I feel it is to a large degree, but within certain limits. I am able to do my best and excel at many pursuits in my life. For instance, returning to my studies has largely been possible due to a level of convenience afforded because of working on campus. Working on campus, I have been able to take courses at virtually any time of day, and knowing that my husband is willing to help at home has allowed me to concentrate on my coursework. Would I have been as apt to return to college if a long commute was necessary, if night classes were the only option, if I were financially unable to pay tuition, or if there had been no one willing to help care for my son? Very likely not. Such an opportunity has brought my educational goal within reach. Davis and Moore wrote of **degrees of opportunity** in their functionalist discussion of principles of stratification. The idea of **mobility**, or the ability to change one's position or rank within a system, is one mode or type of variation in stratified systems (235). Hence, my opportunity to advance myself occupationally through education is possible because I am part of a relatively **open** or mobile system, which allows for such movement. Also, the opportunity to attend college, whether taken or not, is itself a source of power. According to Davis and Moore, "The control of the avenues of training may inhere as a sort of property right in certain families or classes, giving them power and prestige in consequence" (234). The authors' idea that **social inequality** is a society's way of making sure only the best people for important positions indeed fill those positions somewhat corresponds with Weber's writings on bureaucracy. On this I will elaborate more later.

Marcuse wrote in *One Dimensional Man* of **false needs**, or those that are not actually needs, but wants generated by society and the media (393). Until this time I have thought of economic freedom as being able to afford everything my family feels they need; however, Marcuse defines **economic freedom** as "…freedom from the daily struggle for existence, from earning a living." (392). I also agree that people have misguidedly come to define themselves through their material possessions, and I do not believe there is such a thing as economic freedom in the United States today. Unfortunately, a person must participate in the system to earn a living, but the level of participation can be largely at the individual's discretion. I was profoundly struck by the film *Affluenza* and its depiction of the U.S. as a society caught up in consumerism and the desire to obtain material possessions. I was able to relate to every aspect of the film, but especially with the idea that consumerism is contagious and that people today are suffering an overload of debt and anxiety. I feel that society is showing me through the media what and who I should be. In magazines and on television I see the slim, attractive, successful, professional woman in stylish clothes standing in a beautiful kitchen, making a gourmet dinner for her family with a happy baby on her hip—after which she will load into a new sport utility vehicle and take her son to a cub scout meeting for which she prepared all of the refreshments… from scratch. In my reality, I ride home in a used minivan trying to identify the latest squeaking noise, to trip over a toy in my disheveled kitchen while wearing budget clothing because my son needs the clothes worse than I do, trying to figure out what to make for dinner because I forgot in our morning rush to thaw anything out, with a grumpy toddler pulling on my leg, suddenly remembering that I forgot to make pies for the church dinner three days ago. Yet, at the end of the evening when I pick up a magazine and see a picture of the "together" woman, I somehow feel that what I'm seeing is achievable. I also know now, upon introspection, that as long as I buy into that picture I am a potential consumer, "buying" much more than simply products but also an idea of what society expects of me. The same idea that defies all common sense plagues many women like myself—the conflict between what is possible in everyday life and what society tells us happiness and success are supposed to look like. I can see that I am largely resembling Nietzsche's **ultimate man**, seeking happiness in "things" no matter how temporary that happiness will be. The difficulty is that being aware is not enough—breaking these societal ideals and becoming the **overman** is extremely hard to do (93). Weber's view of **bureaucracy,** from a **conflict theory** perspective, centers on the idea of impersonal, hierarchical organizations where individuals are in competition for available positions. This competition is largely due to the degree of **specialization** required of various positions, which is demonstrated through training and the ability to pass special examinations (Weber 115). The higher an individual's position in the hierarchy, generally the higher their **salary** and hence their **social prestige**, as employees within a bureaucratic system are paid for their position or **status** rather than for the work completed (Weber 117). Weber also addresses the waning of the "**cultivated man,**" a man of a time when education was the pursuit of knowledge rather than specialized training (123). In my personal experience with our modern bureaucratic world I have found a great deal of support for what Weber has written. While I have enjoyed several of my college courses, pleasure is not the most powerful motivator for me, rather it is the reality that my obtaining a Bachelor's degree will give me greater choice in securing career positions which would be otherwise unavailable. Such positions, their salaries, and benefits, will allow me to improve my family's **style of life**, when I can help to provide more for my husband and children. But how many of my family's needs are truly needs?

If having it all is such a struggle, why bother? From an **exchange theory** perspective, Blau would argue that in turn for my efforts I am receiving some sort of reward. The rewards described can be "extrinsic rewards, which are tangible things, such as money, and intrinsic rewards, which are intangible, such as love or respect" (Blau, in Farganis 295). It is apparent that through education and a successful career I receive both types of rewards; **extrinsic rewards** such as money or pay will allow me to help provide for my family, and the **intrinsic reward** of respect will advance my professional status. Being successful at home offers intrinsic rewards such as the love of my family, and the respect of my husband for being his partner and a good mother to our children.

While there are many hurdles to leap in my effort to balance family and career, the greatest struggle is an internal one. My desires to be a good mother while having a personally satisfying career are constantly in conflict with one another. Even as Parsons had stated that women are taught their domestic role early in life, it also seems to me to be true that much of a woman's role as mother and caretaker is natural. No matter how important it is that I work or how good my daycare provider is, I will always feel that I should be the one taking care of my children. When my son is sick or injured, I feel physical discomfort—not his pain exactly, but a deep internal reaction to his pain. One scene in the film *Erin Brockovich* brought tears to my eyes because I could feel the main character's pain. One night on her way home from work, Brockovich calls home to talk to her boyfriend and babysitter about how her children's day has gone. She cries as he tells her that the baby spoke her first word that day, and how amazing it was to witness such an event. This mother had missed an important moment, much as I did when my son took his first steps at daycare and instead of seeing it myself I was told about it second-hand. Moments like those will never come again.

When a mother must contribute financially, the search for quality daycare is an agonizing one. The mother who is already feeling guilt at having to place her child in someone else's care is also (in most cases) primarily responsible for securing that care. Our society is not currently providing an affordable, adequate supply of daycare for the huge demand that exists. Daycare providers are paid low wages and given little respect for the work they do. Why does such an important service continue to go unprovided? In her article, "Children Left Behind: Why We Need a National Child-Care Program, Now More Than Ever" (2002) Stephanie Mencimer states that the main reason why the daycare issue does not demand attention is that the lack of active voters among parents of young children allows politicians to focus on other issues without fear of repercussion. This paired with our nation's ideal of personal responsibility contributes to parents' private struggle to find a safe place for their children during working hours. It seems that this problem will remain until its effects are felt by politicians themselves.

"A RICH CHILD OFTEN SITS IN A POOR MOTHER'S LAP."—DANISH PROVERB

Having now had the opportunity to exercise my **sociological imagination**, I reflect upon the challenge in my everyday life and the larger societal forces that contribute to that challenge. I have begun to develop a new outlook on my balance of family and career. The goal to obtain a satisfying career that will allow me non-monetary benefits such as flexibility of my work schedule, while also being able to contribute more to my family financially, is a respectable goal to have. At this point in my life I have to work, so I might as well have some freedom in choosing a job I will enjoy. However, any jobs I take during my career will be chosen with my children in mind, as it is the time spent with them that is most important, and their childhood will no doubt go by quickly.

As parents, my peers and I need to feel there is power in our votes for making our needs known to those in power. As we are all "working" mothers, women must recognize that many of us are facing the same struggles and challenges, and perhaps be supportive rather than competitive and judgmental of one another. It is admittedly difficult to fight the urge to try and be more like the "together" woman than our neighbor. Our society also needs to "reward" stay-at-home mothers so that such a choice is seen as valid and respectable. Employed mothers' balancing act may be made easier if quality daycare was made available at an affordable price. Consequently, if daycare providers were better compensated for the important service they provide, perhaps more people would be willing to enter the field of childcare. In the workplace, women do not want easier jobs or special treatment—they need understanding and flexibility. These women need not been seen as selfish, but rather as providers for their families who are respected for the many important things they do each day.

If American society cannot cure its "affluenza," I can at least attempt to treat mine. It is possible to have some and not all, and to be okay with what is affordable within my family's means. This is perhaps the most important lesson I can learn, as what I choose to do about consumerism will be an example for my children and influence how they live their own lives.

Perhaps most importantly, we must recognize that women's struggle to balance career and family is not their struggle alone. Happy women make happy wives, mothers, and workers. Men must take an active part in their roles as husbands, fathers, co-workers, employers, voters, and/or lawmakers. All of society is affected by the plight of working mothers, because all of society is affected by what kind of adults our children will become. Children really are our future, and it is time to decide what kind of world this will become.

"The only way to predict the future is to have power to shape the future." — Eric Hoffer, The Passionate State of Mind (1954).

REFERENCES

Chapin, Nancy. (2002). "Honor Thy Father and Mother," *Human Architecture, Journal of the Sociology of Self-Knowledge*, Volume I, Number 2, Fall, pp. 47-54, Okcir Press, Endicott, NY.

Davis, Kingsley and Wilbert E. Moore. (1945/2000). "Some Principles of Stratification," *Readings in Social Theory, The Classic Tradition to Post-Modernism, Third Edition*, pp. 228-236, compiled by James Farganis, Vassar College and New School University, McGraw-Hill, USA.

Farganis, James. (2000). "Exchange Theory," *Readings in Social Theory, The Classic Tradition to Post-Modernism, Third Edition*, pp. 294-296, Vassar College and New School University, McGraw-Hill, USA.

Farganis, James. (2000). "Feminist Theory," *Readings in Social Theory, The Classic Tradition to Post- Modernism, Third Edition*, pp. 369-371, Vassar College and New School University, McGraw-Hill, USA.

Farganis, James. (2000). "Friedrich Nietzsche: Reason and Power," *Readings in Social Theory, The Classic Tradition to Post-Modernism, Third Edition*, pp. 91-94, Vassar College and New School University, McGraw-Hill, USA.

Marcuse, Herbert. (1964/2000). "One-Dimensional Man," *Readings in Social Theory, The ClassicTradition to Post-Modernism, Third Edition*, pp.387-400, compiled by James Farganis, Vassar College and New School University, McGraw-Hill, USA.

Margulies, Emily. (2002). "From Anti-man to Anti-patriarchy," *Human Architecture, Journal of the Sociology of Self-Knowledge*, Volume I, Number 2, Fall 2002, pp. 1-8, Okcir Press, Endicott, NY.

Mead, George Herbert, "Mind, Self and Society," *Readings in Social Theory, The Classic Tradition to Post-Modernism, Third Edition*, pp. 160-178, compiled by James Farganis, Vassar College and New School University, McGraw-Hill, USA.

Mencimer, Stephanie. (2002). "Children Left Behind: Why We Need a National Child-Care Program, Now More Than Ever," *The American Prospect*, Volume 13, Issue 23, December, p. 29, The American Prospect, Inc.

Parsons, Talcott. (1942/2000). "Age and Sex in the Social Structure of the United States," *Readings in Social Theory, The Classic Tradition to Post-Modernism, Third Edition*, pp. 236-246, compiled by James Farganis, Vassar College and New School University, McGraw-Hill, USA.

Roth, Stephanie. (2002). "For the Love of Our Many Lives," *Human Architecture, Journal of the Sociology of Self-Knowledge*, Volume I, Number I, Spring, pp. 53-61, Okcir Press, Endicott, NY.

Schoen, Robert et. al. (2002). "Women's Employment, Marital Happiness, and

Divorce," *Social Forces*, Volume 81, Issue 2, December, p. 643, University of North Carolina Press.

Shutz, Alfred. (1967/2000). "Common-Sense and Scientific Interpretation of Human Action," *Readings in Social Theory, The Classic Tradition to Post-Modernism, Third Edition*, pp. 313-339, compiled by James Farganis, Vassar College and New School University, McGraw-Hill, USA.

Simmel, Georg. (1950/2000). "The Metropolis and Mental Life," *Readings in Social Theory, The Classic Tradition to Post-Modernism, Third Edition*, pp. 149-157, compiled by James Farganis, Vassar College and New School University, McGraw-Hill, USA.

Smith, Dorothy. (1990/2000). "Women's Experience as a Radical Critique of Sociology," *Readings in Social Theory, The Classic Tradition to Post-Modernism, Third Edition*, pp. 372-380, compiled by James Farganis, Vassar College and New School University, McGraw-Hill, USA.

Wallace, Ruth A. and Alison Wolf. (1999). "Peter Berger and Thomas Luckmann: The Social Construction of Reality," Contemporary *Sociological Theory, Expanding the Classical Tradition, Fifth Edition*, pp. 276-283, George Washington University and University of London, Prentice Hall, Upper Saddle River, NJ.

Weber, Max. (2000). "Bureaucracy," *Readings in Social Theory, The Classic Tradition to Post-Modernism, Third Edition*, pp. 114-136, compiled by James Farganis, Vassar College and New School University, McGraw-Hill, USA.

Films:

"Affluenza." (1997). KCTS-Seattle and Oregon Public Broadcasting.

"Billy Elliot." (2000). Universal Pictures.

"Erin Brockovich." (2000). Universal Pictures.

"Multiple Personalities: The Search for Deadly Memories." (1994). Home Box Office.

"Twelve Angry Men." (1957). MGM.

Links in the Chain:
Untangling Dysfunctional Family Ties

Ira Omid

To achieve **self-knowledge**, we must look both within and outside ourselves to focus on and understand why we are the way we are. It seems that we must first sort through our many different **selves** within to determine which our true self is. We need as well to wade through the **norms** and **mores** that depict what is expected of us. That said, we are required to evaluate the very nature of our souls, not just our presentations of our selves in public. Our **sociological imagination** depends on our perception of our realities both within and without.

As the saying goes, if you don't know where to begin, start at the beginning. A few pieces of relevant background information about my life may be useful in this regard. Without such knowledge the reader may not adequately understand the unique nature and interplay of **micro and macro** forces shaping my personal life.

I was born out of wedlock in the early 1970s into a large, **dysfunctional** family. My father had five children from his previous marriage, with whom he had no visitation rights. It has been explained to me by my mother that this is why I exist today, i.e., as a sort of consolation prize for him. The theory presented to me was that he would not feel the absence of those children of his former life if he had children with her in his new life. My immediate family also included seven siblings from my mother's first marriage. I think my mother married at eighteen to escape her role as mother, not just a sibling, to her brothers and sisters after her mother abandoned them. My grandmother made this decision because of my grandfather's alcohol dependence and physical abuse. My grandmother took only one child with her, who remains institutionalized in a hospital to this day—a common practice at the time for those who suffered from birth defects.

The four youngest siblings from my mother's first marriage lived with her and my father. Given their actions, we seemed not to be welcome additions to the family. The sibling rivalry our existence induced resulted in a more hostile, tense environment. Presently all of our siblings continue to refer to us as half-sisters, if we are politely acknowledged at all.

My mother's children made it obvious that they were resentful that they had to live with my father versus their own. To this day, they do not accept her position on their divorce. Their father was an abusive alcoholic whom our mother had to escape from, or die trying. Those who were older and had also married young, with children, did not have much contact with either of their parents. However, to hear them speak of him, their father was a victim and should have been crowned with a halo. Also, the older children have accused my father, rather than their own father, of abusing our mother.

My mother alleges—and outside sources confirm—that my mother's first husband would work long enough to earn money to sit at a local bar, holding all the household's money and making my mother sit and watch him drink it away while she pleaded with him for hours to have enough money to buy some milk or bread to feed their children. Other accounts include her having to walk to the local grocery store and beg for groceries on loan until her next paycheck arrived so the children would not starve. Their allegations against my father include attempted murder by injecting our mother with needles, putting a rope around her neck and beating her in her sleep. In contrast to the many accounts of abuse and neglect inflicted by their father, this and other lesser allegations have not been corroborated with witnesses, police reports, or even pictures.

I cannot recall them taking in my mother or any of us in response to these allegations. I must question the idea that if they knew this was occurring, why did they do nothing to assist her? They did not contact the police or the Department of Social Services to perform an investigation. They did not come to the house to bear witness (as I had done) to the (non-existent) needle pricks, rope burns, or bruises. They did not help her plan an escape of any kind. They certainly did not advise her to get mental health counseling. They did not see our Saturday night ritual of homemade pizza and ice cream and other demonstrations of harmony among them. We might see them at a family funeral or wedding, but that was all. So, since they did not live with them and I did, I have to question their motivation for saying that he had abused her. I must also allow for the possibility that it did occur, however, because the truth has many sides to it.

From an early age my mother has shared with me that she would not be alive today had she remained married to her first husband. Her life had been endangered by frequent beatings to unconsciousness, exhaustion, malnutrition, and attempted murder by choking. Several miscarriages and several children resulted from repeated episodes of rape. However, the feelings of their children altogether did not go unnoticed by either of my parents. My mother would plead with them, crying and begging for their forgiveness for a sin she did not commit. (Much like, I assume, she had done with her husband and possibly her father.) My father understood he was not welcomed and why, but did not give up on the idea of being a parent that would be there for them. I do not doubt that he considered leaving his home—many stepparents do. I also do not doubt that many things could—and should—have been done differently.

The undercurrent of sibling rivalry led to hostile and physical aggression toward my younger sister and I since we were the product of our parents. In other words, we were to blame for keeping them together. Our **role** was to become the targets upon which they could project their fears and insecurities. Since my father was a strong and muscular man, he would appear to be a powerful and intimidating force to reckon with. Since he was easy to frustrate, but did not leave us behind, he would have to be punished for remaining with my mother through his children. Also, someone would benefit from their revenge if they were punished, sometimes corporally, for not performing their chores or not responding appropriately to what they had been told by either of my parents. I can recall vividly many examples of such behavior. Their insubordination, physical acts against my parents, my sisters, and myself were acts that demonstrated how they felt about their lives. These acts were irrationally violent yet effective ways of meeting their petty purposes. For example, if they requested to spend the night with a friend and were denied, it would be decided privately by them that it was our fault. We were to suffer because they felt that as younger children we received whatever we asked for—which was not true. Actually, as younger children we had less perks but different responsibilities to perform around the home. To be fair to my parents, we also received lectures, grounding, and had privileges taken away for discipline; this was because we were younger, not because we were their own common flesh and blood. We needed to learn and understand the rules, plus we were not pushing them to resort to corporal punishment. (I am not saying that I agree with the use of corporal punishment though.) It was not **nepotism** which motivated my parents to deal with us differently. Many households have a different disciplinary structure for teenage children versus preschool children, *as they should.* The age gap has not been represented accurately in their estimation of abuse. Age had to be factored in to the equation then and it should remain so now.

Understandably my younger sister had a little more protection from my mother because as the youngest child she was with her the most—because she needed to be. I admit to spending a lot of time with our mother, assisting her in chores that never seemed to end, even assimilating her helping personality to try to keep the peace. My relationship with our mother and my actions aggravated the other children and made them even more opportunistic in their efforts. Their feelings regarding inequity and favoritism were reinforced unfortunately. To this day they know I am still close with our mother and my father. Any thoughts or secrets our parents have shared with me about the past remain a secret. I cannot share certain things about the past or the future with my brothers and sisters, as it would only hurt them. I will not do so until they are truly ready to listen to the truth as my parents saw it. They need to be able to put themselves in others' shoes—to understand others' perspectives and common sense ways of knowing and acting in the world, as **phenomenological sociologists** aim to do.

They also need to behave as mature adults. As many are parents now I hoped they would have realized by now the stress of being a parent, the love and commitment necessary to be a *good parent*, not to mention the added pressures of being step-parents in a mixed family environment. I would also hope they could realize how my father's many headaches were caused by more than the stress of our family's situation. He has since had to have a brain tumor removed before it became inoperable. It does not absolve anything that occurred. However, having similar headaches myself, and knowing two of his daughters have required surgeries for multiple brain tumors—not to mention having a stepchild myself—I can see how difficult it must have been for our parents. My situation pales in comparison to their lives.

Looking at my own personality I tend to take it another step backward. I often wonder what makes a man commit to a woman with seven children that were not his own, even after he had been married, divorced, and was the father of five children? What makes a woman raise seven children of her own, after raising her brothers and sisters? Why did the pattern of abuse and alcoholism repeat in her life? And why did they then have two additional children despite financial hardship and a crowded house and yet still not be wed? These are questions I cannot answer. If I were to put myself in their places I could only make assumptions. If I were to ask them now I might receive two very different answers.

The film *Twelve Angry Men* portrays how the same occurrence or situation set before the members of the jury are interpreted and acted upon differently by them. I believe no two people will recall the same event in the same way. My parents' perspectives and my siblings' perspectives will no doubt vary from mine. Having performed interviews and interrogations professionally in the past, I have proved this theory time and again.

The **conflict** that results from **inequity** within a mixed family can be illustrated by using my older sister as an example. As the youngest daughter of my mother's first marriage she had little contact with her father. Not having contact with her father made her feel **alienated,** feeding her low self-esteem. She felt she was not equal to the others who did know their father, but was also not equal to my younger sister and I who have known our father from birth. My mother had left her father when she was an infant, so my father was the only true father she had known. However, as she aged she was transformed from being one of the young ones that was being bullied by the others for her relationship with my father, to being a manipulative bully herself. She has hung on to the idea that she had been kept from knowing her father by my parents. She does not feel her father rejected her. She has never dealt with the realization that he never sought visitation with her. She has also mentally blocked out her own history of not just being a victim of physical and sexual abuse, but a perpetrator as well.

She continues to live a life where she appears to literally enjoy fighting with others. As a result, she and other siblings have repeatedly been in unsuccessful relationships and have strained relationships with their own children, not just with each other. The majority has married, divorced, and remarried with additional children being brought into the world. As a result, I no longer seek to keep in touch with many of them because I simply cannot keep score among their disagreements. I do not restrict them from my world; however I do not often invite them into it either.

Recently, my younger sister lost custody of her three boys due to abuse and neglect in the home. Their father admits to some of the allegations; however, he does not willingly attend counseling or parenting classes. The court mandated my brother-in-law to attend parenting classes and anger management therapy, but my sister has yet to acknowledge she played an active part in the abuse and neglect. Therefore she is not able to receive the help she desperately needs because she is unwilling to admit her guilt. She was not an innocent bystander, those children were. In an ironic twist, the older sister that was such a bully to us was the one called upon to take in the three children. The boys knew her, so familiarity was to her advantage; however, our past crept into their future. Since my younger sister still resents how she was treated, she does not act maturely and responsibly. Stress from both sides is painfully obvious whenever I speak with any of the adults or children involved. The children no longer wish to return to their home but I know Family Court will award custody to their parents eventually. The cycle of abuse needs to end and it has a chance of doing just that if the right people say the right things at the right time—and mean what they say.

The film *The Matrix* has an interesting premise regarding a software program that implies a world of free will while really intentionally forcing subjects into playing out a predetermined role. You might consider the Matrix an artificial reality within reality. This relates to my life as it seems I was also placed artificially into a dysfunctional family to serve a purpose as my father's consolation prize. The idea that we humans could be so manipulated, for the best and worst of intentions, is a horrible realization. The pattern was set in place even before I was born. We seem to be born into a role in which we had no say, like paper dolls. The idea of predestination has escaped my attention while growing up. Excuses for dysfunctional behavior were offered in terms of environmental factors, two broken homes trying to make one. At least that is what I have been offering as an explanation to myself, until maturity taught me at a young age that *people also make choices*.

Partly because of such choices, however, I have been assaulted verbally, physically, mentally, and emotionally throughout my childhood and adult life. Any innocence I had was robbed of me when others exercised their free will to sexually plunder my body by the time I attended elementary school. You might consider this submission to abuse as an **irrational choice** if you didn't know anything about why they did what they did. I sought to understand it and not just cope with it. My mother explained to me that my brothers and sisters were just "jealous" of us. That seemed like a generic parental response, which did not console or appease me. So, I required myself to break out of this seeming predetermination. Like Oprah Winfrey's character, Sophie, in the movie *The Color Purple*, I need to know that despite fighting with my family one day I will not have to fight in my own house.

As a young child I needed to know if I was strong enough to live through this experience just as my mother had done—except, perhaps quite selfishly, I wanted to do so without the same consequences. I did not wish to repeat the nervous breakdowns, depressions, broken bones, broken homes, and altered perceptions of others in general. I did not wish to apologize to my children because they are unhappy with the choices *I made*. This was my dysfunctional family's life and a legacy left to us; though I had to tell myself it wouldn't have to become *my* life.

Regrettably, I bought into the projection. I promised myself and my mother that we would not continue to live this way if we did not continue to live with my father. I believed our everyday interactions were undeniably a product of our environment. As a result of my immaturity and 'free will' my mother tried to scrimp and save money to allow us to run away from our situation. In convincing her to take us out of the pressure cooker we called home I incorrectly thought that the issues of sibling rivalry and abuse would deteriorate. (This is something I have kept from everyone but my mother, until now.)

Before this could occur my father's ex wife passed away. The children she had with her second husband remained with him. The youngest daughter and youngest son that she shared with my father came to live with us. We inherited these two strangers with problems of their own. Adding two more children to the mix created additional difficulties. Beyond the fact that there was financial hardship during the 1970s and a large family had to make do with even less, how dare we have two parents that are alive when their mother had died? They didn't know their father. They didn't realize he could only stare at them through the schoolyard fence at recess while on his lunch hour. They had never met my mother or us. They didn't know any of us at all, yet they had preconceived notions about us. They too attacked us for our relationship with *their* father since he was their father first.

My mother was very good to them, as my father had tried to be to her children. This produced another dimension to the sibling rivalry issue. Again, her children accused my mother of favoritism from her first marriage. Yet, she and my father tried to continue to spread themselves too thin for all those who needed them. Needless to say, the great escape was not going to happen. Eventually the pressure cooker we were living in exploded beyond recognition.

My teenage brothers from my mother's first marriage decided they had had enough of my father and his children. My mother could not convince them to stay. One of her daughters took in the older son after he attempted to throw a punch at my father during an argument over alcohol consumption. Within a year a neighbor took in the younger son after he received corporal punishment for not performing a chore, not putting away a bicycle when he had been told twice to do so and uttering a vulgar expression in retaliation to my father. The punishment was physically drastic and my father was out of line. Belts are to be worn around the waist as a fashion accessory, not as a handy tool to abuse someone. I do not condone shoving my brother to the floor with his hand twisted behind his back. On the other hand, I also do not condone the behavior of my brothers toward my parents, my sisters, or myself.

As for my brothers and sisters from my mother's first marriage, those who did not live with us claim they mothered us. Those who abused us claim they did not. The perpetrators also actually romanticize the abuse they received by telling us they endured beatings for us as well as for each other. My brother recently told me that he would kick my father while he beat my other brother just to beat on him for a while. As stated earlier, no two people are going to recall the same event(s) in the same manner.

All of my mother's children now speak to my father when they see him, but have never apologized for not giving him their respect. I do not honestly know if he ever apologized to them either. Perhaps this will never happen among them. It is possible that one day they will understand what it must have been like for our parents when their own children speak of their parenting skills, or lack thereof. I can only hope for a more positive, if not more progressive outlook about their upbringing.

I will never hope for an outcome that is utopian, since a perfect place does not exist among imperfect people. Not even in my imagination would I dare to dream of such a thing happening. Despite the frequent attempts to undermine my parent's authority and love for each other, my parents remained together for thirteen years. They were never married though. My mother said long ago that marriage never came up. One day when I felt I needed to ask why they had never married my father stated he bought her a ring and she refused his proposal. Whom should I believe? My response to that is, who cares? I only say that because it does not rewrite historical fact to offer an opinion now.

My mother remarried a much older widower approximately a year and a half after we left our home. Due to this union, *I would now know what being a stepchild felt like*. I also inherited a much older stepbrother and stepsister. They are still treating my mother, siblings, and myself as though we are white trash looking to steal away their inheritance from them. My family is a lot of things, but not that. (They know nothing of our past.)

As for my father, only after my brother and sister moved out from my father's house did he remarry. I have since met and dealt with two stepmothers, both of which he has since divorced and both of which brought additional stepchildren to the already complicated family. My father now lives with another divorced woman, yet keeps his own residence. She also has grown children, whom I have heard many nice things about but am yet to meet. My father has been with this woman nearly two years as far as I know.

As an alternative to all this negativity, I can honestly say I can empathize with both victims and abusers in some capacity regarding domestic violence cases. *Please don't misunderstand me; I do not condone, excuse, justify, or support such behavior!* But I can do more than sympathize with these people. I can understand the underlying tension, apprehension, insecurity, and longing for control that I feel could be the root cause of abuse that occurs. I can also relate to the people in the film shown in class about **multiple personality disorder**. I know exactly what Gretchen, John, and Barbara mean when they sometimes don't want to be touched. I also understand why they look inward to another personality when they seek certain strengths to deal with difficult situations. I believe that their destructive alter-egos would rather harm them than let someone else do it again to them.

Further, I know from my childhood that those abused can become abusers themselves. I can only suppose that that is the reason why an uncle who married into the family also molested me and was accused of molesting other female cousins. Could he have been himself victimized as a child? We need to acknowledge that possibility and try to help abusers heal, not just attempt to rehabilitate them before they create other victims and/or abusers. If we live in denial as my aunt does and do not reach out to them they are going to suffer consequences such as being isolated, allowing them to have more freedom to commit such acts as a result. If we keep our friends close, and our enemies closer we could know who is doing what, where, when, and for what reason. Obviously, resentment can easily be extracted from this equation. Frustration brings up other questions… Would it be too much of a stretch to ask if *any* individual would have to heal himself or herself had a group protected that person in the first place? At what point would the group deny responsibility? Would it be at a certain age? Would it include a legal threshold? Would it be at a point at which no glory and only blame would result from accountability? Having said that you might develop a better understanding of why I have my views and why I have made certain decisions in my life.

In my adult life I have pursued a career in the Human Services field. Criminal Justice seemed to be a proper nitch when I attended college in the early 1990s. During that time I participated in internships with a local attorney's office and a Probation Department's Juvenile Division. Both of these had a tremendous impact upon my thinking. This was an opportunity to do a lot of soul searching.

I was considered to be someone who could be of some assistance to those in need. I worked full time, often at two jobs, but I did not gain employment in the local Human Services field until the late 1990s. I became a 911 Operator, otherwise known as a Public Safety Dispatcher, for a local Sheriff's office. Listening skills became key again, but I had to separate myself from the callers as I had done with my own family "clients" in the past. To a fault, I wanted to know more about the situation and learn of the outcome of each call. I left that wonderful job in pursuit of a position in which I could indulge that curiosity but be of even more help to the client at the same time. As a result I was on unemployment for the first time ever. Appropriately, the soul searching continued.

After two months, I found an even better job. I worked as a Crime Victim's Advocate for a local Crisis Intervention Agency. I also substituted as a Homeless Shelter Advocate. It was an almost perfect match for my skills. I had been open and honest about my past with the staff, which was liberating instead of shameful. In my disclosure, a firm exception were the clients. It would be inappropriate to have shared it with them. Prior to these two positions, I had only shared it with others on a need-to-know basis.

When 9-11-2001 rocked the world it restructured our agency. My part-time position was consolidated with another position, raising the educational requirement to a Bachelors degree. I had four years of college credits but in the form of two Associates degrees in Applied Sciences. So, after having a much-needed surgery I attended a local college to get my degree. I hope to return to a position with the same enthusiasm as I had in the past. I really miss helping people, despite the inherent stress of this type of work. It is questionable that I can return to this field, however, because not everyone would view my past as an asset instead of a liability.

In the film *Erin Brochovitch*, Erin also proved herself to be worthy of acceptance despite a downtrodden past of regrets. This was not because of sympathy for her, but was due to the extent to which she sought *justice for others.* The film was based on a true story and not the work of a talented scriptwriter, so I can only hope that the reality of justice prevailing in the film can also prevail in the real life of other victims throughout this world. Nobody truly *wants* to be a victim! Epitaphs are not given a volume discount for etching that word on tombstones. People can gain from being a victim in certain respects; however, this does not mean people desire to be victims in the first place. Love and abuse do not have to be exchanged for benefits to result. They can be so embedded in a person's life that they may be passed on to future generations as well. Just as a child does not ask to be born, they do not ask to be abused either.

I continue to ask and attempt to answer several key questions regarding my life to date. My past includes abuse that even my parents do not know about. I have kept it from them mainly because I was afraid of their reaction. They may never learn of it and I may never regret not sharing it with them. Ultimately, I need to live without the pain, shame, and regret that stems from such experiences. Exposing my childhood for what it was is only one option. Using it to an advantage, i.e., to have empathy for others, is another alternative. However, a third option, perpetuating the cycle is an unacceptable option for me.

Through counseling, education, and self-evaluation I have accomplished several key things in my life. I am not repeating some of the old mistakes made by others before me. I did not marry young and have children just to divorce, remarry and have additional children. I have no addictions and I do not abuse or depend upon any substances. I am not unfaithful and I do not have on again, off again intimate relationships. I do not raise my hand on others unless I am waving at someone. Nor do I look upon my parents as saints or sinners.

I have a higher education, but am I a scholar? Do I scientifically observe and evaluate my world around me using objective procedures? Am I giving myself credits that I do not deserve? Wouldn't an intellectual be far too intelligent to live a life like mine?

I need to question several of my other decisions. For example, I had an acquaintance that terrorized me as a stalker in college at age nineteen. I did have a brief relationship with a man who might very well have abused me physically had I remained with him. I had also briefly dated someone I believe might have been married (I have no proof of this, just a strong suspicion). After all that, I also contemplated accepting a proposal from someone whom I had had a long-term relationship with. Later I believe he suffered from depression and became suicidal. I also realized he eventually turned to using marijuana and alcohol to dull his pain.

I do not wish to know of any of their whereabouts now, although I am curious as to how to answer the questions that haunt me relating to them. How did I attract these troubled men (I have never sought out male companionship)? Why did I deal with it as long as I did? What made me think they were appropriate people to have in my life? How did I believe I could make it better for them when it kept getting worse for me? Was there an unrealistic part of me that believed I could actually help them? Or was I merely appeasing them as I had done with bullies and various other manipulators throughout my life? To answer these questions I have had to search within myself and essentially perform an autopsy of my life.

In answering these questions about myself I have been left with other questions. For instance, I have been monogamously involved with my boyfriend since late November 1994. He is older than I and is divorced with one child. Both he and his daughter were born into a dysfunctional family as well. Even though we live together as though we are husband and wife, I have yet to accept his many marriage proposals. I operate on the theory that if I never get married I can never get divorced. I do not wish to be divorced since I take the marriage vows very seriously. I also do not wish to have children born out of wedlock, as my parents and some siblings have done. Nor do I wish to have a mixed family with some children living with me while other children might live with an ex-spouse for whatever reason. In fact, to tell the truth it would be fine with me if I never give birth to children. I say that because there are so many children out there who could use a better life, beginning with a better living environment. These personal conflicts within me create a contradictory lifestyle.

For example, I have often entertained thoughts of becoming a foster parent. However, this has a catch: you should be either 'completely single' or 'completely married.' In other words, I must demonstrate that I am happily and faithfully married or happily unmarried. Either way I must show that I can offer a stable home, with little risk of change to it that might impact the child(ren) negatively. For instance, do I like where I live? Is there enough room for the child(ren) to live there comfortably? What is the relationship between my spouse and myself? Are my spouse and family receptive and supportive to the idea of another family member(s) joining them? Do I get along with my neighbors? Am I considered fit to be a mother by my family and close friends? Do I have a proper support system in place to assist me with the child(ren)?

Also, they would need to know of my history. The powers that be may not want to chance having a formerly abused person become a guardian of a child. As noted above, my personal experience and professional training has taught me that abusers were often victims in the past. It would serve in the best interest of the child to investigate me. It would also serve them well to gain access to the psychiatric evaluations I passed in order to gain employment with two agencies.

Further, as a foster parent wouldn't I be exposing my boyfriend's child to yet another 'mixed up child' and a 'mixed up family life'? She already has a complicated life as it is. Her father and stepfather are not the fathers of any of her sisters. She has a younger sister and an older sister. Since none of these girls has the same father I would be perpetuating the mixed family that I very much want to avoid (as her mother has done, as a product of yet another mixed family.) Yet I want to help someone out because that is the right thing to do. Which way do you go when there are more right answers than wrong, when almost all of the choices *feel* wrong?

So when I try to not make the same choices as my parents or siblings, in a way *I have*. Most notably I live in sin, despite believing in the merits of marriage. Like my parents and some of my siblings I am involved with someone who has been divorced and is a parent. How exactly have I *differentiated* myself from the old patterns? Is it that I am only one of two that has yet to marry? Could it be that I do not believe in divorce? Or is it because I have no child(ren) of my own, or desire to have any? What truly sets me apart and allows me to be *different*?

I honestly did not set out to be better than anyone else. I just want to be someone who lives better as an adult than as a child. I have no desire to be of a higher **social class** with the added pressures of maintaining an identity based on **status symbols**. I do not wish to suffer from **Affluenza**, a social disease described in the film by the same name, with symptoms of greed, insatiable materialism, and debt in pursuit of an illusion of happiness. I do not need to be what Nietzsche called the "Ultimate Man" where status and self-worth are gauged by the accumulation of material possessions and wealth. I do not believe power and wealth are based upon tangible trinkets. I believe power and wealth come from an understanding of yourself and of what truly matters to *you* in your life. Just because I want a simple life does that entitle me to one? Is it possible to deserve a simple life and never achieve one, despite lifelong efforts? Will I ever experience an inner peace when there may never be one within my family? Where (and when) do I ever separate myself from my family's influence? Can it be done by simply changing the environment? I have to question this since there are days that I feel like the only change I have made is a change in venue. So, how will I define a simple life when I have not known one?

Also, in my own little world why do I rent rather than own a home? Why do I continue to turn down my boyfriend's marriage proposals? Do I promote a mature relationship but not foster one in any way, with anyone? Why do I have the strong belief that people should not share bank accounts? Is it really because I think that everyone should be responsible for their own credit rating? Am I truly saving my unborn children from a confusing and uncomfortable life in this world by not giving birth? Or do I justify this to myself to avoid my commitment and trust issues? Which choices can I make without repeating the same mistakes I have made and those of people around me? Who around me can offer himself or herself as a positive role model?

Women that I have looked up to still struggle alone despite having been married until death parted them from their (only) spouse. My social reality includes friends that are my age, are married with children, divorced with children and unwed with children. I have looked at their parents and often wondered what their lives must have been like while growing up in what they might call a "normal" household. Is there such a thing as a *normal* family? I would like to think so after having grown up the way I did.

How can I truly help others after all this has gone on in my life? For some reason, close friends and previous employers believe I can. Part of me firmly believes it could be the best outcome of this crazy life of mine. I could choose to use it to motivate myself to assist others, and thereby assist myself. I still may cringe a little when explaining my past to those who need to know it, but I have accepted it as a part of me.

The HBO documentary *Multiple Personalities* concluded by suggesting that sharing secrets with doctors and other caring selves is the first step toward healing. Releasing details such as these can be uncomfortable for victims. It takes courage to explore oneself honestly. It makes the discloser to become volnurable to others' judgments. A look of pity could make someone regret telling her or his side of the story. Also, a certain amount of betrayal could be felt for revealing such personal details publicly. A family's existence is a private matter. In saying this, I admit I myself feel I have offered too much information. I have had to convince myself that if it helps someone else, I should continue to speak of it, as long as it serves as a benefit to others. This is yet another way to elevate my personal troubles to the level of public issues to be reflected upon and discussed by others. Conversely, it is important to understand how public issues become personal troubles. There is no better practical way to exercise one's **sociological imagination**.

As much as I want to believe that we construct our own social reality, with our own free will, in the end I am left in agreement with several of the previous contributors to *Human Architecture, Journal of the Sociology of Self-Knowledge*. In her article, "Struggles and Predicaments of Low-Income Families and Children" (2002), Jennifer Van Fleet acknowledges the impact of her environment by describing the role parents play in a child's life. "Children are easily influenced by what their parents tell them or by how their parents act when they are around them" (Van Fleet 37). In "Honor thy Father and Mother," Nancy Chapin also echoes this sentiment as well when she writes, "Parents are transmitters of attitudes that the child adopts in forming a self-image. Our personal narratives are initially largely constructed through our relationships with our parents or other significant adults. The relationship that we form with our parents is elemental to the concept of self, forming the base of our identity" (Chapin 45).

My early childhood environment also included poverty. Like Chapin's tale of her life, I can not escape the impact poverty has had on my upbringing, on the relationship with my parent(s) and in having and/or raising children. I can relate to the struggle to make ends meet while not enduring the added pressures of another mouth to feed even in my present life, yet I was the additional mouth to feed while living in the poorest county of New York State during the economic crisis of the 1970s. Our family did have many wants and needs not met because of financial restrictions, but I have to say that in all fairness, we developed adult-like independence at an earlier age and have been self-sufficient with limited resources ever since. There were parts of our childhood that made us stronger, more resourceful, and smarter than others around us, despite the heartaches and lack of 'glory days.'

Through my childhood experience I can also relate to the anxiety and vulnerability expressed by Peter Dai in his journal article, "Why is P Afraid to Love a Woman?" (2002). Like him, I can trace some of my commitment phobias to my past. There are other similarities between us though. I too do not attribute one particular act or one specific person to be the factors that have shaped my life into what it is now. As mentioned earlier, as much as I would like to have complete and total control over my life, it is self-evident that there are other forces acting on it. My decisions are based upon experiences that are built upon those of others.

Related to this, Stephanie Roth offers an excellent point in her article, "For the Love of Our Many Lives" (2002). Similar to my mother, her mother also had a troubled relationship with her grandparents and went on to have a relationship with a man Roth described as "controlling." We need to acknowledge the impact of broader social relationships on our personal life. We need to expand our understanding of those relationships that extend beyond our microsocial relationships within ourselves and our families. Our personal realities can not be fully understood until we look at the broader social environment.

In conclusion, I try to forgive my past but not forget my past. I must continue to acknowledge and explore where I have come from. I cannot cope and move forward without continuing to rely on a truthful assessment of my past. Yet, I need to also continue to look forward and accept responsibility for my own actions and choices. I must not take my good times for granted. I must realize that good people are capable of doing bad things. And I must remember that everyone deserves a second chance. Above all, however, I need to acknowledge again the power of choice. I need to make informed decisions based on a clear understanding of the uniquely personal as well as broader social forces shaping my life. Among all the selves I have internalized from the far and near past, my true self is that which continues to educate, cultivate, and empower herself in order to make informed choices in life.

REFERENCES

Chapin, Nancy. (2002). Honor thy Father and Mother. *Human Architecture: Journal of the Sociology of Self-Knowledge*, I, 2, Fall, pp. 47-54.

Dai, Peter. (2002). Why Is P Afraid to Love a Woman? *Human Architecture: Journal of the Sociology of Self-Knowledge*, I, 1, Spring, pp. 18-25.

Grosskope, Barry. (1999). *Forgive Your Parents,*

Heal Thyself. New York: The Free Press.

Roth, Stephanie. (2002) Good Mother / Daughter Hunting: A Process of Self-Healing. *Human Architecture: Journal of the Sociology of Self-Knowledge*, I, 1, Spring, pp. 45-52.

Van Fleet, Jennifer. (2002) Struggles and Predicaments of Low-Income Families and Children. *Human Architecture: Journal of the Sociology of Self-Knowledge*, I, 2, Fall, pp.37-46.

Witkowski, Aaron. (2002) Children: The Unheard Society. *Human Architecture: Journal of the Sociology of Self-Knowledge*, I, 1, Spring, pp. 111-119.

Films:

"Affluenza." (1997). Bullfrog Films.

"The Color Purple." (1985). Warner Studios. Based upon Alice Walker's novel The Color Purple.

"Billy Elliot." (2000). Universal Pictures.

"Erin Brockovich." (2000). Universal Pictures.

"The Matrix." (1999). Warner Brothers.

"Multiple Personalities: The Search for Deadly Memories." (1994). Home Box Office.

"Twelve Angry Men." (1957). MGM.

Marx, Gurdjieff, and Mannheim:

Contested Utopistics of Self and Society in a World-History Context[1]

M.H. (Behrooz) Tamdgidi

This presentation is more an exercise in theorizing history (in this case the dialectics of world-history and utopistic praxis) than in historiography, though I am not sure if the two can really be separated and dualized as such. My concern here is with contested identities (in a world-history context) of not just who we are, but who we can and should be. What attracted me to this panel topic was in fact the ways in which it could accommodate comparative and cross-disciplinary discourses of self and world on one hand and theory and practice on the other. Above all, however, from the standpoint of my applied sociological interest in comparative utopistics, it allowed me to problematize and historicize the taken-for-granted notion of "contestation" itself, questioning whether identities *have to be* contested, even if they have undoubtedly been so, throughout millennia.

In what follows I will try to share with you in outline the argument advanced in my dissertation research titled "Mysticism and Utopia: Towards the Sociology of Self-Knowledge and Human Architecture" (Tamdgidi 2002). Therein, I have explored the utopistic theories of Karl Marx, G. I. Gurdjieff, and Karl Mannheim as contested efforts towards the good life in self and society within a world-historical framework. I argue that the three approaches—representing western utopian, eastern mystical, and academic movements—are fragmented microcosms of an otherwise singular creative human search for the good life. Their mutual alienations, I argue, are rooted in fragmented philosophical, religious, and scientific ideologies which have emerged in conjunction with the broad historical transitions of ancient civilizations to classical political, medieval cultural, and modern economic empires. Human architecture and the sociology of self-knowledge are then introduced as creative conceptual, curricular, and pedagogical efforts beyond the contested terrains of fragmented utopistics in favor of a just global society.

"Utopistics" is a term recently coined by Immanuel Wallerstein denoting "the serious assessment of historical alternatives, the exercise of our judgment as to the substantive rationality of alternative possible historical systems. It is the sober, rational, and realistic evaluation of human social systems, the constraints on what they can be, and the zones open to human creativity. Not the face of the perfect (and inevitable) future, but the face of an alternative, credibly better, and historically possible (but far from certain) future. It is thus an exercise simultaneously in science, politics, and morality" (1998a 1-2). I use the concept with certain important qualifications, however.

---

1. An earlier version of this paper was presented to a gathering of sociology faculty at UMass Boston in March 2003. I'd like to take this moment to thank them all for their support. The present paper is a revised version presented to the "Contested Identities in a World-History Context" panel of the World History Association Conference, held June 26-29, 2003, at Georgia State University, Atlanta, Georgia. I would like to thank Fakhri Haghani, the organizer and chair of the panel for making it possible for me to share this brief summary of my dissertation research with a broader audience.

Notice: Copyright of *Human Architecture: Journal of the Sociology of Self-Knowledge* is the property of Ahead Publishing House (imprint: Okcir Press) and its content may not be copied or emailed to multiple sites or posted to a listserv without the copyright holder's express written permission. However, users may print, download, or email articles for individual use.

First, utopistics in my view must simultaneously deal with macro and micro processes, with broad structural concerns as well as everyday interactive issues. Second, it must eschew ethnocentrism and actively embrace comparative approaches across cultural traditions. Third, it must involve both rigorous assessment and actual application. Utopistics, in my view, is the comparative applied sociology (or historiography—reflective and creative) of the good life—of realistic seeking of optimally better selves, persons, communities, and worlds. The utopistic approach to applying sociology moves beyond either the mainstream or merely oppositional/anti-systemic modes of resolving concrete everyday problems; it seeks positive self and social change by the example of its alternative methodological, theoretical, practical, and inspirational innovations and solutions.

My purpose here is to use Marx, Gurdjieff, and Mannheim as representative doors for entering the stratified building rooms of theories we have inherited from modern or traditional, western or eastern, spacetimes, critically assessing their usefulness in helping us effectively move beyond our inner and broader social contestations and alienations in favor of the good life. I will conclude with my translation of another representative example from the mystical poetry of Rumi with a brief note on his poetic utopistics in a world-historical context—one in which the audience is simultaneously one's own selves, the face-to-face "others," and all future (and in remembrance all past) human generations.

I

I begin my reflections on Marx's theories of social stratification and revolution with the perceived stereotyped assumptions some carry, in the context of a deeply materialistic culture, that upper classes are happy when underclasses are not. In other words, the implicit value-judgments of our stratification theories, including those of oppositional ideologies as advanced by Marx, is that somehow being upper-class equates with happiness and being lower-class does not—hence, the struggle to overthrow one type of class privilege (private property) in favor of another type of class privilege (collective property as owned by the victorious proletariat), in the hope that the latter will eventually lead to the disappearance of class distinctions in general in the course of a transition under the dictatorship of the proletariat. The underlying assumption of such a stratification theory of liberation, therefore, is that we need to change the form of property ownership (from individual and private to social and public) in order to rid society of the ills of class division. What is problematized, in other words, is not the "possessive" attitude towards things, material or otherwise, in the first place. When a Native American says, for instance, "Earth does not belong to us, we belong to earth," he or she is not contrasting private with public property, but questioning the very possessive attitude of humanity towards things, individual or collective—in this case towards the whole of nature and earth. Conversely, however, Marx's "Workers of the World, Unite! You have nothing to lose but your chains, but you have a world to win!" still carries the message that the goal is to possess the world albeit collectively, NOT to become free from possessiveness itself—as Fromm or Adorno would suggest, liberating ourselves from the "have" attitude towards things in favor of the "being" attitude, away from the fetishism of things, from being habituated and attached to things, from being dominated and controlled by things. Marx may have espoused a challenge to the bourgeois form of materialism and property ownership, but his proletarian materialism, apart from the latter's philosophical content, still shared with the bourgeoisie the notion that human happiness involves primarily material wants, and that human liberation ultimately originates from and must be guided by a concern for material interests and objectives. Marxism, after all, was a western artifact.

Marx's mature theory of stratification and revolution is based on an assumed dualized and stratified primacy of nature over humankind, of economy and politics over culture, of matter over mind, of materialism over idealism. The dualistic framework of these oppositions are strongly present in the mature Marx (a distinction between mature and young Marx is necessary of course, for the young Marx, influenced by Hegel, believed that the solution lies in neither materialism nor idealism, but in a humanism which sees humanity as part of nature, endowed with its powers). If mind was seen as a part of matter without any predetermination attached to the latter aspect, then we may have found education, literature, or poetry to have been at least as significant a weapon to wage the war for the good life as the weapon of the arms. The most troubling aspect of Marx's theory of stratification and de-stratification (through the agency of a revolutionary proletariat) was its self-fulfilling prophetic logic which played into the hands of a materialistic bourgeoisie which equated material possessions (albeit in collective ownership) with the human liberative agenda. That human liberation inherently is about liberation *from* unconscious attachment to things, ideas, feelings, sensations, relations, and processes, that human liberation is about the power of the mind over matter, of intelligence and rational self-knowledge and determination over purely "material" interests to possess things, was regrettably repressed in the transition from the young to the old Marx.

Through a critical revisitation of how Marx constructed his theory of social stratification and revolution, I have tried to show how inherently inconsistent his theoretical framework was in all its three political, economic, and philosophical components. I have argued that the thesis of the dictatorship of the proletariat is inherently a contradiction in terms, since the propertyless class that assumes political supremacy inherently metamorphises into a collectively property owning class whose characteristics cannot be, as even predicated by the theoretical framework of Marx's own historical materialism, the same as the pre-revolutionary class. Note here that I am not arguing for the historical contingency of a misguided or degenerated proletariat in Soviet Union, China, or elsewhere, but I am saying that the very theory of a proletarian dictatorship is inherently a contradiction in terms and thereby flawed. The proletariat that assumes, in part or even as an ideally international whole, political supremacy and collective ownership of the social means of production cannot by definition remain a propertyless, hence a proletarian class.

On the economic front, I have also argued that the very formulaic representation of Marx's theory of the falling general rate of profit in capitalism is a demonstration of the fact that the transition from capitalism to socialism or communism can never be a purely economic act and thus objectively inevitable, but cultural and political self-awareness and organization of all classes, including the revolutionary class, are equally (if not more) important factors that can determine whether or not a transition will take place at all. Culture is not a superstructure flying overhead, but actually a potentially determining material productive force. The mechanistic "laws of motion of society" theorization of the inevitability of transition built into Marx's stratification and revolution theories, in other words, is inherently flawed for it relegates such a possibility to the a priori and predetermined forces of an objectively developing economic agency.

The dualism of economy/politics vs.

culture, I further argue, was rooted in another fatal inconsistency in Marx's philosophical arsenal, which has escaped the gnawing teeth of even the most critical of post- or ex-Marxists, i.e., the dualism of idealism vs. materialism. What I find quite perplexing in my autopsy of Marx, is that at the very same time Marx and Engels were preoccupied with rescuing human social imagination from mechanistics of formal Aristotelian logic espousing either/or argumentations—favoring instead a dialectical logic of identity of opposites—they increasingly fell trapped in the argument that dialectical method must itself be *either* idealist *or* materialist. The primacy of matter over mind can only thrive in the ontological environment of dualized matter/mind conceptions, since otherwise, if mind is seen as a part of matter, as a material force of specific nature and vibration itself, then the predetermined and universal primacy of one over the other would become a tautological argument.

I have much respect for Marx, and in many ways, as he advised through Engels, to be fateful to him is not to be a Marxist, i.e., not to be habituated to his thought and methods as levers for construction of truth. My critique of Marx is a self-critique in more personal terms as pursued in more detailed in my dissertation. Time does not allow me to dwell more on this personal side or on my critical revisitation of Marx's theory of history, but what I like to convey here is the proposition that Marx's sociology of stratification based on which he constructed the edifice of his applied sociology of revolution, was itself dualistic and stratified. The very "building" or "three storeys" metaphor used by Marx to construct his "guiding thread" and revolutionary paradigm in terms of economic base and politico-legal and ideological superstructures was an inherently dualized architectural construct. In such a metaphor, what exists on one floor, say in the foundation, cannot be at the very same time present in other floors. Culture and knowledge cannot be economic and political forces, economy cannot be a cultural artifact, and radical revolution cannot be based on purely cultural, educational, or artistic strategies. In the dissertation I have exhaustively deconstructed this stratified architectural metaphor in Marx, still a common schema used subconsciously in even non-Marxist social scientific discourses, in the hope of a radical remodelling of our subconscious visual artifacts in favor of more humanistic architectural pursuits to bring about creative social change simultaneously in personal and world-historical spacetimes.

My self-critique of Marx's theory is not of course to be interpreted as a reversion back to mainstream sociological theories and practice, not historically as a reversion back to the outdated modes of capitalist organization of the workforce, but as an effort to search for alternative methodological and theoretical tools needed in favor of the good life. The defeat of Marxist theory, as Marx himself would have proclaimed in his political writings, is not a defeat of revolution, but the defeat of our own shortcomings and hesitations in pursuing it. In this case, the obstacles were hesitations to see oneself and one's own theories as being implicated in the social reality we try to change for the better, an approach which was inherently missing from Marx's objectivist, nineteenth century classical scientific, paradigm of social change. Marx's era was one in which social science was still emerging from the midst of philosophical argumentations. Being trained in philosophy himself, Marx had a deep-seated propensity to approach his science of revolution from a philosophical point of view, involving pre-conceived ideological argumentations—of course packaged and legitimated in a framework conducive to proletarian interests and revolutionary projects. Despite Marx's considerable contributions to social science, at its roots his paradigm was a philosophically inspired western utopian project.

Paradoxically, however, Marx's drive to seek an "objective" and scientific framework to pursue utopistics was made at the expense of the individual self-reflexiveness that has traditionally been, somewhat, the preoccupation of philosophical tradition, albeit in abstract forms. Society for Marx was about interpersonal relations, while the intrapersonal reality was seen at best as an automatic product of the outer social reality and conflicts. Social stratification was perceived as that between assumed "individuals," whereby each person could easily be boxed into this or that class, group, or party, if not sitting between the chairs of major social classes—as in the case of the petty-bourgeoisie. Marx's view of society was atomistic and Newtonian, not relativist and quantal, not based on relationality of selves that cross skin boundaries of visible bodies. In his theory of stratification, it was not possible as a matter of rule for the same person to belong to multiple class groupings. It was no wonder then that revolutionary change was sought primarily in outer interpersonal relations only, and not simultaneously in the intrapersonal class, gender, race, and ethnic stratifications of our selfhoods and psychologies. Such a theorization, of course, was predisposed to allow the possibility and necessity of social change through violence, for economic, political, or ideological powers could be more or less easily boxed into separate persons who could raise and use arms against one another. That the person could be simultaneously a member of dominated and dominating classes, oppressor and oppressed, discriminating and discriminated, etc., would have required much more than waging a ruthless struggle against the so-called "other." It would have involved serious preoccupations with self-reflectiveness and change within—would have involved serious needs to theorize not only a sociology, but a self-reflective social psychology of revolution. It is certainly true that later theorists, especially the Critical Theorists of the Frankfurt School filled significant gaps in Marxist theorizing about the self and social psychology of revolution; however, it is important to still note the difference between the sociologies and social pyschologies of *others'* selves on one hand, and the sciences of *self*-knowledge and *self*-change found elsewhere such as in the eastern cultural traditions.

To borrow and revise Marx's eleventh thesis on Feuerbach, "Marxists interpreted and/or changed the *world* in various ways; the point, however, is to *begin with oneself*."

II

Gurdjieff, a strange Caucasian mystic of the late nineteenth and early twentieth century, who has been acknowledged by Jacob Needleman, a specialist in religion studies, to be one of the founding sources of the so-called New Religious Movements of the past century, had a lot to say, and theorize, about the inner fragmentation of the human psyche. He was an Ashokh (or Ashikh/Ashegh, meaning lover, as Persian or Azeri speakers know them in the region), but extraordinarily trained with traditional sciences of human psyche, skills of hypnotic conditioning, and also the arts of mystical dance and music. It is sad that we academics sometimes allow "disciplined" vocabularies and labeling practices to exclude many non-academics from entering our theoretical and curricular rooms. Of these limiting and fragmenting architectural practices in our educational landscapes I will say more later. Here I would like to describe how wrapped in all sorts of deliberately constructed mystical sayings, Gurdjieff's theory of the self advocates viewing human individuality not as an assumption, but as a destination of the journey of human life course. Calling humans "three-brained beings," he proposes a view of the person as an ensemble of hundreds if not thousand of selves, clustered around three main centers of gravity which he labels as physical, intellectual, and emotional centers. The fragmentation of these centers via all sorts of buffers, or what modern psychology would label as "defense mechanisms," coincides with the fragmentation of human consciousness into its so-called instinctive (or unconscious), waking conscious, and subconscious realms, relatively separate and independent functioning of which allows the possibility and propensity of the organism to become habituated, addicted, and attached to things, to live in illusion, to live in sleep in waking life, to be a machine in human guise, to be a prisoner of an illusively free life.

Using the allegory of a carriage driven by a horse in which the box symbolizes the body, driver the mind, the horse the emotions, and the passenger the master self supposedly in charge of the whole system, Gurdjieff argues that the human organism is often fragmented into a box broken down needing lots of greasing and repairs, the driver mind being almost always sleepy and drunk, the emotional horse wild and out of control with its constant desires for food and sex, and the master passenger literally absent from the scene altogether. The shafts connecting the physical box with the emotional horse, the reins connecting the emotional horse to the driver mind, and the brake lever connecting the driver mind to the physical box, symbolize for Gurdjieff three qualitatively different modes of communication among the three centers of the organism—but these too are broken down and imbalanced, making the person powerless to know and change her or his physical, intellectual, or emotional habits. The organism has been originally designed for supernatural journeys, but is alas broken down traversing wasteful terrestrial byroads. The interstellar transport system that is the human organism is actually so fragmented and absent of singular, individual will, that it confuses any passerby outside or passing self inside for being its "true self," letting her or him in as a temporary master passenger, to be soon replaced by another temporary will. In this contemporary so-called "man" in quotation marks, the self that sets the clock at night to get up early in the morning is almost always not the self that actually gets up in the morning, but one who decides to shut the alarm and go back to sleep again. No one knows who or what one really is.

Human alienation for Gurdjieff has a practical and specific meaning, the separation and the alienation of our multiple selfhoods from one another, such that the liberation of the organism must necessarily involve conscious labor and intentional suffering of self-knowledge and transformation by a deliberately evoked and trained, fourth, observing self which is the seat of the future permanent and unified "I." Only such a unified organism in which the three centers actually communicate and blend with one another really has the right to say "I am" and "I do." The ordinary human organism does not "do," things are simply done to her or him. In ordinary everyday life, we all are each "We"s. Multiplicities of selves are not merely maladies of extreme pathological conditions, but a fact of everyday life for each and every one of us, its architecture varying across body organisms depending on their make-up and degree of efforts made in self-knowledge and change. Gurdjieff's enneagram of 21 human personalities, overly misused and popularized today, is actually constructed to take account of the varied forms of architecture of the inner landscape of selves. The sociologist George Herbert Mead, of course, agreed that in a sense "multiple personalities" are normal. But the difference here is that for Gurdjieff there is no presumption that the internalized selfhoods automatically converge in adulthood to form a unified individual self-identity. For Gurdjieff, actually the opposite happens as a rule, since the very process of individuation requires the person's own volition to pursue the task of alchemical self-knowledge and change. We of course all know those so-called "mood swings" we encounter in our every day lives, moods which Gurdjieff would literally associate with multiple selfhoods manifesting themselves according to the blind necessities of everyday time and space. In this sense, of course, Gurdjieff's eastern mysticism predicts much of modern sociologies of symbolic interaction including those of Blumer and Mead, predates Goffman's dramaturgical theory of social life as a theater, and in many ways predicts (and I would venture to claim surpasses in all practicality of its healing strategies) much of Freudian theories of the subconscious and modern psychology. Sadly, our eurocentric prisms often prevent us from acknowledging in our cherished academic disciplines the pioneering work of non-westerns.

Gurdjieff's mysticism, as I have understood it, and aside from its otherwise serious problems and contradictions which I have also exhaustively identified in my dissertation, has an important message for our applied and clinical theories of self and social change. This importance is as much about the inner nature of stratification of our assumed and supposed "individualities" into multiple selfhoods, as it is about undermining the very textbook definitions we have about society, and thereby sociology as the study of society. Any sociology textbook today defines society as a system of relationships or interactions among individuals, or groups of individuals. This would be like the early classical scientific view of nature as a system of bodies, of molecules, or at best of atoms. But further insight, as we know, led us to a different view of matter and of nature, as a system of subatomic elements and currents, which established a drastically different view of the universe while subsuming the earlier atomistic view into itself. Likewise, by relaxing our a prior and ahistorical assumptions of our unified and singular individualities in favor of recognizing our inner multiplicities, we may be able to form a new definition of society not as a system of individual interactions, but as a system of interactions of multiple selves, products of our contradictory, fragmented, alienated, and stratified socializations, which once formed confront one another as fragmented selfhoods. As Mead has argued, once a self arises from the context of our socializations, it takes a life of its own. There is no reason why the "individual" must be our assumed unit of analysis and point of departure for defining society and social interaction.

If we adopt an alternative definitional framework for society, and thereby of sociology as the study of it, many "social" phenomena that appear as inexplicable become rather easily understood. Our severely depressive mood changes, the loving mothers who suddenly drawn their children in bathtubs, the friendly but unexpectedly homicidal neighbors, the quiet kids who suddenly bomb their classrooms and schools, are not exceptions to our supposedly singular individualities, but extreme examples of our common lot as clusters of multiple and fragmented selfhoods, caught in the illusive shell of our alleged individualities with the aid of equally illusive ideologies of individualism, but in reality living the life of fragmented selfhoods easily manipulatable by all kinds of advertising, television sitcoms, mass media news, and glamour and fashion industries, not to speak of afflictions with all sorts of habituations to food, money, fame, sex, power, wealth, drugs, alcohol, and nicotine substances. Despite its ideological rhetoric, capitalism does not individuate persons, but fragments them into landscapes of fragmented and alienated selfhoods, within and without. Colonialisms do not have to always take place at the macro level of nation-states and civilizations. Imperialism has long discovered, as Michel Foucault has aptly reminded us, of the micro and intrapersonal industries of control and inner colonialism. "Divide and Rule" is not only useful in classical or neo-, or even post-colonial geometries of nation-states. It also works in the micro geometries of divided and controlled selfhoods. How can we be singularly willful and indivisible "individuals" but not be able even to drop our coffee drinking habits!?

It is the tragic story of modern human organism to be caught in a world-wide colonized web of multiple selfhoods, intra, inter, and extrapersonal, with respect to oneself, to others, and to our natural and built environments. Gurdjieff's theory, albeit its shortcomings and misuses suffered at the hands of its inventive guru, and despite its mystical religious wrappings and—as in most mystical teachings—dependent and hypnotic modalities of teacher-student relationships, gives us an alternative, eastern, approach to utopistics. Where Gurdjieff fails is the separation and the stratification he introduces between this inner realm of human life and that taking place inter- and extrapersonally in relationship to others and the environment. The interplay of the inner and broader, micro and macro, social stratifications of the human life is thereby ignored in his mystical paradigm. As in most religions, for Gurdjieff the suffering in the broader social life is a given, a fact and fate to be reckoned with as an inevitability against which the human soul is to be tested, purified, and forged towards human inner salvation, in this world and in the thereafter. As Marx focused on the broader sociality and lost sight of the inner sociality of human organism, Gurdjieff loses sight of the broader sociality and the role it plays in the origination and perpetuation of human inner fragmentations and alienations. The self and the world are thereby themselves separated from one another in their respective western and eastern doctrines, each failing to notice and thereby to rectify one or another side of the totality of human social reality which needs to be criticized in theory and revolutionized in practice.

III

Western utopistics is concerned with how to possess and control the world, being caught in cycles of strivings for private and/or collective possession of its resources, cultural artifacts, and instruments of power. Eastern utopistics, however, in its mystical varieties in particular, problematizes that very possessive attitude towards worldly objects, positing that attachments to the world are not only the root causes of all suffering, but also the impediments to seeking and exercising knowledges that can alone facilitate human spiritual perfection. Karl Mannheim, to whom I turn now, would perhaps argue that each of the above provides only a one-sided perspective on how to pursue the good life, their rational kernels becoming more fruitful when synthesized integratively into optimally rational formulations about the utopistics of self and society. But, how can the utopistics of self and broader social world be forged into a singular theoretical framework?

In my study of Mannheim, I have tried to revisit not only the contributions of Mannheim's sociology of knowledge, but also the self-defeating elements of his arguments, in the hope of rescuing the essence of his invaluable insights regarding general conceptions of ideology and "collective unconscious" as the fundamental problem of our age. The "social origins of knowledge" thesis built into Mannheim's perspective, which was rooted in Marx's theory of material determination of consciousness, can only thrive in a conceptual and theoretical environment where knowledge is divorced and separated from social existence. If we say social existence determines our consciousness, as stated the thesis of Mannheim's sociology of knowledge, this would turn tautological if we consider our knowledge, our ideas, our culture, to be a part and parcel of that social existence. The dualism of society and knowledge, therefore, in contrast to a part/whole dialectical conception of them, allows a primacy to be attached with one rather than another aspect of the dichotomy. Hence, we have a sociological perspective whereby we always seek to find the "social origins," not recognizing that our own ideas, views, and cultural artifacts may as well be the origins of old or new and alternative social arrangements. Although Berger and Luckmann's notion of "social construction of reality" has become a commonsense sociological perspective nowadays, even then we shrug from creative sociological theorizing and practice of alternative and utopistic social arrangements, big or small, under the pretext of engagement in "scientific" study of facts and figures about the reality of our social stratifications.

Despite the above shortcomings, however, Mannheim made a great contribution to the sociological theory of ideology, by introducing his what he called "general conception of ideology," i.e., the notion that in our socio-political discourses we become increasingly aware that not only our adversaries, but even ourselves are unconsciously biased and thereby ideological. Mannheim advanced the notion that the problem of collective unconscious is the greatest challenge and obstacle in the path of scientific social knowledge and transformation. Thereby, by encouraging sociologists and social scientists alike to turn their gaze as well inward, he introduced a significant self-reflexive element into utopistic theorizing and practice. Nevertheless, because of his all-universal materialist theoretical environment inherited from Marx, his generally "objectivist" social scientific framework, and also his eschewing of the individual as a unit of analysis (given his sociological training and bias) Mannheim in effect disarmed the intellectual from being personally self-reflective and thus self-transformative. His borrowed "detached intellectuals" theorization was to be sure a self-defeating argument within a paradigm of "social origins of knowledge;" but I have argued that it did not have to be self-defeating in a more dialectical environment in which knowledge is as much the origin of self and social reality as it is its product. Theories of social stratification, if pursued for their own sake, run the risk of becoming self-fulfilling prophecies when applied to everyday social problems and solution strategies. Sociologists as intellectuals, in their teaching and research, no matter how dedicated, may become embroiled so much in interpreting, albeit critically, the stratified class, gender, race, and ethnic nature of capitalist society, that they inadvertently become a perpetuator of them and the belief that there is something to be gained by pursuing upward mobilities in either of its bourgeois or proletarian varieties. It will perhaps take some effort in the sociologies not just of knowledge but of *self-knowledge*, on the part of the academics themselves, faculty or student, to realize that stratifications of our inner and broader social lives are two sides of the same coin tossed around by the Wall Street and Microsoft managers of the postmodern information society.

Social stratification is not simply about the amount of possessions or savings in bank accounts. It is not a state of things, but a relational process taking place without and within. It is about the nature and quality of our experiences as human beings. Social and self stratifications cannot exist apart from one another. To break the chain of our macro social structural slaveries, we cannot jump over our own knees, so to speak, but need to understand and practically change the micro structural slaveries shaping our everyday inner lives and psyches, here and now.

IV

The contested theoretical identities of Marx, Gurdjieff, and Mannheim in search of the good life, eastern or western, are not isolated efforts in world-historical context. On the contrary, as fragmented voices finding their way into our contemporary imaginations they encapsulate the three broad world-historical movements of western utopianism, eastern mysticism, and the academia. Using a nonreductive dialectical conception of world-history in contrast to the conceptions espoused respectively by Marx, Gurdjieff, and Mannheim, I have tried to construct an alternative view of world-history as a grand human architectural project of building inner and global human harmony. World-history is viewed as a long-term and large-scale process of splitting of the intra- and inter/extrapersonal realms of human life into a habituated eastern vs. western civilizational dualism whose transcendence has been, and will necessarily be, dependent upon conscious and intentional creative human effort. World-history is conceptualized as a process of nomadization, ruralization, urbanization, and subsequent rise and disintegration (partly as a result of the first major, Indo-European, nomadic invasions of the south) of ancient civilizations, followed by a long era of imperial reintegrations of the world through increasingly synchronous periods of classical political domination, medieval cultural conversion, and ultimately modern economic exploitation for which the second major (central Asian and north European) nomadic invasions paved the way. The modern world-system is a result not only of the ascendance of an economic form of imperial integration of the world, but of the invention of a new phenomenon in world-history which may best be characterized as "collective imperialism." Postmodernity and globalization today are expressions of the deepening structural crisis of the modern world-system of collective imperialism.

Pointing out that world-history has experienced not one, but two major renaissances—during 600-400 BC and A.D. 1300-1500—each of which followed a long and devastating process of nomadic invasions of the south marking respectively the fall of ancient civilizations and the rise of modern economic imperialism, I have argued that the settled-nomadic dialectic in fact lies at the root not only of the north-south, but also of the east-west, nomenclature in world-historical discourse. The by and large failing eastern and western renaissances signified conscious and intentional human efforts at integrating the fragmented philosophical, religious, and scientific dimensions of human creativity which emerged after the fall of ancient civilizations and reinforced by classical, medieval, and modern empires. This fragmentation has essentially involved and perpetuated a dualistic spatiotemporal distanciation of the intra- and inter/extrapersonal dimension of social knowledge and transformation, manifested in the lop-sided emergence of oppositional utopian, mystical, and academic traditions in humanist utopistics. The structural crisis of the modern world-system involves both the self-destructive tendency of collective imperialism *and* the potentially self-transforming power vested in human creative powers to invent new humanist renaissances on a global scale capable of critically reintegrating the lopsided utopian, mystical, and academic fragments of humanist utopistics in search of alternative self and broader social systemicities in the midst of the existing order, here and now. In the world-historical dialectics of eastern mystical and western utopian traditions, academia has played a determining role—for better or worse. The failed renaissances of the past also signify failed academic efforts at defragmenting the philosophical, religious, and scientific disciplinarities. A fragmented and "disciplined" academia, still in the grips of matter/mind, self/society, and theory/practice dualisms will continue to fail in fulfilling its mission of reintegrating the essentially creative powers of humankind in favor of the good life.

One may view Marx's western utopianism, Gurdjieff's eastern mysticism, and Mannheim's academic sociology of knowledge as mutually alienated and lop-sided philosophical, religious, and scientific fragments of humanist utopistics in modern times. The projection of human creative powers onto "objective laws (or origins) of motion of nature or history," "supernatural" agencies, or select elites of remarkable intellectuals or party cadres, represents the degree to which the very world-historical agencies for human de-alienation have themselves grown alienated from one another. The failing conscious and intentional shocks of the two major eastern and western humanist renaissances of the 4th-6th centuries BC and of 13th-15th AD in bringing about a lasting dialectical synthesis of the three polarized and failing fragments of utopistic endeavor, I argue, has given rise in the modern period to the "antisystemic" mode of seeking social change which by its very nature of spatiotemporally distanciating the actual means from the promised ends of social change has also proven to be an exercise in failure.

The way out of this world-historical impasse, I argue, is inventing new humanist renaissances involving far-reaching and integrative alternative-"civilizational" dialogues across utopian, mystical, and academic fragments of humanist utopistics. The answer lies in conscious and intentional reclaiming and reconstitution of humanist utopistics—informed by a view of human society as a singular spatiotemporal ensemble of diverse intra-, inter-, and extrapersonal self relations, and exercised by example in the midst of life in the context of creative, self-de-alienating, self-harmonizing, and globally self-expanding movements beginning from the personal here and now. Only through dialectical transcendence of philosophically perpetuated religious vs. scientific teleologies of world-historical change in favor of a conscious and intentional humanist teleology arising from the creative powers of human beings themselves can substantively rational and real advances be made towards building inner and global harmony. "Human architecture" is the art of imaginative design and construction of alternative spatiotemporal dialecticities between the personal self-identities here and now and long-term, large-scale, world-historical change.

In my dissertation I have tried to demonstrate that all philosophical, theoretical, and practical dualisms—which emanate from dichotomizations of reality into matter and mind, and result in alienating self and social knowledges and praxes—can be effectively transcended through their re-articulation as diverse manifestations of part-whole dialectics. Developing and applying an architectural approach to sociology, I advocate the abandoning of "house storeys" and similar metaphors still subconsciously fragmenting psychosociological and historical analyses. The habituated common sense definition of society as "multiple" ethno-national and/or civilizational systems of relations among "individuals"—based on ahistorical presumptions of human "individuality"—is rejected in favor of its definition as a singular world-historical ensemble of intra-, inter-, and extrapersonal self relations. It is argued that human life can be harmonious only when it is a world-system of self-determining individualities. Towards this end, the sociology of self-knowledge is proposed as an alternative research and pedagogical landscape for building de-alienated and self-determining human realities.

The proposed sociology of self-knowledge and human architecture—twin fields of inquiry involving research on and practice of spatiotemporal dialectics between here-and-now personal self-identities and world-historical social structures—are exercises in applied sociology beginning in the social spacetimes of our classrooms. They are meant to introduce students to applied sociology not simply in theory, but in the practice of their globally self-reflective research as part of their curricular assignments. I use audiovisual media and particularly feature films to evoke not just the intellectual, but also the emotional and sensual selves of students in their learning experience. I have found a reverse micro to macro, present to past, ordering of sociological theories to be an invaluable strategy in exposing students to rather abstract theoretical discussions. Seeing no dualism between teaching and research, I approach teaching itself as a most important exercise in applied sociological research. For me, practicing what C. Wright Mills called the sociological imagination is not simply a motto but is an actual practical guide to be pursued by students first in the laboratory of their global self-research assignments throughout the semester. Examples of students' works chronicled in the journal *Human Architecture: Journal of the Sociology of Self-Knowledge* attest to the plausible value of such a pedagogical strategy in teaching applied sociology across diverse course offerings.

I have argued, more exhaustively in the dissertation and more briefly in the foregoing, that the root cause of practical failures in ending our self and social stratifications is to be sought in the habituated structures of our theoretical frameworks, world-historically inherited in terms of various dualisms of mind/matter, self/society, theory/practice, and east/west. Recognizing the significance of challenges posed by the subconscious as a mediating region between mind and matter, redefining society and sociology in terms of interaction of selves rather than of presumed "individuals," adopting both micro/macro and integrative (not just selective or even eclectic) approach to various classical or contemporary social theories, and being open to comparative cultural diversity in our theorizing efforts, I argue, would provide a much more fruitful theoretical environment for the advancement of utopistics. To dehabituate from the alienating self and social structures preventing us from achieving social justice, we need to find ways to dehabituate ourselves from dualistic theoretical practices. We do not stand apart from the contested theoretical identities of the good life we have inherited from the past in world-history context; to recognize this and to move beyond contestation in favor of open and detached dialogues would be a prerequisite for bringing about effective change in favor of the good life, without and within.

V

One crowd in religion ponder their way,
One crowd in science supposedly stay,
I fear one morning town crier shouts,
"The way's neither! O gone astray!"

—Omar Khayyam

If anything, Khayyam's quatrain above speaks to the heart of our contested identities in a world-history context. Our contested identities habitually framed in philosophy, religion, and science, have often sidelined art and artistic endeavors from assuming hegemonic standpoints in the formulation of our theories of and strategies for change. Why not stop at this point of interpreting our selves and world in predetermined frameworks and start creating new ones in the here and nows of our inner and interpersonal lives? Really, what makes us not see Omar Khayyam (or Rumi, similarly), for instance, as social psychologists, sociologists, historians, and applied social theorists? Why can't our sociologies and historiographies be poetic, and expressed in diverse art forms? Why do we not see Rumi, who is more globally popular than ever today, as an applied sociologist, social psychiatrist, and inner and world historian, in his own right? Why should sociology and historiography not be at the same time utopistic in substance, and artistic in form?

The Song of the Reed which opens Rumi's book of spiritual couplets is another voice crying humankind's alienated and contested identities in search of loving reintegration and fulfillment in world-history context. This song with which I would like to conclude my presentation is actually a three-fold song, woven delicately with one another as in a Persian carpet destined for a mystical flight towards the good spiritual life. The meaning, the feeling, and the sensations are the three equally significant and vital elements of the poem, aimed at evoking, awakening, blending, and "cooking" our souls towards the experiencing of inner and global unity that can only be a precondition for experiencing the cosmic self-knowledge sought after in the mystical tradition. The three-foldness of the Song of the Reed is of the essence for the eastern civilizational utopistics of which it is a part. To bridge it with the thoughts, feelings and sensibilities of a western audience engaged in western utopistics of varied kinds—i.e., searching in their own western ways for the good life around the globe and outside themselves—requires not one, not two, but a triple translation of its context, content, and form elements.

Western free-verse translations of Rumi's Song of the Reed miss the whole point of his applied social psychology and psychiatry when they omit its tropological rhyme from its truncated and overrationalised substantive meaning. The song is directed not just to one, but to all the three physical, intellectual, and emotional centers of the human organisms comprising his audience. The meaning of the poem in terms of the alienation of humankind and the need for efforts to give up worldly habituations in favor of the good spiritual life is of course one of the layers of the poem directed at the intellectual center of our organism, to what comprises our waking consciousness. The reed metaphor, on the other hand, and all the subtle and complex tropological symbolisms associated with the metaphor is directed at our emotional center, speaking to it in terms of the language of visualizations, which is the primary language of communication with our subconscious mind. Finally, the couplet form and rhythm of reed's song as expressed in the poem is a crucial third layer of the poem, directed at our sensibilities of hearing, sight, and movements, aspects of the physical center of our organism. The three-fold nature of the poem in the original is, in short, of paradigmatic relevance to the very thesis of the poem, which is the need of human beings to free themselves from habituations and addictions of the earth in favor of the good spiritual life. It is the fragmented and independent functioning of the three centers in the human organism, and the alienated multiple selfhoods resulting from it, that makes possible the perpetuation of habituated and addictive behaviors in the human organism. Rumi's seeking a "torn-torn, longing" heart is meant to evoke our emotional sensibilities to join the whirling dance of his spiritual journey. His references to the distinction between soul and body, the limits of our ear and tongue and eye sensibilities, are meant to evoke our physical selfhoods to tune in to his reed's song. His evoking our curiosities about his secret is meant to evoke our higher intellectual selves to embark on the journey of cosmic self-knowledge and change.

Rumi's Song of the Reed is not simply preaching to us, but through the actual unfolding of his poem's threefold architecture is participating in helping us transform our identities towards freedom from enslavements to worldly objects. He is speaking not only to our conscious but to our unconscious and subconscious minds, i.e., to the three-fold minds of our intellectual, physical, and emotional selves simultaneously, seeking to tear apart the veils and buffers that separate the three centers from one another and all of them from lessons of world-history, preventing us from realizing the utter sleepiness, imprisonment, mechanicalness, and enslavement of our ordinary lives as alienated selves. The "secret" alluded to in the poem, i.e., the separation of body and soul, the inner alienation of human physical, intellectual, and emotional selves, is the fundamental and paradigmatic essence of the poem, a secret that is paradoxically being given to us on the humble platter of spiritual food by Rumi without our eyes and ears being able to "get the clue," so to speak. The voice of Rumi is another contesting identity in world-history context whose aim is to do away with contestations altogether in favor of the good life through the unitary experiencing of human and cosmic love.

Imagine a ceremony in the presence of Rumi, where one hears the soothing cries of reeds in the background. Rumi suddenly interrupts them and sings his own reed's song:

Listen to how *this* reed is wailingAbout separations it's complaining:
"From reedbed since parted was IMen, women, have cried my cry
"Only a heart, torn-torn, longingCan hear my tales of belonging
"Whosoever lost his essenceFor reuniting seeks lessons
"In the midst of all I criedFor the sad and happy both sighed
"But they heard only what *they* knewSought not after the secrets *I* blew
"My secret's not far from this, my cryBut,   eye or ear catch not the light if don't try
"Body and soul each other do not veilBut there is no one to hear *his soul's* tale"
What arises from the reed is fireWhoever lost it, is lost entire
What set the reed on fire is love, loveWhat rages in reed is nothing but love, love
Reed comes of use when lovers departIt's wailing scales tear love's veilings apart
Like reed both poison and cure, who saw?Like reed comrade and devote, who saw?
Reed tells of the bleeding heart's talesTells of what mad lovers' love entails
With the truth, only seeker's intimateAs the tongue knows only ear's estimate
Days, nights, lost count in my sorrowPast merged in my sorrow with tomorrow
If the day is gone, say: "So what! go, go!But remain, O you pure, O my sorrow"
This water's dispensable—not for the fishHungry finds days long without a dish
Cooked soul's unknowable if you're rawThen there is no use to tire the jaw
Break the chain, . .. be free, ... O boy!How long will you remain that gold's toy?!
Say you have oceans, but how can you pourAll oceans in a single day's jar, more & more?!
The greedy's eye-jar will never fill upNo pearl, if oyster's mouth doesn't give up
Whoever tore his robe in love's affairTore free of greed, flaw, and false care
Joy upon you! O sorrowful sweet love!O the healer! healer of ills! love! love!
O healer of the vain, of our shameO Galen in name, Platonic in fame!
Earth's whirling in heaven's for *love*, loveHills' whirling round the earth's for *love*, love
Love's the soul in hill! It's *love* in the hillThat brought hill down and Moses the chill!
If coupled my lips with friends' on and onI'll tell tales, like reed, long, long
Uncoupled, though, these lips will cease wails Lose tongue, though remain untold tales
When the rose is dead, garden long goneNo canary can recite her song long
The lover is veiled, beloved's the allVeil must tear to hear beloved's call
If you do stay away from love, hear, hear!Like a wingless bird you'll die, fear, fear!
How can I stay awake and see the roadIf lover's light shine not on my abode?
Love always seeks ways to spread the light Why, then, does your mirror reflect a night?
Your mirror takes no tales, if need to know, 'Cause your rust keeps away all lights' glow.

SUGGESTED BIBLIOGRAPHY

Adorno, Theodor W. 1967. "The Sociology of Knowledge and Its Consciousness." In *Prisms*, London: Spearman.

Adorno, Theodor W. 1973. *Negative Dialectics.* New York: Seabury Press.

Bailey, Leon. 1994. *Critical Theory and the Sociology of Knowledge: A Comparative Study in the Theory of Ideology.* New York: Peter Lang.

Baker, George and Walter Driscoll. 1992. "Gurdjieff in America: An Overview." In *America's Alternative Religions.* SUNY Press, Albany.

Berger, Peter and Thomas Luckmann. [1966] 1967. *The Social Construction of Reality: A Treatise in the Sociology of Knowledge.* Garden City, NY: Doubleday & Company, Inc.

Bourdieu, Pierre, and Loic J. Wacquant. 1992. *An Invitation to Reflexive Sociology.* Chicago: The University of Chicago Press.

Bourdieu, Pierre. 1998. *Practical Reason: On the Theory of Action.* Stanford: Stanford Univ Press.

Bourne, Russell, series editor. 1966. *Great Ages of Man: A History of the World's Cultures.* New York: Time Incorporated.

Brook, Peter. (director). 1978. Feature Film: "Meetings with Remarkable Men." New York: Remar Productions, Inc.

Buford, Thomas O. 1995. *In Search of a Calling: The College's Role in Shaping Identity.* Macon, Georgia: Mercer University Press.

Cohen, G. A. 1978. *Marx's Theory of History: A Defense.* Princeton, New Jersey: Princeton University Press.

Collins, Randall. 1998. *The Sociology of Philosophies: A Global Theory of Intellectual Change.* Cambridge, Massachusetts: The Belknap Press of Harvard University Press.

Coser, Lewis. 1968. "Knowledge, Sociology of." Pp. 428-435 in *The International Encyclopedia of the Social Sciences.* New York: The Macmillan Company and The Free Press.

Curtis, James E. and John Petras, eds. 1970. *The Sociology of Knowledge: A Reader.* New York and Washington: Praeger Publishers.

Deikman, Arthur J. 1982. *The Observing Self: Mysticism and Psychotherapy.* Boston: Beacon Press.

Deikman, Arthur J. 1990. *The Wrong Way Home: Uncovering the Patterns of Cult Behavior in American Society.* Boston: Beacon Press.

Driscoll, J. Walter and the Gurdjieff Foundation of California. 1985. *Gurdjieff: An Annotated Bibliography, with an introductory essay by Michel De Salzmann.* New York: Garland Press.

Driscoll, J. Walter. 1999. *Gurdjieff: a Reading Guide,* Los Altos, California: Gurdjieff Electronic Publishing. (purchasable at http://www.gurdjieff.org/G.htm)

Engels, Frederick. [1888] 1970. "Ludwig Feuerbach and the End of Classical German Philosophy." Pp. 335-376 in *Karl Marx and Frederick Engels: Selected Works.* Moscow: Progress Publishers.

Engels, F. 1976. *Dialectics of Nature.* Moscow: Progress Publishers.

Finch, Henry Leroy. 1996. "Gurdjieff and the Modern World." Pp. 8-29 in *Gurdjieff: Essays and Reflections on the Man and his Teaching,* edited by Jacob Needleman and George Baker. New York: Continuum.

Foucault, Michel. 1972. *The Archeology of Knowledge and the Discourse on Language.* NY: Pantheon Books.

Foucault, Michel. 1995. *Discipline and Punish.* Translated by Alan Sheridan. NY: Vintage/Random House.

Foucault, Michel. 1973. *Madness and Civilization: A History of Insanity in the Age of Reason.* Translated by R. Howard. NY: Vintage/Random House.

Fromm, Erich. [1956] 2000. The Art of Loving. NY: HarperCollins.

Fromm, Erich. [1976] 1996. To Have or To Be. NY: Continuum.

Garaudy, Roger. [1964] 1967. *Karl Marx: The Evolution of His Thought.* New York: International Publishers.

Gulbenkian Commission. 1996. *Open the Social Sciences: Report of the Gulbenkian Commission on the Restructuring of the Social Sciences.* Stanford: Stanford University Press.

Gurdjieff, G. I. [1933] 1973. *Herald of Coming Good: First Appeal to Contemporary Humanity.* New York: Samuel Weiser Inc.

Gurdjieff, G. I. 1950. *All and Everything: Beelzebub's Tales to His Grandson.* First Edition. New York: Harcourt, Brace and Company.

Gurdjieff, G. I. 1973. *Views from the Real World: Early Talks of G.I. Gurdjieff.* New York: Arkana/Penguin Books.

Gurdjieff, G. I. [1963] 1985. *Meetings with Remarkable Men.* New York and London: Viking Arkana.

Gurdjieff, G. I. [1981] 1991. *Life is Real Only Then, When "I AM."* New York and London: Viking Arkana/Triangel Editions, Inc.

Gurdjieff, G. I. 1992. *All and Everything: Beelzebub's Tales to His Grandson*. Second Edition. New York and London: Viking Arkana/Triangle Editions, Inc.

Habermas, Jurgen. 1973. *Theory and Practice*. Boston: Beacon Press.

Harvey, David. 1990. *The Condition of Postmodernity*. MA: Basil Blackwell.

Harvey, David. 1996. *Justice, Nature & the Geography of Difference*. Oxford: Blackwell Publishers Ltd.

Harvey, David. 2000. *Spaces of Hope*. Berkeley: University of California Press.

Harvey, David. 2001. *Spaces of Capital*. London: Routledge.

Haschak, Paul G. 1994. *Utopian/Dystopian Literature: A Bibliography of Literary Criticism*. Metuchen, N.J., & London: The Scarecrow Press, Inc.

Hegel, G. W. F. 1975. *Hegel's Logic*. Translated by William Wallace with foreword by J. N. Findlay. Oxford: Clarendon Press.

Hegel, G. W. F. 1969. *Hegel's Science of Logic*. Translated by A. V. Miller. London: Humanity Books.

Hoffman, John. 1976. *Marxism and the Theory of Praxis*. New York: International Publishers.

Hopkins, Terence K., Immanuel Wallerstein, and Associates. 1982. *World-Systems Analysis: Theory and Methodology*. Beverly Hills: Sage Publication, Inc.

Horkheimer, Max. 1947. *Eclipse of Reason*. NY: Seabury Press.

Horkheimer, Max. 1974. *Critical Theory: Selected Essays*. NY: Seabury Press.

Horkheimer, Max. 1990. "A New Concept of Ideology?" Pp. 140-157 in *The Sociology of Knowledge Dispute*, edited by Volker Meja and Nico Stehr. London and New York: Routledge.

Horkheimer, Max and Theodor W. Adorno. 1972. *Dialectic of Enlightenment*. NY: Seabury Press.

Horton, Robin and Ruth Finnegan, eds. 1973. *Modes of Thought: Essays on Thinking in Western and Non-Western Societies*. London: Faber & Faber.

Kateb, George. [1963] 1972. *Utopia and Its Enemies*. Schocken Books.

Kateb, George. 1968. "Utopias and Utopianism." Pp. 267-70 in *The International Encyclopedia of the Social Sciences*, edited by David L. Sills, vol. 16. New York: The Macmillan Company and The Free Press.

Kateb, George. [1967] 1972. "Utopias and Utopianism." Pp. 212-215 in *The Encyclopedia of Philosophy*, vol. 8. New York: Macmillan Publishing Co., Inc. & The Free Press.

Kettler, David and Volker Meja. 1993. "Introduction." In *From Karl Mannheim*, edited by Wolff. Kurt H. New Brunswick: Transaction Publishers.

Kettler, David and Volker Meja. 1995. *Karl Mannheim and the Crisis of Liberalism: The Secret of These New Times*. New Brunswick and London: Transaction Publishers.

Kettler, David, Volker Meja and Nico Stehr. 1984. *Karl Mannheim*. New York: Tavistock Publications.

Kuhn, Thomas S. 1962. *The Structure of Scientific Revolutions*. Chicago: The University of Chicago Press.

Kumar, Krishan. 1991. *Utopianism*. Minneapolis: Univeristy of Minnesota Press.

Lefebvre, Henri. 1991. *The Production of Space*. Translated by Donald Nicholson Smith. Oxford: Blackwell.

Lenin. V. I. [1913] 1968. "The Three Sources and Three Component Parts of Marxism." Pp. 62-67 in *Marx, Engels, Marxism*. Moscow: Progress.

Lenin, V. I. 1977. *Philosophical Notebooks*. In *Collected Works*, vol. 38. Moscow: Progress Publishers.

Lenin, V. I. 1977. *Selected Works*. Moscow: Progress Publishers.

Levin, Jerome David. 1992. *Theories of the Self*. Washington: Hemisphere Publishing Corporation.

Lukacs, Georg. [1923] 1971. *History and Class Consciousness: Studies in Marxist Dialectics*. Translated by Rodney Livingstone. Cambridge, Massachusetts: MIT Press.

McCarthy, E. Doyle. 1996. *Knowledge As Culture: The New Sociology of Knowledge*. New York: Routledge.

McLellan, David. 1977. *Karl Marx: His Life and Thought*. New York: Harper Colophon Books.

McLellan, David. 1979. *Marxism after Marx: An Introduction*. New York: Harper & Row Publishers.

McMurtry, John. 1978. *The Structure of Marx's World-View*. Princeton: Princeton University Press.

Mannheim, Karl. 1990. "Competition as a Cultural Phenomenon." In *The Sociology of Knowledge Dispute*, edited by Volker Meja and Nico Stehr. London and New York: Routledge.

Mannheim, Karl. 1936. *Ideology and Utopia*. Translated by Louis Wirth and Edward Shils. New York: Harcourt Brace and Company, Harvest Books.

Mannheim, Karl. [1940] 1981. *Man and Society in an Age of Reconstruction*. London: Routledge Kegan & Paul.

Manuel, F. E. and F. P. Manuel. 1979. *Utopian Thought in the Western World*. New Jersey: Humanities.

Marcuse, Herbert. 1990. "Sociological Method and the Problem of Truth." Pp. 129- 139 in *The Sociology of Knowledge Dispute*, edited by Volker Meja and Nico Stehr. London and New York: Routhledge.

Marcuse, Herbert. 1954. *Reason and Revolution: Hegel and the Rise of Social Theory*. NY: Beacon Press.

Marcuse, Herbert. 1955. *Eros and Civilization: A Philosophical Inquiry into Freud*. Boston: Beacon Press.

Marcuse, Herbert. 1958. *One-Dimensional Man*. Boston: Beacon Press.

Marcuse, Herbert. 1958. *Soviet Marxism: A Critical Analysis*. NY: Vintage Books.

Markovic, Mihailo. 1974. *From Affluence to Praxis*. Boston: Beacon Press.

Marx, Karl. 1967a. *Capital*. Vol. 1. New York: International Publishers. Ninth 1979 printing.

Marx, Karl. [1859] 1970. *A Contribution to the Critique of the Political Economy*. Edited with and Introduction by Maurice Dobb. New York: International Publishers.

Marx, Karl. [1859] 1970. "Preface." Pp. 19-23 in *A Contribution to the Critique of the Political Economy*. Edited with and Introduction by Maurice Dobb. New York: International Publishers.

Marx, Karl. 1970. "Letter to F. Mehring," dated July 1893, 1858, pp. 495-497 in *Karl Marx and Frederick Engels. Selected Works*, vol. 3. Moscow: Progress Publishers.

Marx, Karl. 1973. *Grundrisse: Foundations of the Critique of Political Economy*. New York: Vintage Books.

Marx, Karl. 1975. "Letter to Engels," dated January 14, 1858, pp. 93 in *Karl Marx and Frederick Engels. Selected Correspondence*. Moscow: Progress Publishers. Third revised edition.

Marx, Karl and Frederick Engels. Vol. 1:1969, Vol. 2:1969, Vol. 3:1970. *Selected Works*. Moscow: Progress Publishers.

Marx Karl and Frederick Engels. 1975. *Selected Correspondence*. Moscow: Progress Publishers. Third revised edition.

Marx, Karl and Friedrich Engels. 1978. *The Marx-Engels Reader*, edited by Robert C. Tucker. 2nd edition. New York: W. W. Norton & Company.

Marx, Karl and Frederick Engels. 1975-. *Collected Works*. New York: International Publishers.

Marx, K., Frederick Engels, and V. I. Lenin. 1978a. *On Dialectical Materialism*. Moscow: Progress Publishers.

Marx, K., Frederick Engels, and V. I. Lenin. 1978b. *On Communist Society*. Moscow: Progress Publishers. Third revised edition.

Mead, George Herbert. 1934. *Mind, Self and Society*. Chicago, Illinois: University of Chicago Press.

Mead, George Herbert. 1938. *The Philosophy of the Act*. Chicago: University of Chicago Press.

Mead, George Herbert. [1959] 1981. *The Philosophy of the Present*. Chicago: University of Chicago Press.

Meja, Volker and Nico Stehr, eds. 1990. *The Sociology of Knowledge Dispute*. London and New York: Routhledge.

Meja, Volker and David Kettler. 1993. "Introduction." In *From Karl Mannheim*, by Kurt H. Wolff, New Brunswick: Transaction Publishers.

Merton, Robert K. [1949] 1957. *Social Theory and Social Structure*. Glencoe, Ill.: The Free Press.

Mills, C. Wright. 1940. "Methodological Consequences of the Sociology of Knowledge." *American Journal of Sociology* 46:316-330.

Mills, C. Wright. 1953. *Character and Social Structure: The Psychology of Social Institutions*. New York: Harcourt Brace Jovanovich.

Mills, C. Wright. 1959. *The Sociological Imagination*. New York: Oxford University Press.

Moore, James. 1991. Gurdjieff: *The Anatomy of a Myth*. Rockport, Massachausetts: Elment.

More, Sir Thomas [1516] 1965. *Utopia*. New York: Penguin Books.

Mukherjee, Ramkrishna. 1978. *What Will It Be?: Explorations in Inductive Sociology*. Durham, North Carolina: Carolina Academic Press.

Mumford, Lewis. 1941. *The Story of Utopias*. New York: Peter Smith.

Needleman, Jacob. 1993. "G. I. Gurdjieff and His School." Pp. 359-379 in *Modern Esoteric Spirituality* (part of the series *World Spirituality: An Encyclopedic History of the Religious Quest*) edited by Antoine Faivre and Jacob Needleman. London: SCM Press Ltd.

Needleman, Jacob. 1996. "Introduction." Pp. ix-xii in *Gurdjieff: Essays and Reflections on the Man and his Teaching*, edited by Jacob Needleman and George Baker. New

York: Continuum.

Negley, Glen. [1977] 1978. *Utopian Literature: A Bibliography with a Supplementary Listing of Works Influential in Utopian Thought*. University Press of Kansas.

Nicoll, Maurice. 1985. *Psychological Commentaries on the Teaching of Gurdjieff & Ouspensky*. Volume One. Boston & London: Shambhala.

Ouspensky, P.D. 1949. *In Search of the Miraculous: Fragments of an Unknown Teaching*. New York: Harcourt Brace Jovanovich Publishers.

Pilcher, Jane. 1994. "Mannheim's Sociology of Generations: An Undervalued Legacy." *British Journal of Sociology* 3:481-495.

Popper, Karl, R. 1963. *The Open Society and Its Enemies*. 2 vols. New York: Harper Torchbooks.

Popper, Karl, R. 1970. "The Sociology of Knowledge." Pp. 282-306 in *The Sociology of Knowledge: A Reader*, edited by James E. Curtis and John Petras. New York and Washington: Praeger Publishers. (Reprinted from *The Open Society and Its Enemies*. 2 vol. NJ: Princeton University Press. 1963).

Remmling, Gunter W. 1975. *The Sociology of Karl Mannheim: With a Bibliographical Guide to the Sociology of Knowledge, Ideological analysis, and Social Planning*. London: Routledge & Kegan Paul.

Rosdolsky, Roman.1977. *The Making of Marx's 'Capital.'* London: Pluto Press.

Rumi (Molana Jalaleddin). *Masnavi-e Ma'navi* (Spiritual Couplets).

Scheler, Max. 1978. *Problems of a Sociology of Knowledge*. Translated by Manfred S. Frings, edited and with an introduction by Kenneth W. Stikkers. London: Routledge & Kegan Paul.

Shannon, Thomas Richard. 1989. *An Introduction to the World-System Perspective*. Boulder, San Francisco, & London: Westview Press.

Shun, Kwong-loi. 1995. "Chinese Philosophy." Pp. 130-132 in *The Oxford Companion to Philosophy*, edited by Ted Honderich. Oxford: Oxford University Press.

Shils, Edward. 1968. "Mannheim, Karl." Pp. 557-562 in *The International Encyclopedia of the Social Sciences*, edited by David L. Sills, vol. 16. New York: The Macmillan Company and The Free Press.

Shils, Edward. 1995. "Karl Mannheim." *The American Scholar* 64, 2, Spring: 221-235.

Singer, Peter. 1995. "Hegel, George Wilhelm Friedrich." Pp. 339-343. in *The Oxford Companion to Philosophy*, edited by Ted Honderich. Oxford: Oxford University Press.

Snodgrass, Mary Ellen. 1995. *Encyclopedia of Utopian Literature*. Santa Barbara, California: ABC-CLIO.

Soja, Edward. 1993. "History: Geography: Modernity." Pp. 135-150 in *The Cultural Studies: A Reader*, edited by Simon During. New York and London: Routledge.

Speeth, Kathleen Riordan. 1989. *The Gurdjieff Work*. NY: Jeremy P. Tarcher/Perigee.

Stark, Werner. 1958. *The Sociology of Knowledge: An Essay in Aid of A Deeper Understanding of the History of Ideas*. Glencoe, Ill.: The Free Press.

Stark, Werner. [1967] 1972. "Sociology of Knowledge." Pp. 475-478 in *The Encyclopedia of Philosophy*, vol. 7. New York: Macmillan Publishing Co., Inc. & The Free Press.

Tamdgidi, Mohammad H., ed. 1997. *'I' in the World-System: Stories From An Odd Sociology Class, (Selected Student Writings, Soc. 280Z: Sociology of Knowledge: Mysticism, Utopia, Science)*. Limited Edition. Binghamton: Crumbling Façades Press.

Tamdgidi, Mohammd H. 1999. "Ideology and Utopia in Mannheim: Towards the Sociology of Self Knowledge," Presented at the History of Sociology Refereed Roundtable Session of the American Sociological Association, 94th Annual Meeting, August 6-10 1999, Chicago. Reprinted in Human Architecture: Journal of the Sociology of Self-Knowledge, Fall, 2002, 120-139.

TTamdgidi, Mohammad-Hossein. 2002. "Mysticism and Utopia: Towards the Sociology of Self-Knowledge and Human Architecure (A Study in Marx, Gurdjieff, and Mannheim)." Ph.D. Dissertation, Binghamton University (SUNY).

Tamdgidi, Mohammad H. 2001. "Open the Antisystemic Movements: The Book, the Concept, and the Reality" *Review*, XXIV, 2:301-338.

Taylor. C.C.W. 1995. "Socrates." Pp. 836-837 in *The Oxford Companion to Philosophy*, edited by Ted Honderich. Oxford: Oxford University Press.

Thayer, H.S. [1967] 1972. "Pragmatism." Pp. 430-436 in *The Encyclopedia of Philosophy*, vol. 6. New York: Macmillan Publishing Co., Inc. & The Free Press.

Tillich, Paul. 1990. "On Ideology and Utopia." Pp. 107-112 in *The Sociology of Knowledge Dispute*, edited by Volker Meja and Nico Stehr. London and New York: Routledge.

Tucker, Robert, C., ed. 1978. *The Marx-Engels Reader*. 2nd edition. New York: W. W. Norton & Company.

Turner, Bryan S. 1995. "Karl Mannheim's Ideology and Utopia." *Political Studies* XLIII:718-727.

Turner, Bryan S. 1998. "Preface to the new edition." In *Ideology and Utopia*. London: Routhledge.

Vazques, Adolf S. 1977. *The Philosophy of Praxis*. Prometheus Books.

Vigadski, Vitalis. 1974. *The Story of a Great Discovery: How Karl Marx Wrote "Capital."* Abacus Press.

Wallerstein, Immanuel. 1974. *The Modern World-System, I: Capitalist Agriculture and the Origins of the European World-Economy in the Sixteenth Century*. New York & London: Academic Press.

Wallerstein, Immanuel. 1979. *The Capitalist World-Economy*. Cambridge: Cambridge Univ. Press.

Wallerstein, Immanuel. 1989. "Culture as the Ideological Battleground of the Modern World-System," *Journal of Social Studies*, XXI, 1:5-22.

Wallerstein, Immanuel. 1990. "Braudel on Capitalism, or Everything Upside Down." In *Modern Age - Modern Hitorian*. Edited by Ferenc Glatz, Budapest.

Wallerstein, Immanuel. 1991a. *Unthinking Social Science: The Limits of Nineteenth Century Paradigms*. Cambridge: Polity Press.

Wallerstein, Immanuel. 1991b. *Geopolitics and Geoculture: Essays on the Changing World-System*. Cambridge: Cambridge Univ. Press.

Wallerstein, Immanuel. 1996. *Historical Capitalism with Capitalist Civilization*. London and New York: Verso.

Wallerstein, Immanuel. 1998a. *Utopistics: Or, Historical Choices of the Twenty-First Century*. New York: The New Press.

Wallerstein, Immanuel, ed. 1998b. *Mentoring, Methods, and Movements: Colloquium in Honor of Terence K. Hopkins by His Former Students*. Binghamton: Fernand Braudel Center (co-publisher: Ahead Desktop Publishing House).

Wallerstein, Immanuel. 1999. *The End of the World As We Know It: Social Science for the Twenty-First Century*. Minneapolis: University of Minnesota Press.

Wallerstein, Immanuel. 2000. "Where Should Sociologists Be Heading?" *Contemporary Sociology* 29, 2:306-308.

Weber, Alfred. 1927. *Ideen zur Staats- und Kultursoziologie*. Karlsruhe.

Weber, Max. [1930] 1958. *The Protestant Ethic and the Spirit of Capitalism*. Translated by Talcott Parsons, New York: Charles Scribner's Sons.

White, Hayden, V. [1967] 1972. "Feuerbach, Ludwig Andreas." Pp. 190-2 in *The Encyclopedia of Philosophy*, vol. 3. New York: Macmillan Publishing Co., Inc. & The Free Press.

Williams, Raymond. 1958. *Culture and Society: 1780-1950*. Harmonsworth: Penguin.

Williams, Robin M., Jr. 1966. "Some further Comments on Chronic Controversies." *American Journal of Sociology* LXXI, May:717-21.

Wilson Organ, Troy. 1975. *Western Approaches to Eastern Philosophy*. Athens, Ohio: Ohio University Press.

Wolff, Kurt H. 1983. "A Preliminary Inquiry into the Sociology of Knowledge from the Standpoint of the Study of Man." In *Beyond the Sociology of Knowledge: An Introduction and a Development*. New York: University Press of America.

Wolff. Kurt H. [1971] 1993. *From Karl Mannheim*. New Brunswick: Transaction Publishers.

Young, T. R. 1972. *New Sources of Self*. New York: Pergamon Press Inc.

Young, T. R. 1990. *The Drama of Social Life: Essays in Post-Modern Social Psychology*. New Brunswick: Transaction Publishers.

Young-Eisendrath, Polly and James A. Hall. 1987. *The Book of the Self*. New York and London: New York University Press.

Zurcher, Louis A., Jr. 1977. *The Mutable Self: A Self-Concept for Social Change*. Beverly Hills: Sage Publications.

Notes on Contributors

Colin Campbell, is a freshman in Biology at SUNY Oneonta. He was enrolled in Socl. 100-01, "Introduction to Sociology," during the Spring 2003 semester. **Abstract:** "This paper is about shyness and the effect it has on people and society as a whole. I explore several facets of shyness including its causes, effects, and possible "cures" to help people overcome their fear of social interaction. I utilize several examples from outside sources such as films and books watched and read either in or outside class. I relate this to my life, as I was (and am) afflicted with deep shyness stemming from childhood events."

Charles (pen name), is an undergraduate student at SUNY Oneonta. He was enrolled in Soc. 100-02, "Introduction in Sociology," during the Spring 2003 semester.

Jennifer S. Dutcher, is a senior majoring in Sociology at SUNY Oneonta. She enrolled in Socl. 313, "Perspectives and Theories in Sociology," during the Spring 2003 semester. **Abstract:** "The struggle to balance family and career is a difficult one. A delay in college education makes simultaneously achieving success in family, employment, and part-time study especially challenging. Ideas of what women's roles are and how they should be carried out are formed by observation of one's own parents and other significant individuals. Because society is a complex web of relations, each cohort has the power to affect the society of its successors. Through the media, society has established an unattainable idea of what a working mother should be, and the bar has been set high. Mothers' employment outside the home must deal with the bifurcation of consciousness, because many household duties will continue to fall upon women's shoulders, as does the difficult task of securing quality childcare. Americans have been consumed by "affluenza," and the resultant drive to fill their lives with material goods has left them spending more and enjoying less. Women have grown to want more than a job—they are instead pursuing careers that provide self-satisfaction as well as a paycheck. As women realize their strengths, it will not be enough to adequately fill their roles; rather they will strive to succeed in every aspect of their lives. "

M. Goltry, is a senior majoring in Psychology and minoring in Sociology at SUNY-Oneonta. She was enrolled in Socl. 313, "Perspectives and Theories in Sociology," during the Spring 2003 semester. **Abstract:** "Throughout everyone's life, there is a constant struggle to find oneself. My search for true self-identity began in middle school, when I went through some physical changes, such as weight gain. When the other children in school picked on me, I attempted to change myself in order to fit with their expectations. The sociological perspectives of symbolic interaction, theories of rational choice, exchange theory, and others shed light on my situation on a micro level. On the macro level, the sociology of the body and functionalism came into play. Throughout my struggle both the forces acting upon me from a personal standpoint and outside cultural forces taught me an important lesson concerning the significance of inner beauty. Although I am still striving to find myself, my middle school experience gave me great insight, and brought me closer to my goal of self-discovery."

James McHugh, is a freshman at SUNY Oneonta majoring in Political Science. He enrolled in Socl. 100-02, "Introduction to Sociology," during the Spring 2003 semester. **Abstract:** "In my paper I draw parallels to how society has shaped my life, how every other member has been shaped, how the universal norm doesn't apply to the individual, and how it can be overcome."

Notice: Copyright of *Human Architecture: Journal of the Sociology of Self-Knowledge* is the property of Ahead Publishing House (imprint: Okcir Press) and its content may not be copied or emailed to multiple sites or posted to a listserv without the copyright holder's express written permission. However, users may print, download, or email articles for individual use.

Emily Margulies, is a junior in Sociology at SUNY Oneonta minoring in Criminal Justice. She enrolled in Socl. 313, "Perspectives and Theories in Sociology, " during the Spring 2003 semester.

Neo Morpheus (pen name), is an undergraduate senior at SUNY Oneonta.

Megan Murray, is a senior at SUNY Oneonta majoring in Elementary Education. She was enrolled in Soc. 100-01 during the Spring 2003 semester. **Abstract:** "This paper describes the events that can cause anxiety in young adults and college age students. It discusses the process through which I came to realize I was suffering from Generalized Anxiety Disorder. This diagnosis has changed my outlook on life. Through a journey of self-exploration using micro and macro perspectives in sociology I realized that many factors could influence a person's life, including mine."

Ira Omid (pen name), was a senior in Sociology at SUNY Oneonta during the Spring 2003 semester. **Abstract:** "For the exercise in the sociology of self-knowledge, one must liberate the sociological imagination. I explore the role of domestic violence in the past, present and future of a family's life. Despite conscious efforts to the contrary, some mistakes have been repeated. The following is one person's view, within a multiple micro/macro theoretical perspective, of the impact her dysfunctional family life has had on her life."

Anna Schlosser, is a senior majoring in Psychology at SUNY Oneonta. She enrolled in Socl. 100-02, "Introduction to Sociology," during the Spring 2003 semester.

Jillian E. Sloan, is a junior majoring in Psychology and Child & Family Studies at SUNY Oneonta. She enrolled in Socl. 100-02, "Introduction to Sociology," during the Spring 2003 semester. **Abstract:** "In this paper I explore issues concerning religion, materialism, individualism, and more. These topics are explored from both a micro and macro perspective. My main question is: Is it possible in an individualistic nation to raise a child without religion to become a self-sufficient, moral member of society? This question leads to many other ideas and debates. How do relationships affect one's identity? How important is the role of a family in early childhood experience? Is religion the best way to measure moral character?"

M.H. (Behrooz) Tamdgidi, Ph.D., has taught courses at Binghamton University (SUNY) and SUNY Oneonta. He will serve as Assistant Professor of Sociology at UMass Boston beginning in Fall 2003.

Sherry Wilson, is a junior majoring in Business Economics at SUNY Oneonta. She was enrolled in Soc. 100-02, "Introduction to Sociology," during the Spring 2003 semester. **Abstract:** "My entire life I have been confronted with the challenge of being shy. As a result of being shy, I find that I only talk to the people that I already know and I have trouble forming new relationships. When I am in a situation to form a new relationship, I will conform to the views of the other person to avoid having to defend myself. I understand the ways in which to overcome my fears; however my battle is an ongoing one that simply takes time."

www.ingramcontent.com/pod-product-compliance
Lightning Source LLC
Chambersburg PA
CBHW080402030426
42334CB00024B/2964